EMOTIONS AND BODILY RESPONSES

A Psychophysiological Approach

BEHAVIORAL BIOLOGY

AN INTERNATIONAL SERIES

Series editors

James L. McGaugh

Department of Psychobiology
University of California
Irvine, California

John C. Fentress

Department of Psychology
Dalhousie University
Halifax, Canada

Joseph P. Hegman

Department of Zoology
The University of Iowa
Iowa City, Iowa

Holger Ursin, Eivind Baade, and Seymour Levine (Editors), Psychobiology of Stress: A Study of Coping Men

William W. Grings and Michael E. Dawson, Emotions and Bodily Responses: A Psychophysiological Approach

Enoch Callaway, Patricia Tueting, and Stephen H. Koslow (Editors), Event Related Brain Potentials in Man

In Preparation

Larry L. Butcher (Editor), Cholinergic-Monoaminergic Interactions in the Brain

EMOTIONS AND BODILY RESPONSES

A Psychophysiological Approach

WILLIAM W. GRINGS

Department of Psychology
University of Southern California
Los Angeles, California

MICHAEL E. DAWSON

Gateways Hospital and Community Mental Health Center
Los Angeles, California

ACADEMIC PRESS   New York   San Francisco   London   1978
A Subsidiary of Harcourt Brace Jovanovich, Publishers

2/1980
Psych.

ACADEMIC PRESS, INC.
111 Fifth Avenue, New York, New York 10003

United Kingdom Edition published by
ACADEMIC PRESS, INC. (LONDON) LTD.
24/28 Oval Road, London NW1 7DX

Library of Congress Cataloging in Publication Data

Grings, William Washburn, Date
    Emotions and bodily responses.

    (Behavioral biology series)
    Bibliography: p.
    1. Psychology, Physiological. 2. Emotions.
I. Dawson, Michael E., joint author. II. Title.
III. Series. [DNLM: 1. Emotions. 2. Psy-
chophysiologic disorders. WL103 G876e]
QP360.G75   152.4   77−25730
ISBN 0−12−303750−6

Contents

Preface   ix

A Glossary of Terms and Abbreviations   xi

1

Overview of Emotions and Bodily Responses   1

Historical Perspective and Issues   2

Some Basic Physiological Principles   6

Bodily Reactions Accompanying Emotion   12

Conclusions and Outline of This Book   24

2

Stimuli that Cause Bodily Responses   27

Simple Environmental Stimuli   27

Task-Related Stimuli   31

Fear-Producing Stimuli   33

Internal Self-Generated Stimuli   36

Complex Social Stimuli   37

The Effects of Set and Attitude on Responses to Stimuli   41

Conclusion   45

3

Individual Differences and Bodily Responses — 47

Autonomic Balance   48
Individual-Response Stereotypy   50
Personality Tests and Bodily Responses   52
Conclusion   64

4

Behavior Disorders — 65

Anxiety   66
Depression   69
Psychopathy   72
Hyperkinesis   75
Schizophrenia   77
Summary and Conclusions   82

5

Physiological Arousal and Performance — 87

Arousal and Bodily Responses   87
Arousal and Motor Performance   89
Arousal and Sensory Performance   94
Arousal, Learning, and Memory   97
Arousal and Acting Out Aggression   101
Conclusion   103

6

General Behavioral States — 105

Sleep   106
Stress   110
Relaxation   113
Desensitization of Fears   118
Conclusion   122

7

Psychosomatic Disorders   **123**

Necessary Conditions Hypothesis	124
Specific Attitude Hypothesis	125
Response Specificity Hypothesis	130
Other Interpretations	132
Experimental Psychosomatics	133
Conclusion	135

8

Learning of Bodily Responses   **137**

Types of Learning	137
Pavlovian Conditioning	139
Instrumental Conditioning	145
Biofeedback Training	149
Conclusion	152

9

The Detection of Deception   **153**

Procedures and Techniques	154
Physiological Measures	156
Test Validity	159
Theories of Bodily Changes during Deception	163
Legal Status	165
Conclusion	167

References	169
Author Index	183
Subject Index	189

Preface

This book presents an introduction to the principles of psychophysiology as they relate to bodily responses and emotions. The emphasis is on the study of human subjects and on those bodily responses that can be measured from the periphery of the body without the use of invasive techniques. This approach necessarily omits some important bodily changes that accompany emotions, such as biochemical changes, which can only be measured by invasive techniques. Nevertheless, a variety of bodily responses (e.g., heart rate, blood pressure, blood volume, electrodermal responses, muscle tension, and brain waves) can be measured from the periphery of the human body. Such responses are the focus of this book.

This volume was written for students, clinicians, and researchers who would like to become familiar with the basic methods, data, and concepts that relate bodily responses to emotional states. This relationship is of interest to a wide range of disciplines in the behavioral and biological sciences—including biology, medicine, psychiatry, psychology, and physiology. We have tried to address the material to readers with these various backgrounds, without presupposing a specialty in any of them. Preliminary drafts of this book have been used as a text for two psychology courses. One, entitled Psychophysiology of Emotion, at the University of Southern California was accompanied by a laboratory, which served to introduce the procedures of research involving psychophysiological measurement. The other, entitled Motivation and Emotion, was given at California State University, Los Angeles.

This volume consists of nine chapters that cover the following material: Chapter 1—presents an overview of some basic physiological principles and recording techniques; Chapter 2—discusses some of the types of stimuli that cause changes in bodily responses; Chapter 3—relates individual differences in personality and emotional factors to differences in physiological responses; Chapter 4—relates differences in bodily responses to the major forms of psychopathology; Chapter 5—discusses the relationship between bodily responses and behavioral performance; Chapter 6—relates general states such as sleep and stress to bodily responses; Chapter 7—reviews the bodily responses that accompany psychosomatic illnesses; Chapter 8—discusses the modification of bodily responses by various learning techniques, including Pavlovian conditioning, instrumental conditioning, and biofeedback training; Chapter 9—presents the application of bodily responses to the detection of deception.

The principles that guided our selection and presentation of material were (a) the representativeness of current research activity, (b) the intrinsic interest level for the reader, (c) conciseness, and (d) readability. In regard to this last principle, a glossary of terms and abbreviations used in this volume follows this preface.

A Glossary of Terms and Abbreviations

$\overline{A}$ Autonomic Balance Score
AEP Average Evoked Potential
AER Average Evoked Response
ANS Autonomic Nervous System
BPM Beats Per Minute
BV Blood Volume
CER Cortical Evoked Response
CNS Central Nervous System
CNV Contingent Negative Variation
DBP Diastolic Blood Pressure
DR Defensive Response
EEG Electroencephalogram
EKG (ECG) Electrocardiogram
EMG Electromyogram
EOG Electrooculogram
GSR Galvanic Skin Response
HR Heart Rate
HRL Heart Rate Level

MAP Muscle Action Potential
OR Orienting Response
PC Palmar Conductance
PP Pulse Pressure
PNS Parasympathetic Nervous System
PV Pulse Volume
RA Respiratory Amplitude
REM Rapid Eye Movements
RR Respiration Rate
SBP Systolic Blood Pressure
SCL Skin Conductance Level
SCR Skin Conductance Response
SNS Sympathetic Nervous System
SPL Skin Potential Level
SPR Skin Potential Response
SRR Skin Resistance Response
SSS Sensation Seeking Scale

1
Overview of Emotions and Bodily Responses

The concept *emotion* covers a wide spectrum of behavior and experience. It is readily identified in personal conscious awareness, for it represents the intense experiences of joy and pleasure, or of fear and anger. The concept may be extended to include more prolonged states of *mood*, or less specific states like *feelings* or *affect*. Here are represented likes and dislikes and reactions of pleasantness or unpleasantness. When qualities of personality are described in terms of their characteristic emotional or feeling tone, reference is made to *temperament*. For example, an individual may be described as of even temperament, or stormy temperament.

This book is about bodily reactions associated with emotions. More specifically, it is about those particular bodily reactions, such as heart rate, brain waves, and blood pressure, that can be measured from intact, healthy, and feeling people while they are in different situations and experiencing different emotions. We will therefore focus on the particular responses that can be measured from the periphery of the body rather than the physiological and chemical changes that usually can be measured only by invasive techniques, such as implanting electrodes within the body.

The material reviewed in this book comes from various sources. The primary scientific disciplines from which the material is drawn are the fields of *psychophysiology* and *psychobiology*. As the terms imply, these disciplines are concerned with the interrelationships between psychological states (such as emotions) and physiological responses.[1]

In this first chapter we will briefly: (a) put the issue of the relationship between bodily reactions and emotions into historical perspective, (b) review a few basic principles of physiology, and (c) identify the bodily responses that will be discussed in later chapters.

HISTORICAL PERSPECTIVE AND ISSUES

From man's earliest conjectures about behavior, the notion of "emotional experience" has been present. The idea that bodily reactions are intimately involved with emotions can be found in the writings of the ancient philosophers and poets. Even today, our language is replete with references to this relationship. For example, we use phrases like: "red with rage," "butterflies in the stomach," "cold sweat," "trembling with fear," and the like to describe emotional distress.

As efforts were made to define precisely the term *emotion* several ingredients were seen as necessary to a comprehensive definition.[2] One of them clearly involved the presence of unique bodily activity. Others referred to conscious experience and to provoking stimulus conditions. Young (1961) defined emotion as "an acute disturbance of the individual, psychological in origin, involving behavior, conscious experience and visceral function." Hunt's (1941) definition was broader in scope:

> In certain emergency situations of biological significance to the organism, usually involving the blocking of some vital drive or some threat to the well-being of the organism, there is an interruption of the current behavior with the appearance of innate responses of a patterned nature. These responses are particularly noticeable in the viscera, but also contain peripheral elements and may be accompanied by specific conscious content [p. 250].

One important outcome of early conjectures about physiological reactions and emotions has been the realization that there is a subtle relation between feeling states and bodily activity. Psychophysiology is the research specialty that is concerned with studying these relations. One of psychophysiology's major activities has been to manipulate behavior factors, like emotional stimuli and experiences, while observing the re-

---

[1]The subject matter of the relatively new discipline of psychophysiology was discussed by Ax (1964). The differences between physiological psychology and psychophysiology were reviewed by Stern (1964).

[2]Readers interested in an historical account of efforts to define the concept of emotion will find one in Young (1973).

sultant effect upon bodily responses that could be objectively measured from outside the body—responses like pulse rate, blood pressure, palmar sweating, muscle tension, and brain wave activity. Psychophysiology, then, provides one particular approach to the study of emotions—one that emphasizes emotion–bodily-response relationships.

What are the specific relationships between bodily reactions and emotional experiences? Historically, two general views regarding this relationship can be identified. The first view maintains that bodily reactions play a controlling function in emotions, that they to some degree control and determine what we feel. The second view posits that bodily reactions are secondary effects of emotions and, while they do not control emotions, they can be used as indicators of emotion.

Controlling Function of Bodily Reactions

One of the earliest and most influential theories that proposed a controlling function of bodily reactions on emotions was the James–Lange theory. This theory was developed in the 1880s by the American psychologist William James and the Danish physiologist C. G. Lange, independent of one another. Broadly stated, the James–Lange theory held that consciousness of certain bodily reactions is the essential element in emotional experience. That is, some stimulus situations produce certain bodily reactions (e.g., pounding of the heart and other visceral responses) and the perception of these reactions *is* the emotion. James (1890) expressed the theory in the following way:

> Common sense says, we lose our fortune, are sorry and weep; we meet a bear, are frightened and run; we are insulted by a rival, are angry and strike. The hypothesis here to be defended says that this order of sequence is incorrect, . . . that the more rational statement is that we feel sorry because we cry, angry because we strike, afraid because we tremble [pp. 449–450].

What James is saying is that we feel emotional because we sense our body reacting. According to this view, bodily reactions and the perception of those reactions are controlling factors in the experience of emotions. It can be seen that without bodily reactions there would be no emotion. It also follows that each different emotion must be accompanied by different bodily reactions.

The James–Lange theory was seriously criticized and challenged in the late 1920s by Walter Cannon. Central to Cannon's criticisms were the following points: (*a*) When the bodily reactions that typically occur in emotion are prevented from occurring (as with transection of the spinal cord and vagus nerve, and removal of the sympathetic nervous system) emotional behavior in animals is not visibly altered. (b) The same bodily reactions occur in all emotions, hence these changes cannot produce qualitatively different emotions. (c) The viscera have fewer sensory nerves than other structures, hence people are typically unaware of the physiological processes occurring there. (d) Bodily reactions have a relatively long latency period, whereas reaction time for emotional responses is often much shorter. (e) Drugs, like adrenalin, that produce bodily reactions do not necessarily produce emotional reactions. Partly out of disenchantment with the James–Lange theory, Cannon developed his own neurophysiological theory of emotions, called the Cannon–Bard theory. This theory emphasized the role of subcortical structures, such as the thalamus and hypothalamus, in emotions.[3]

The James–Lange theory might seem to have been completely discredited by Cannon's criticisms. However, the evidence reported by Hohmann (1966) cautions us against too quickly discarding it. According to the James–Lange theory, a complete lesion in the spinal cord will reduce emotional experiences because such lesions would reduce messages from the viscera reaching the brain. Cannon posits that such lesions would have no effect on emotions as the thalamus and hypothalamus are not affected by spinal cord lesions. He reported that dogs with such lesions still reacted emotionally, although he pointed out there is no way to know whether the animals actually "felt emotion." Consistent with the James–Lange theory, however, human patients with spinal cord lesions reported feeling less anger, fear, and sexual excitement after the lesion than before. However, all of the patients still reported acting emotional. As one patient who had a lesion comparable to that referred to by Cannon, reported:

> Sometimes I act angry when I see some injustice. I yell and cuss and raise hell, because if you don't do it sometimes, I learned people will take advantage of you, but it just doesn't have the heat to it that it used to. It's a mental kind of anger [Hohmann, 1966, p. 151].

There are many contemporary theories of emotion. Strongman (1973) describes 20 such theories in his introductory chapter. While only a portion would be called psychophysiological theories, most involve two fundamental features: (a) an evaluation of environmental events as of vital significance to the organism, and (b) the presence of bodily activity that the person sees or perceives in terms of these significant events.

One example of an explanation of emotional experience in terms of physiological reactions and cognitive interpretations is suggested by the

---

[3]Neurophysiological theories and research findings regarding emotion have been reviewed by Glass (1967) and Grossman (1967).

following experiment, which was reported by Schachter and Singer (1962). Bodily reactions were manipulated by injecting college students with a drug (epinephrine) that causes physiological changes (e.g., increases in heart rate) and injecting others with a placebo. Cognitive factors were varied by accurately informing some of the students that the injection would cause bodily reactions while not informing others. All students were then left in a waiting room with an experimental accomplice who tried to make the subjects feel either euphoric or angry. The emotional reactions of the students to the accomplice were then rated by an observer.

Two important sets of results were observed in this experiment. First, students who knew that their physiological reactions were due to the injection (the informed group) showed fewer emotional reactions than students who had no ready cognitive explanation for their physiological reactions (the noninformed group). This indicates that cognitive factors play an important role in emotions. Second, students who were injected with the placebo and who experienced few or no physiological reactions, exhibited fewer emotional reactions than students who were injected with epinephrine. This suggests that bodily reactions also play an important role in emotions. Schachter and Singer concluded that in order for there to be a full-blown emotional experience, bodily reactions must occur and the person must believe that these reactions are due to the environmental stimuli. Thus, in this experiment (a) subjects who did not have bodily reactions (the placebo group) failed to have emotional experiences, and (b) subjects who thought that their bodily reactions were due to an injection and not environmental stimuli (the informed group) also failed to have full-blown emotional reactions. Material in later chapters will further illustrate how both bodily responses and cognitive factors interact to produce emotional reactions (see also Schachter, 1971).

Indicating Function of Bodily Reactions

A second theory regarding the role of bodily reactions in emotions is one that interprets these reactions as useful indicators of emotional states.[4] Different emotional states are assumed to be associated with different types and patterns of bodily reactions. This assumption is

[4]The distinction between controlling and indexing functions of bodily responses in regard to emotions was made by Mandler (1962). Investigators who think that different emotions are not associated with different peripheral bodily reactions frequently support an *activation theory of emotions*. Advocates of this activation theory consider concepts such as level of activation and level of arousal to be of more scientific value than concepts such as fear, anger, etc.

rooted in the common experience that different emotions (e.g., joy and sorrow, love and hate) feel different and therefore must differ physiologically. Thus, this theory assigns specific indexing functions, but not controlling functions, to bodily reactions.

Although our personal experience may lead us to believe that different emotions are associated with different bodily reactions, the research results do not strongly support this hypothesis. There are several reasons for this. First, "true emotions" are difficult to manipulate in a laboratory situation. How does one go about creating strong feelings of fear, anger, love, hate, etc. in the laboratory? Second, it is impossible to measure all the relevant bodily reactions simultaneously. Thus, failure to find physiological differences between different emotions only indicates that negative results apply to the particular responses measured in that study.

Ax (1953), however, did find evidence of physiological differences between two strong emotions: anger and fear.[5] In order to produce anger in the laboratory situation, the experimenter was very rude, critical, and insulting to the subjects. In order to produce fear, mild shocks were given to the subjects, sparks began to fly from the instrument to which the subject was attached, and the experimenter exclaimed with alarm that there existed a dangerous short-circuit. Of the 14 physiological measures obtained, 7 were significantly different between the anger and fear situations. For example, the increase in diastolic blood pressure was greater during anger than fear whereas the increase in the number of muscle tension potentials was greater during fear than anger.

Before taking a look at more details of research relating bodily activity and emotional behavior, some review of physiology is necessary, as well as a closer look at some of the response systems to be considered. First, brief attention will be paid to the way the nervous system contributes to emotion and to the control of bodily activity. Then, the most frequently used responses will be described with special emphasis on how they are measured.

SOME BASIC PHYSIOLOGICAL PRINCIPLES

The nervous system of higher organisms can be classified into two major sections, the *central nervous system* (CNS) and the *autonomic nervous system* (ANS). The central nervous system consists of the brain and spinal cord. The principal functions of the central nervous system are to receive and process sensory information and to regulate bodily

[5]Also see Funkenstein (1955) and Schacter (1957).

movements. The autonomic nervous system consists primarily of nerves that lie outside the CNS, although some of the autonomic nerves originate in the CNS. The principal function of the autonomic nervous system is to regulate the internal and relatively involuntary responses (e.g., those of the viscera and glands) that are associated with emotions.

The Central Nervous System

The basic building block of the CNS is the *neuron* (nerve cell). The CNS consists of over 10 billion of these neurons. The typical neuron consists of three parts: the dendrites, the cell body, and the axon. When a neuron is stimulated, there is an electrical charge called a *nerve impulse.* The nerve impulse travels along the dendrite to the cell body and then down the axon away from the cell body. When the nerve impulse reaches the end branches of the axon, adjacent neurons become stimulated and in this way the nerve impulse is transmitted up and down the CNS.

The end branches of the axon, however, do not actually make direct physical contact with the adjacent neurons. The place where the axon of one neuron comes in close proximity to the dendrite of another neuron is called a *synapse.* When the nerve impulse reaches the endings of the axon, there is a release of chemical transmitters which cross the synaptic cleft and these chemicals stimulate the next neuron. Several different chemical transmitters have been identified, some of which will be mentioned in the discussion of the autonomic nervous system.

Neurons are not distributed randomly in the CNS. Instead they occur as well organized structures (with connections to other structures) with rather specific functions. For example, there are certain areas of the cerebral cortex that have specific sensory and motor functions. Electrical stimulation to these areas of the cortex can cause sensations and movements. Some of the important brain areas involved in emotion have been identified, but the total integrated picture is not fully understood. One well-documented fact is that surgical removal of the cerebral cortex will cause animals to become hyperexcitable. The decorticate animal will become over-reactive and fly into a rage at the slightest provocation. However, the decorticated animal's attack is poorly directed toward the provoking stimulus and is shortlived. Cannon called this type of behavior *sham rage.*[6]

This fact suggests that the cerebral cortex normally inhibits certain subcortical "emotional centers." Thus, when the cortical inhibitory mechanisms are removed, the inhibitions are also removed and the ani-

---

[6]The differences between sham rage and "normal" rage are described in many physiological psychology textbooks (e.g., Morgan, 1965).

mal becomes "over-emotional." More selective surgery has shown that removal of the cingulate gyrus (which lies just below the neocortex, see Figure 1.1) will cause the sham rage, but removing only the neocortex does not. In fact, removal of only the neocortex (leaving the cingulate gyrus untouched) will produce an unusually placid or nonemotional animal. It would appear, therefore, that the cingulate gyrus has a primary inhibitory function over the lower emotional centers.

One of the most important subcortical emotional centers is the *hypothalamus* (see Figure 1.1). The hypothalamus is a relatively small collection of neurons near the center of the brain. Stimulation of the posterior portion of the hypothalamus can elicit a variety of emotional responses. For example, stimulation of the posterior portion of the hypothalamus in an animal that has an intact cortex can elicit a rage reaction that, unlike sham rage, is well-directed toward the instigating stimulus. If the posterior hypothalamus is surgically removed, the animal will show only partial or fragmentary emotional responses.

Although the hypothalamus is an important center for the integrated expression of emotions, it is not the only brain site involved.

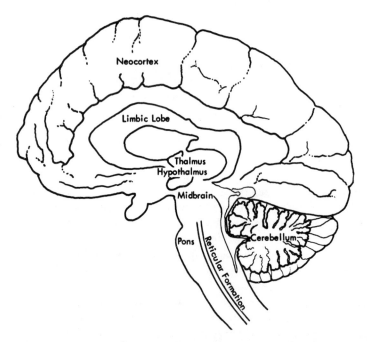

FIGURE 1.1. Schematic diagram of the human brain sectioned along the median plane.
[Reprinted with permission of Macmillan Publishing Co., Inc. from *Sleep: An experimental approach* by W. B. Webb. Copyright © 1968 by Wilse B. Webb.]

Surgical removal and stimulation of other subcortical structures can also alter an animal's emotional reactions. These additional subcortical structures constitute a complex neural circuit called the *limbic system* (e.g., see the limbic lobe in Figure 1.1). This system is part of the evolutionarily "old brain" and lies just above the thalamus and includes portions of the thalamus. The specific structures, and their interconnections, which make up the limbic system are beyond the scope of the present book.[7] The interworkings of the neocortex, limbic system, and hypothalamus are not fully understood and much remains to be learned.

The Autonomic Nervous System

The autonomic nervous system is subdivided into two branches, the *sympathetic nervous system* (SNS) and the *parasympathetic nervous system* (PNS). These two branches differ in both function and structure. The SNS is functionally associated with bodily responses that mobilize the energies of the organism, get it ready to meet a threatening object with fight or flight, or prepare it to "meet emergencies," as different authors have characterized it. It tends to be more active during stress and strong emotions. The PNS, on the other hand, serves to conserve energy, to slow down certain bodily responses. The PNS is more active during relaxation and rest. Most important is the fact that the two branches work together and complement one another in maintaining a balance of bodily function (homeostasis).

The SNS nerve fibers leave the spinal cord in the middle region (see Figure 1.2). Most of these fibers go directly into the sympathetic chain (also called sympathetic ganglia) where they synapse with other nerves. The nerve fibers that come from the spine and go into the sympathetic chain are called *preganglionic fibers.* The nerve fibers that leave the sympathetic chain and then go to the organs are called *postganglionic fibers.*

The PNS nerves leave the spinal cord in the upper and lower regions (see Figure 1.2). The PNS nerves do not synapse in the sympathetic chain, instead they synapse near the organ they influence. The most important of the parasympathetic nerves, the *vagus nerve*, leaves at the base of the brain (the medulla) and travels down through the chest and diaphragm to the heart, lungs, stomach, pancreas, kidney, and intestines. The lower parasympathetic fibers go to the colon, bladder, and reproductive organs.

While some organs are innervated by only one division of the ANS (e.g., as can be seen in Figure 1.2, the sweat glands, peripheral blood

---

[7]The anatomy as well as behavioral functions of the limbic system and hypothalamus are reviewed by Guyton (1976).

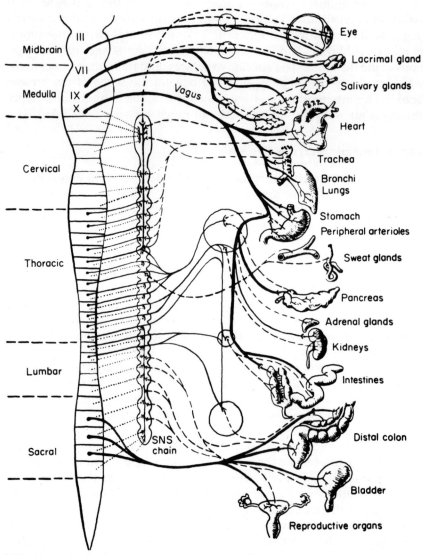

FIGURE 1.2. Schematic diagram of the autonomic nervous system. The sympathetic division is made up of those fibers that leave the spinal cord in the middle region (dashed lines and thin solid lines). The parasympathetic division consists of those fibers originating from the upper and lower parts of the spinal cord (thick solid lines). [From Sternbach, 1966.]

vessels, and adrenal glands are innervated solely by the SNS), most organs are innervated by both the SNS and PNS. In those cases, the SNS and PNS branches usually produce opposite reactions. Among the most significant of the bodily reactions produced by the SNS are pupil dilation, inhibition of salivation (causing a dry mouth), secretion of sweat (causing clammy hands), constriction of blood vessels in the periphery of the body (causing cold hands and feet), dilation of blood vessels in the muscles and brain, increased heart rate, increased blood pressure, and inhibition of digestive processes. Among the bodily reactions produced by the PNS are pupil constriction, increased salivation, decreased heart rate, decreased blood pressure, and increased digestive processes.

There are many other significant differences between the two branches of the ANS. One set of differences arises from chemical and hormonal factors like the nature of the neurotransmitter substance active at the synapse. The predominate chemical transmitter in the parasympathetic system is acetylcholine (Ach) and the system is sometimes described as *cholinergic*. The SNS is termed *adrenergic* because the postganglionic fibers are energized by noradrenaline (also called norephinephrine). Similar chemical relations also occur at higher levels of the nervous system. For example, some central nervous system structures involved in emotion, like the hypothalamus, are in some regions adrenergic and in others cholinergic, in the sense of being controlled by acetylcholine, norepinephrine, and related chemicals.

The intimate interaction of hormones and the ANS is seen in other terminologies. The vagus nerve (a PNS nerve) is closely associated with secretions of the pituitary gland and pancreas. As a result the PNS is sometimes referred to as a vagal–insulin system. As such it is contrasted with the sympathetico-adrenal system, which emphasizes the close association of sympathetic activity with secretions of the adrenal gland.

Although study of the role of anatomical and chemical determiners of emotional behavior is very important to full understanding of bodily responses and emotion, the field is detailed and extensive. Since the present treatment is very limited in scope, the interested reader is referred to more complete discussions.[8]

---

[8]Reference material on the autonomic nervous system varies widely in orientation and comprehensiveness. Netter (1962) emphasizes medical illustrations. Other sources are schematic (e.g., Weil, 1974) whereas still others emphasize clinical concepts (e.g., Appenzeller, 1976). For students of psychology the best source is contained in textbooks of physiological psychology (e.g., Deutsch & Deutsch, 1966; Grossman, 1967). Some such texts (e.g., the last two mentioned) devote a chapter or more to the physiological basis of emotion. Also, see Candland, Fell, Keen, Leshner, Plutchik, and Tarpy (1977).

BODILY REACTIONS ACCOMPANYING EMOTION

Six Primary Responses

Many bodily responses may occur during emotional states. The six responses referred to most often throughout this book will now be reviewed. They are (a) heart rate, (b) blood pressure, (c) blood volume, (d) electrical properties of the skin (electrodermal responses), (e) muscle potentials, and (f) brain waves (electroencephalogram). These bodily responses can be recorded on an instrument called a *polygraph*. A polygraph is used to record a number of bodily changes simultaneously on a moving strip of paper in the form of ink tracings. The measuring techniques and physiological control of each of these responses will now be presented.

HEART RATE

The heart is a muscular organ slightly larger than the fist. It serves as a pump, circulating blood through the body with each muscular contraction (heart beat). When the heart relaxes, blood flows into the heart from the veins, and when the heart contracts, blood is expelled out into the arteries.

The most common psychophysiological measure of heart activity is *heart rate* (HR). Heart rate is usually expressed in units of beats per minute (BPM).[9] The adult human heart normally has a rate of approximately 70 BPM, although the rate can fluctuate from over 100 BPM to less than 50 BPM as a result of emotions or other factors. Both the sympathetic and parasympathetic divisions of the ANS influence heart rate (see Figure 1.2). Stimulation of the sympathetic division accelerates heart rate while stimulation of the parasympathetic division decelerates heart rate.

Contraction of the heart muscle is associated with changes in electrical potentials. The electrocardiogram (abbreviated EKG or ECG) is a measurement of these electrical potentials produced by the heart during contraction. The EKG can be measured by placing electrodes on both sides of the body and recording the voltage changes associated with the pumping action of the heart. A polygraphic recording of the EKG is shown in the top portion of Figure 1.3. The large spikes, called R waves, represent the heart beats. Heart rate can be measured by counting the number of R waves per unit of time. Heart activity can also be measured

[9]The recording techniques and mechanisms involved in heart rate have been reviewed by Brener (1967).

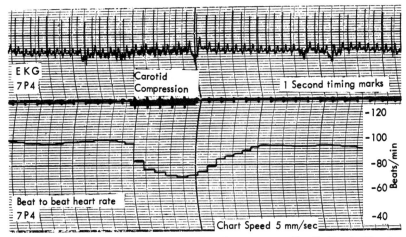

FIGURE 1.3. EKG recording (top) and cardiotachometer recording (bottom). [Courtesy of Grass Instrument Company, Quincy, Massachusetts.]

by calculating the interval between the successive R waves (called either the interbeat interval [IBI] or heart period (HP]).

However, a more convenient method of measuring HR involves using a device called a *cardiotachometer*. This device can be triggered by the EKG electrical signal which then produces a printout that is proportional to the time since the last heart beat. Thus, HR can be read more directly by the cardiotachometer. The bottom portion of Figure 1.3 shows the cardiotachometer printout controlled by the EKG signal above. The figure shows a clear HR deceleration (going from about 100 to 70 BPM) followed by an acceleration (going from 70 to about 95 BPM) in the cardiotachometer printout.

BLOOD PRESSURE

The force of the heart beat drives blood through the large arteries and then to the smaller capillaries. Each time the heart contracts (pushing blood out to the arteries), there is an increase in the pressure of the blood against the walls of the arteries. Each time the heart relaxes (filling with blood), there is a decrease in this pressure. The maximum pressure that occurs when the heart contracts is called *systolic blood pressure* (SBP), while the minimum pressure that occurs when the heart relaxes is called *diastolic blood pressure* (DBP). The difference between the systolic blood pressure and the diastolic blood pressure is called *pulse pressure* (PP).

Human blood pressure can be measured with a device called a sphygmomanometer. This device consists of an inflatable cuff that is wrapped around the upper arm over the brachial artery. The cuff is filled with air to a point at which the blood cannot flow through the artery. Then the air pressure is slowly reduced until the sound of the blood going through the artery in spurts with each heart beat can be heard (using either a microphone or stethoscope). These sounds are called *Korotkoff sounds*. Systolic blood pressure is the amount of pressure (expressed in millimeters of mercury displacement) at the time the Korotkoff sounds can first be heard. The air pressure is then gradually reduced further until the Korotkoff sounds change and disappear. The reason that the Korotkoff sounds cannot be heard is that the air pressure of the cuff has gotten so low that the blood can now flow continuously. This marks the point of diastolic blood pressure.

Blood pressure can change in rather large degrees with each beat of the heart. The manual sphygmomanometer technique just described can be used to measure blood pressure at only one point in time. Therefore, use of the manual sphygmomanometer can lead to unrepresentative blood pressure values. For this reason, automated techniques, which can measure blood pressure continuously with every few heart beats, have been devised.[10]

The blood pressure of the normal young adult is about 120/80, which means that systolic blood pressure is 120 mm Hg and diastolic blood pressure is 80 mm Hg. However, large changes in blood pressure (usually increases) can accompany emotional states. These changes can be momentary or chronic in duration. Chronic high blood pressure (hypertension) is a major health problem. Essential hypertension, a form of chronic high blood pressure, is thought to be due primarily to chronic states of tension, stress, and anxiety.

Blood pressure is determined by the amount of blood being pumped by the heart and the amount of resistance in the blood vessels (due to their constriction and dilation). The more blood pumped by the heart and the more the blood vessels constrict, the higher the blood pressure. Since blood pressure is dependent upon these various factors, it is determined by both the SNS and PNS divisions of the autonomic nervous system.

BLOOD VOLUME

As just discussed, blood vessels can both constrict and dilate. When blood vessels constrict (called *vasoconstriction*), the volume of blood that

---

[10]Techniques of recording blood pressure are discussed by Lywood (1967) and Tursky (1974). The measurement of arterial *pulse wave velocity* may prove to be a valid indirect index of relative changes in blood pressure on a beat-by-beat basis (Gribbin, Steptoe, & Sleight, 1976).

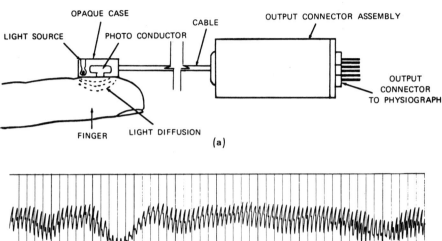

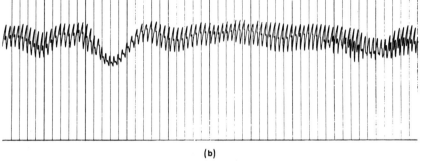

FIGURE 1.4. **(a) A photoelectric plethysmograph.** [Courtesy of Narco Bio-Systems, Inc., Houston, Texas.] **(b) A typical record of blood volume and pulse volume.**

can flow through them is decreased. When blood vessels dilate (called *vasodilation*), the volume of blood is increased. The body contains only a fixed amount of blood (about 5 liters) and the blood is distributed to various organs and muscles depending on the specific demand at the time. For example, blood volume may decrease in the extremities due to vasoconstriction in the hands and feet but increase in the brain due to vasodilation at that location. We can sometimes see this redistribution of blood, for example, when a person blushes with embarrassment or grows pale with fear.

Blood volume can be measured with devices called *plethysmographs*.[11] There are several classes of plethysmographs that differ in their operating principles. One type is called a photoelectric plethysmograph. It works on the principle that light is absorbed into tissue in proportion to the amount of blood contained in the tissue. An illustration of a photo-

[11]The methods of recording blood volume and pulse volume have been presented by Brown (1967) and Cook (1974).

electric plethysmograph is shown in Figure 1.4a. A small beam of light is directed toward an area of skin. The amount of light reflected back from the skin is proportional to the amount of blood in this area of tissue. A light sensitive measuring device (a photocell or photoconductor) is used to measure the amount of light reflected back from the skin. The output of the photocell is then amplified and used as an index of blood volume.

A typical record obtained from a plethysmograph is shown in Figure 1.4b. The individual pulse waves are associated with the pumping action of the heart. The ascending portion of each pulse wave reflects heart contraction and the descending portion reflects heart relaxation. The amplitude of the pulse wave, measured from trough to peak of the wave, is termed *pulse volume* (PV). The overall changes from baseline reflect changes in total *blood volume* (BV). When blood vessels constrict there is usually a decrease in both PV and BV. Conversely, when blood vessels dilate there is usually an increase in both PV and BV.

Blood volume is controlled by the constriction and dilation of blood vessels. Since the blood vessels in the periphery of the body are innervated by the SNS and not the PNS (see Figure 1.2), blood volume responses are useful indices of SNS changes that occur during emotional states.

ELECTRODERMAL RESPONSES

The skin has certain electrical properties that are closely associated with psychological processes such as attention and emotion.[12] The electrical property of the skin that is most commonly measured is the skin resistance response (SRR). The skin resistance is usually expressed as its reciprocal, skin conductance. Skin conductance can be measured by applying a very small electrical voltage across two metal electrodes placed on the skin (usually the palms or fingers). With appropriate instrumentation, one can then measure the basal conductance of the skin (called *skin conductance level* [SCL]) as well as momentary phasic increases in conductance (called *skin conductance responses* [SCRs]). The occurrence of SCRs can be elicited by the presentation of environmental stimuli and SCRs can also occur spontaneously in the absence of stimulation. The later responses are called spontaneous or nonspecific SCRs. The upper portion of Figure 1.5 shows an example of a phasic skin conductance response. During emotional states there is generally an increase in SCL and an increase in the size and frequency of SCRs. In

[12]More information regarding the electrodermal response can be found in Edelberg (1972), Fowles (1973), Grings (1974), and Lykken and Venables (1971). In addition, Prokasy and Raskin (1973) devoted an entire book to the various aspects of this response. It should be noted that another term for electrodermal response is *galvanic skin response* (GSR).

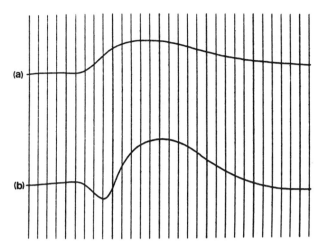

FIGURE 1.5. Simultaneous recording of (a) skin conductance response and (b) skin potential response. [From Grings, 1974.]

other words, the skin usually becomes a better conductor of electricity during emotional states.

The SCL and SCRs are expressed in micromho units. A micromho is one millionth of a mho, and a mho is the reciprocal of ohm, the standard resistance unit (notice that mho is ohm spelled backwards). Since the values are dependent upon the size of the electrodes it is recommended that the units be expressed as micromhos per square centimeter of electrode size. Most SCLs are in the range of 5–20 micromhos/cm^2 while the typical SCR is about 1 micromho/cm^2.

Thus far we have discussed the measurement of tonic SCL and the magnitude of phasic SCRs. Other characteristics of SCRs can also be measured. For example, the amount of time: (*a*) it takes for a response to begin following a stimulus (*latency*), (*b*) from the onset of the response to its peak (*rise-time*), and (*c*) from the peak of the response to its return to the prerevponse level (*recovery time*). In addition, the number of responses that occur within some specified time interval (*response frequency*) can simply be counted. Thus, there are several measures that can be obtained from a recording of skin conductance. Each of these measures can yield important information about the state of the subject.

Another electrical property of the skin is called *skin potential*. Skin potential can be measured without applying any electrical voltage across the skin. Rather, one electrode is placed over an area of skin with a high density of sweat glands (e.g., the palms) and another is placed over an area of the skin with few sweat glands (e.g., the forearm). The difference in electrical potential between the two electrodes can then be measured. As with skin conductance, one can measure the tonic potential difference between the electrodes (called *skin potential level* [SPL]) and the momentary phasic changes in skin potential (called *skin potential responses* [SPRs]). An example of an SPR is shown in the lower portion of Figure 1.5. Notice that the SPR is usually a biphasic response with an initial negative potential change followed by a positive potential change.

The activity of the sweat glands is the primary contributor to the electrodermal measures described. Sweat glands are innervated solely by the SNS postganglionic fibers (note Figure 1.2) and therefore electrodermal measures are useful indicators of SNS activity during emotional states. SNS activity is associated with increased sweat gland activity and this activity in turn is associated with high skin conductance (SCLs and SCRs).

MUSCLE POTENTIALS

Muscle tension is a frequent correlate of emotion and therefore it is desirable to have an objective indicator of skeletal muscle activity. The contraction of muscle fibers is accompanied by electrical potentials that can be measured in various forms. By inserting a fine needle in a muscle, the electrical signal from a single muscle unit can be picked up and recorded. The electrical activity of larger groups of fibers can be recorded without piercing the skin, by simply measuring the voltage from electrodes placed on the surface of the body over the muscle. When measurement is made from electrodes within the muscle the term *electromyogram* (EMG) is commonly used. When measurement is made from electrodes on the surface of the skin above the muscle either the term *surface electromyogram* or *muscle action potential* (MAP) is used.

If electrodes are placed over a muscle group (e.g., the forearm flexor) and the electrical signal is appropriately amplified, each movement of the arm or hand will appear as a burst of activity on the recording (see Figure 1.6). Although the movement may be invisible to the naked eye, it can be recorded electrically. In order to quantify a record like that shown at the top of Figure 1.6, it is possible to count the number of bursts in some time interval, but measuring the amplitude of the response would be difficult and time consuming. To overcome this difficulty, it is common practice to integrate or summate the potential, so that a total amount of electrical activity in a given period of time is graphically registered.

The muscle potential integrator serves as an electrical adding device. There are different ways to achieve such integration. One is called a *contour follower*. It smooths out or averages over time the spikes of mus-

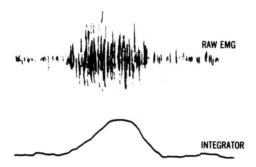

FIGURE 1.6. Muscle action potentials. Raw form and integrated form. [From Coulborn Instruments Applications Manual. Reprinted by permission.]

cle potential. The rise and fall of the recording pen is proportional to the ongoing raw potentials. In the lower portion of Figure 1.6, the rise and fall of the record can be seen to parallel the amplitude of the bursts in the raw EMG record. The EMG is typically quantified in millivolts (thousandths of a volt) or microvolts (millionths of a volt).

Unlike the responses we have discussed up to this point, skeletal muscles are innervated directly by fibers from the CNS and not the ANS. These fibers originate from the spinal cord or, in the case of muscles in the head and face, they originate from the brain stem.[13]

ELECTROENCEPHALOGRAM AND RELATED MEASURES

The brain is constantly emitting small electrical potentials. These rhythmic potentials can be recorded from electrodes placed on the scalp and the result is called an *electroencephalogram* (EEG). These scalp potentials are usually in the neighborhood of 20–50 microvolts.

One of the earliest discoveries made about the EEG was that certain wave frequencies (expressed in cycles per second called Hertz, and abbreviated Hz) occur more often than others (see Figure 1.7). These frequencies were labelled with Greek letters such as: *delta waves* (less than 4 Hz), *theta waves* (4–7 Hz), *alpha waves* (8–13 Hz), and *beta waves* (greater than 13 Hz). Alpha waves are the most common rhythm in the normal awake adult EEG and are associated with a state of relaxation. Beta waves are the next most common and are associated with alert or excited states. Theta waves are not common to the normal awake adult EEG but they are the predominant rhythm in young children. Delta waves also are not common to the normal awake adult EEG but they do occur during certain stages of sleep.

[13]More details regarding muscle potentials can be found in Goldstein (1972).

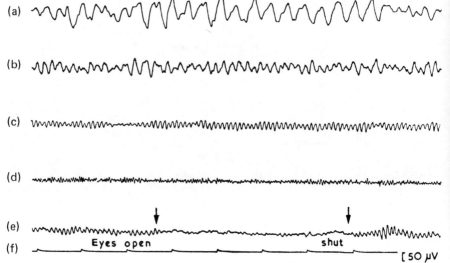

FIGURE 1.7. Examples of (a) delta waves, (b) theta waves, (c) alpha waves, (d) beta waves, (e) blocking of alpha activity by eye opening, and (f) 1-second time marker and calibration. [From Cooper, Osselton, & Shaw, 1969.]

One way of quantifying the EEG is to express the percentage of time that a specific wave frequency is present. Another method is to express the power of the electrical signal in the specific band of frequencies. An important part of this quantification is the specification of the electrode location that was used to record the EEG.

Presentation of a stimulus can elicit responses from the brain called *cortical evoked responses* (CERs). These CERs cannot ordinarily be seen in the EEG tracing since their amplitude is very small (a few microvolts) compared to the ongoing background brain rhythms. However, the evoked response can be measured by presenting the stimulus a number of times and taking an average of the EEG tracings that follow the stimulus presentations. By means of the averaging technique, the random background fluctuations in the EEG cancel out whereas the non-random cortical evoked response signal is added. Thus, the averaging procedure allows one to obtain a clearer picture of the cortical evoked response. Due to this averaging technique, the CER is often referred to as an *average evoked response* (AER) or *average evoked potential* (AEP).

The average cortical evoked response consists of a complex series of positive and negative electrical changes that occur shortly following the presentation of a stimulus. As can be seen in Figure 1.8, the major components of the cortical evoked response are labeled by their polarity

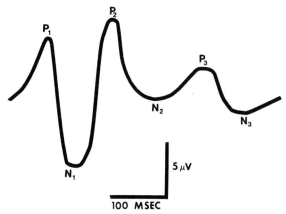

FIGURE 1.8. Average cortical evoked response to an auditory stimulus (P means *positive electrical voltage* and N means *negative electrical voltage*). [Adapted from Satterfield, 1972.]

(positive [P] or negative [N]) and by their sequential order (P1, N1, P2, N2, P3, N3). The appearance of the cortical evoked response will vary depending on the modality of the stimulus (e.g., visual or auditory), the intensity of the stimulus, the location of the recording electrodes on the scalp, and the psychological state of the subject.

One special form of cortical evoked response is a slow wave potential shift that can be recorded from the scalp during the performance of a stimulus–response task. The situation in which this response has been most extensively studied involves the presentation of stimulus pairs where the first stimulus precedes the second stimulus by a few seconds and a manual response (e.g., pushing a button) is required of the subject at the onset of the second stimulus. During the interval between the two stimuli, a slow negative potential appears on the surface of the scalp. The occurrence of this negative potential seems to depend upon the existence of a contingent relation between the two stimuli. For this reason, this response has been termed the *contingent negative variation* (CNV). The CNV is an important response because of its relationship to the psychological processes of expectancy and preparation.

The specific physiological basis of the EEG is not well understood. However, it clearly reflects the summation of electrical activity of many cells in the brain and therefore is a measure of CNS activity and not ANS activity.[14]

[14]The EEG has been reviewed by Shagass (1972) and the CNV was discussed by Tecce (1972).

TABLE 1.1
Summary of Six Major Response Measures

Response system	Primary organ	Unit of measurement	SNS effect	PNS effect	Recording technique
1. Heart rate (HR)	heart	beats per minute (BPM)	increase	decrease	electrodes (placed on both sides of the heart)
2. Blood pressure (SBP, DBP, PP)	heart and blood vessels	millimeters of mercury pressure (mm Hg)	increase	decrease	sphygmomanometer (with pressure cuff wrapped around the upper arm)
3. Peripheral blood volume (BV, PV)	blood vessels	relative change in millimeters (mm)	decrease[a]	none	photoelectric plethysmography
4. Electrodermal skin conductance (SCL, SCR)	sweat glands	micromhos	increase	none	electrical voltage (applied across electrodes on the skin)
5. Muscle potential (EMG, MAP)	skeletal muscles	microvolts or millivolts	none	none	electrodes (placed on the skin above the muscle)
6. Electroencephalogram (EEG, CER, CNV)	brain	microvolts	none	none	electrodes (placed on the scalp)

[a] This table lists only SNS and PNS effects; it is important to remember that determination from parts of the CNS are also important.

Table 1.1 summarizes the material for each of the six bodily responses discussed in terms of their primary controlling organ, unit of measurement, SNS effects, and PNS effects. The recording techniques used to measure each response are also shown.

Five Additional Bodily Responses

Other responses that are importantly related to emotions but less commonly measured will now be reviewed briefly. These additional responses are: (a) respiration, (b) temperature, (c) salivation, (d) pupil size, and (e) gastric motility.

RESPIRATION

The most common measures of breathing are *respiration rate* (expressed in number of breaths per minute), *respiration period* (the time between inspirations), and *respiration volume* (the amount of air inhaled and exhaled). All of these can be measured using a device called a *pneumograph*, which consists of a flexible rubber tube placed around the chest or abdomen. When the subject inhales and exhales, the air in the pneumograph is displaced and this can be electrically recorded. Respiration is regulated by both the CNS and ANS.[15]

TEMPERATURE

Measurements of temperature are typically of two types, *general* or *local*. General temperature can be obtained by using either an oral or a rectal thermometer. Local temperature can be determined by attaching a thermister to specific parts of the body surface (e.g., hands and face). Local temperatures are largely determined by vasoconstriction and vasodilation and therefore are controlled indirectly by the sympathetic division of the ANS.[16]

SALIVATION

Measures of salivation typically reflect the volume of secretion and its chemical composition. The volume can be estimated by weighing cotton balls held in the mouth or by placing a small suction cup over the opening of a salivary duct. The salivary glands are innervated by both the sympathetic division and the parasympathetic division of ANS. Salivary output is inhibited by the sympathetic division and is increased by the parasympathetic division.[17]

---

[15]A discussion of respiration can be found in Stein and Luparello (1967).
[16]For more details on temperature, see Trolander (1967).
[17]The methods of recording salivation have been reviewed by Katz, Sutherland, and Brown (1967) and White (1977).

PUPIL SIZE

The pupil of the human eye can constrict and dilate such that its diameter can range from 1.5 to more than 9 mm. Pupil size can be photographed by infrared movie film. To quantify pupil size, the movie film can be projected on a screen and the size of the pupil in each frame can be measured manually with a ruler or electronically with a photocell. More automated instruments are also available. Pupillary constriction is mediated by the parasympathetic division of the ANS while pupillary dilation is under the control of the sympathetic division of the ANS.[18]

GASTRIC MOTILITY

Activity in the gastrointestinal tract can be measured using a small device that is swallowed. The device may be either a magnet (the field of which can be measured from the surface of the body) or a transmitter (which emits radio signals that can be detected and recorded outside the body). Thus, the rate and intensity of contractions in the stomach and intestines can be recorded and quantified. The stomach and intestines are innervated by both the PNS and SNS.[19]

CONCLUSION AND OUTLINE OF THIS BOOK

The purpose of this chapter has been to provide a general introduction that will help the reader achieve greater understanding of the later chapters. Hopefully, the reader will refer to this chapter for quick reviews of the primary responses, their measurement, and physiological control. Table 1.1 should prove especially useful for review purposes. Also, a glossary of frequently used terms and abbreviations (see page xi) has been included for the convenience of the reader.

All of the physiological responses reviewed in this chapter can be measured in two basic ways: *tonic* (basal) *levels* and *phasic changes*. For example, heart rate can be measured while an individual is resting and then when a stimulus is presented or a task is required. Both measures can yield important information. However, it must be emphasized that the size and even direction of the phasic changes can be affected by the tonic level. This can be presented best by an example. If an individual has a high resting basal heart rate level (e.g., 100 BPM), then an emotional stimulus may produce a phasic increase in HR of only 1 or 2 BPM whereas if the basal level were low (e.g., 60 BPM) then the phasic re-

---

[18]The pupillary response has been discussed by Goldwater (1972) and Hess (1972).
[19]The gastrointestinal system has been reviewed by Wolf and Welsh (1972).

sponse may be much larger (e.g., 20 BPM). The dependence of the size and direction of phasic responses on the initial basal level is called the *law of initial values.*[20] Statistical methods of correcting for initial basal levels have been devised. However, for our purposes, the reader need only remember that the occurrence of phasic changes can be influenced by initial tonic levels. In general, the higher the tonic level the smaller will be the phasic increase caused by a stimulus.

In the subsequent chapters, we will indicate how the types of bodily responses reviewed in this chapter are related to emotions. Following is a chapter by chapter breakdown of topics to be reviewed: Stimulus determiners of these bodily responses (Chapter 2); individual differences in these responses and their relationship to individual differences in emotions and personality traits (Chapter 3); the relationship between these bodily responses and types of behavior disorders (Chapter 4); the relationship of these bodily responses to specific behaviors (e.g., motor performance, learning, and acting out aggression) (Chapter 5); the relationship of these bodily responses to general behavioral states (e.g., sleep, stress, and relaxation) (Chapter 6); the role of these bodily responses in psychosomatic illnesses (Chapter 7); how these bodily responses can be modified by learning experiences (Chapter 8); and the use of these bodily responses in detecting deception (lie-detection) (Chapter 9).

---

[20]The *law of initial values* has been elaborated upon by Sternbach (1966, Chapter 4).

2
Stimuli that Cause Bodily Responses

Chapter 1 identified the principal bodily responses that will be discussed in this book. This chapter will review some stimuli that cause changes in these bodily responses. The types of stimuli to be reviewed are: (*a*) simple environmental stimuli, (*b*) task-related stimuli, (*c*) fear-producing stimuli, (*d*) internal self-generated stimuli, and (*e*) complex social stimuli. The importance of sets and attitudes in determining the physiological responses to stimuli will also be reviewed.

SIMPLE ENVIRONMENTAL STIMULI

Suppose that a soft but novel noise were to occur unexpectedly while you were reading this page. What, if any, physiological responses would be elicited by such a simple environmental stimulus? Surprisingly, a large number of significant bodily reactions would be momentarily elicited. For example, the pupils would dilate, skin conductance would increase, blood vessels in the hand would constrict while those in the head would dilate, the oscillating frequency of the electroencephalogram would increase, heart rate would decrease, and respiration would become irregular.

This set of momentary bodily responses is called an *orienting response* (OR). The OR is a general cluster of physiological responses that occurs in response to a wide range of novel environmental stimuli. It also occurs in a wide variety of lower animals as well as in infant and adult human beings. In addition to the physiological responses just mentioned, you might turn your head toward the source of the noise stimulation. Hence, the OR is considered to be a general alterting response that is associated with the act of attending to environmental stimuli. For this reason, the OR was originally referred to as the "investigatory" or "what-is-it?" response.

One of the characteristics of an OR is that it will become smaller in size and eventually disappear with repeated stimulations. This process of diminishing OR magnitude when the stimulus is repeated several times is called *habituation*. [1] It is a very adaptive process, for it is self-protective to attend to novel or surprising environmental stimuli and it is also adaptive to stop attending to old and familiar stimuli. Variables that affect the amount and rate of habituation include stimulus intensity, stimulus complexity, the perceived importance of the stimulus, and the time interval between stimulus repetitions. In general, the more intense, complex, or important the stimuli, or the longer the time between repetitions, the slower the habituation. Figure 2.1 shows the habituation curves for skin potential responses elicited by tones of five intensities (60, 70, 80, 90, and 100 decibels [dB]). Notice that the rate and amount of habituation is significantly affected by the tone intensity. The most intense tone (100 dB) shows the least habituation whereas the three weakest tones (60, 70, and 80 dB) show the fastest and most profound habituation.

The OR can be contrasted with the *defensive response* (DR). The DR refers to a cluster of physiological responses that occurs in response to very intense or aversive stimuli. The OR and DR consist of many of the same response components, including SCRs. The primary response differences between them are (*a*) the OR involves heart rate deceleration whereas the DR involves heart rate acceleration, and (*b*) the OR involves vasodilation in the head whereas the DR involves vasoconstriction in the head.

In an effort to compare ORs and DRs, Hare (1973) measured bodily responses from 20 female undergraduate volunteers. Half of the volunteers had previously expressed intense fear of spiders while the other

---

[1]The orienting response and its habituation have been extensively studied. One of the most influential papers on the topic was written by the Russian investigator, Sokolov (1960). Another influential article dealing with the heart rate component of the orienting response was reported by Graham and Clifton (1966). A more recent review of the data and theories in this area was written by Graham (1973).

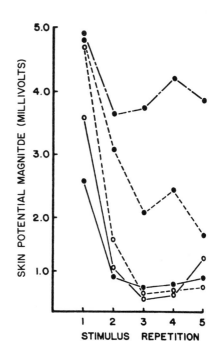

FIGURE 2.1. Skin potential habituation curves to tone intensities of 60 (O———O), 70 (●———●), 80 (O---O), 90 (●---●), and 100 dB (●---●). [Adapted from Uno & Grings, 1965.]

half had expressed little or no fear. Physiological responses were recorded while the subjects observed a series of 24 neutral slides (pictures of common objects and landscapes) and 6 slides of spiders. The results revealed that the subjects who were afraid of spiders responded to the spider slides with heart rate acceleration and a trend toward vasoconstriction in the head. Thus, the spider slides elicited DRs from these subjects. On the other hand, subjects who were not afraid of spiders responded to the spider slides with heart rate deceleration and a trend toward vasodilation in the head, which is consistent with an OR. Thus, ORs were elicited when the pictures of spiders were considered interesting and novel, whereas DRs were elicited when the stimuli were considered repugnant and aversive.

Figure 2.2 shows a portion of a polygraph record obtained from one of the subjects who had expressed a fear of spiders. Shown from top to bottom are heart rate (measured with a cardiotachometer), palmar skin conductance, dorsal skin conductance, cephalic vasomotor response (measured from a photoelectric plethysmograph on the forehead), digital vasomotor response (measured from the thumb), eye movements, and respiration. As can be seen in Figure 2.2, no appreciable response to the neutral slide occurred. The spider slide, however, elicited heart rate

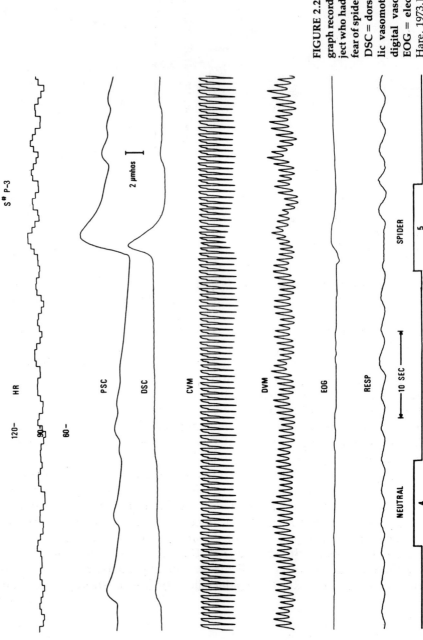

FIGURE 2.2. Portion of a polygraph record obtained from a subject who had expressed an intense fear of spiders. PSC = palmar SC, DSC = dorsal SC, CVM = cephalic vasomotor activity, DVM = digital vasomotor activity, and EOG = electrooculogram. [From Hare, 1973.]

acceleration, large palmar skin conductance responses, vasoconstriction in the forehead, and a brief inhibition of respiration. In short, a DR was elicited by the spider slide.[2]

TASK-RELATED STIMULI

What bodily responses are elicited by stimuli that require the subject to perform a task? Physical tasks (e.g., running or riding a bicycle) are known to elicit momentary increases in heart rate, blood pressure, respiration rate, and skin conductance. But what about tasks that require only mental activity?

In order to study the bodily responses that occur during a mental task, Kahneman, Tursky, Shapiro, and Crider (1969) presented 10 college students with arithmetic problems of varying difficulty. The students were instructed to add either a 0, 1, or 3 to a series of digits. Pupil diameter, heart rate, and skin resistance were recorded while the students solved each problem. As indicated in Figure 2.3, each problem was paced so that a "ready" signal was given at second 1, the instructions to add 0, 1, or 3 were given at seconds 5 and 6 ("task"), the digits were given at seconds 10–13 ("hear"), and the answers were given at seconds 15–18 ("talk"). As shown in Figure 2.3, all three physiological responses indicated sympathetic increases (pupil dilation, heart rate acceleration, and decreased skin resistance) while subjects solved the problems, followed by sympathetic decreases after the subjects gave the answers. In addition, all three physiological responses indicated the greatest sympathetic increases for the most difficult problems ("add 3"). These results indicate that autonomic responses are associated with mental activity and that, moreover, they are associated with the degree of effort involved in the mental activity.

In another study, 94 male college freshmen were given a variety of tasks to perform while heart rate and skin conductance responses were recorded. Two types of tasks were presented: (a) those that required internal mental processes and (b) those that required attention to external stimuli. An example of a task that required internal mental processes involved listening to words spelled backwards and then mentally rearranging the letters and identifying the words. An example of a task that required attention to external stimuli involved observing and noting the colors of a flashing light. The results demonstrated that both types of

---

[2]An extension of Hare's findings using pictures depicting mutilation was reported by Klorman, Weissberg, and Wiesenfeld (1977).

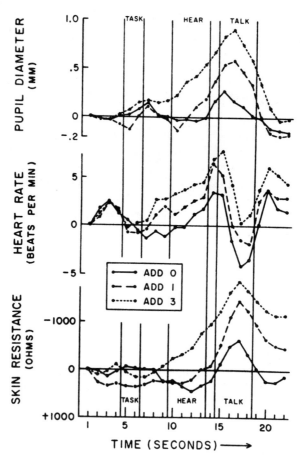

FIGURE 2.3. Second-by-second changes in pupil diameter, heart rate, and skin resistance during stages of solving arithmetic problems. [From Kahneman, D., Tursky, B., Shapiro, D., & Crider, A. Pupillary, heart rate, and skin resistance changes during a mental task. *Journal of Experimental Psychology*, 1969, 79, 164–167. Copyright 1969 by the American Psychological Association. Reprinted by permission.]

tasks produced increases in skin conductance. However, heart rate decreased during tasks that required attention to external events but increased during tasks that required internal mental operations.

Data such as those reviewed above led to the formulation of a provocative hypothesis.[3] Stated most simply, the hypothesis is that intake

---

[3] The data obtained during various environmental intake and environmental rejection tasks were reported by Lacey, Kagan, Lacey, and Moss (1963). The intake–rejection hypothesis has been presented in various sources, for example, Lacey (1967). This hypothesis has been critically reviewed by Hahn (1973).

of environmental stimuli is associated with heart rate deceleration, whereas rejection of environmental stimuli or attention to internal states is associated with heart rate acceleration. This intake–rejection hypothesis is generally compatible with the OR–DR distinction. Novel or interesting stimuli, which the subject intakes, will elicit ORs that are characterized by heart rate deceleration. Intense or aversive stimuli, which the subject rejects, will elicit DRs that are characterized by heart rate acceleration. Probably the most controversial aspect of this hypothesis is the assertion that heart rate deceleration facilitates the intake of sensory information. Thus, this hypothesis predicts that people can see and hear better when their heart rates slow down. Some of the evidence regarding this prediction is reviewed in Chapter 5.

Cortical evoked responses to auditory clicks were measured in another experiment where the task was varied.[4] In the attend task, subjects were instructed to pay attention to the clicks and count the number of occasional clicks that were very faint. In the ignore task, the same subjects were instructed to read a book and to ignore the clicks. It was found that the N_1 and P_2 components of the averaged cortical evoked response (see Figure 1.8 for a review of these components) were much larger to the clicks in the attend task than in the ignore task. In addition, the evoked response to the occasional faint clicks, which the subjects were instructed to count, contained a large P_3 component that was not present otherwise. This late positive wave (P_3) also occurred when an expected click failed to occur. Thus, the P_3 component (also called P_{300} because its average latency is approximately 300 msec) is thought to be an important cortical index of orienting and decision-processes. For this reason, the P_3 component is the focus of much research.

FEAR-PRODUCING STIMULI

Bodily responses have been measured in the presence of fear-producing stimuli, such as stimuli associated with the sport of parachuting. Parachuting provides an unusual opportunity for studying approach and avoidance conflict in subjects under intensely ego-involving circumstances. On the one hand, there is the desire to approach a new adventure but, on the other hand, there is the desire to avoid injury and possible death. The gradients of approach and avoidance tendencies can be measured by recording responses at various times before and after

---

[4] Picton and Hillyard (1974) studied the effects of attention on the cortical evoked response. For reviews of the literature, see Karlin (1970) and Näätänen (1975).

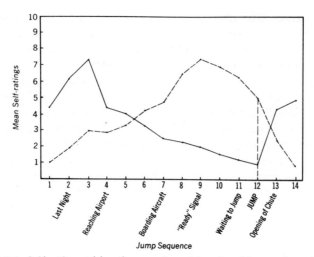

FIGURE 2.4. Self-ratings of fear for experienced (——) and inexperienced (novice) (---) parachutists as a function of a sequence of events leading up to and following a jump. [From Kagan, Haith, & Caldwell, 1971, based on Fenz & Epstein, 1967.]

the parachute jump. As will be shown later, degree of experience is an important variable in determining the steepness of the approach and avoidance gradients.[5]

The relative strengths of gradients were first checked by means of self-ratings by experienced and inexperienced parachutists. Fear of jumping was rated at different time stages before and following a jump. The ratings began the day before the jump, for it had been observed that early enthusiasm often gives way to fear and uncertainty on the day of the jump. Figure 2.4 summarizes the self-ratings of fear at various times before, at, and after the jump for experienced and inexperienced jumpers. The most striking difference between experienced and inexperienced jumpers is not in their degree of subjective fear but rather the time that the peak fear is felt. The inexperienced jumpers are relatively calm at the beginning of the day but become increasingly fearful as the time to jump approaches. The experienced jumpers, however, show their greatest fear at the beginning of the day and then have a decreasing gradient of fear, which reaches its lowest point at the moment of the jump.

These fear gradients suggest important differences between experienced and inexperienced jumpers. The researchers interpreted this dif-

[5]An extensive series of experiments involving arousal and performance in the sport parachuting task was conducted by Epstein and Fenz and their associates. Representative references include: Epstein and Fenz (1962) and Fenz and Epstein (1967).

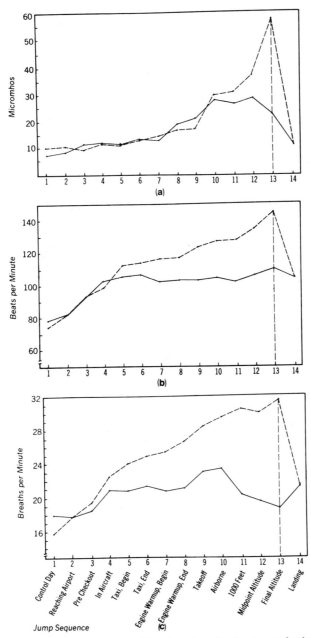

FIGURE 2.5. Responses of experienced (——) and novice (–––) parachutists, as a function of events leading up to and following a jump: (a) skin conductance, (b) heart rate, and (c) breathing rate. [From Kagan, Haith, & Caldwell, 1971, based on Fenz & Epstein, 1967.]

ference to mean that the experienced jumpers work through their fears early in the day and then are able to develop adequate coping mechanisms so as to jump in a fairly relaxed state. The question then becomes: If experience modifies the gradient of subjective fear, will the bodily responses also become controlled in this process?

To answer this question, heart rate, skin conductance, and respiration were measured from two groups of 10 parachutists. The inexperienced (novice) group had made less than 10 static-line jumps and no free-fall jumps. Physiological measurements were made on both groups before boarding the aircraft, throughout the flight of the aircraft, and shortly after landing.

Figure 2.5 shows skin conductance, heart rate, and breathing rate at various points during the jump sequence. The response curves for experienced jumpers level off shortly after takeoff, becoming even lower before the jump; whereas the curves for novices continue to rise up to the point of the jump. These results indicate that fear-producing stimuli cause physiological responses, but that with practice people can learn to keep their physiological arousal levels from becoming excessive.

INTERNAL SELF-GENERATED STIMULI

People's thoughts can affect their mood states. This simple fact has been used to study the relationship between emotions and facial muscle activity (Schwartz, 1975). Subjects were requested to imagine happy, sad, and angry situations for 3 minutes each while surface electromyograms were recorded from four facial muscles. Figure 2.6 shows the location of the four muscle groups that were monitored: frontalis muscles, which are located in the forehead; corrugator muscles, which are in the region of the eyebrow; masseter muscles, which are in the cheek area; and depressor muscles, which are near the mouth and jaw.

It was found that self-generated emotional thoughts were associated with different patterns of facial muscle activity. It should be emphasized that this facial muscle activity was very small, not usually noticeable by merely looking at the facial expression of the subject. Happy thoughts were associated with low corrugator EMG activity (compared to a resting period) and slight increases in the depressor EMG activity. Sad thoughts were associated with increased corrugator EMG activity. Finally, angry thoughts elicited increased muscle activity in all four facial locations, especially in the depressor region. These results indicate that self-generated thoughts can produce discrete bodily reactions and that the facial EMG may prove to be a sensitive method of objectively measuring subtle mood states.

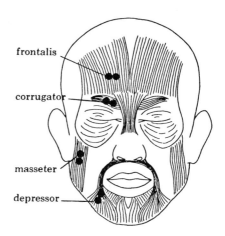

FIGURE 2.6. Location of electrodes used to measure electromyographic (EMG) activity of four facial muscles during different emotions. [From Schwartz, G. E. Biofeedback, self-regulation, and the patterning of physiological processes. *American Scientist,* 1975, *62,* 314–324. Reprinted by permission, *American Scientist,* Journal of Sigma Xi, The Scientific Research Society of North America.]

COMPLEX SOCIAL STIMULI

The relationship of a psychotherapist to a client in the counseling situation is assumed to be highly significant in determining the effectiveness of the therapy. Much of this relationship involves subtle forms of personal–emotional interaction. The effective therapist is not passive but interacting, with definite feelings toward the client and the client's problems. By psychophysiological measurements, simultaneously obtained from both a patient and therapist, some objectification of this interaction process is possible.

Consider a setting appropriate for such observation. A therapy room would be equipped with the necessary lead-in connections for physiological measurements and a microphone for tape recording of conversation. A one-way screen would be used so that an observer could operate tape recording equipment and a response polygraph to obtain a coordinated record of conversation and physiological activity from both the patient and the therapist during a therapy session. The observer would employ some form of sociometric device to rate the interactive behavior of the two individuals.

Such a setting was employed by Di Mascio, Boyd, and Greenblatt (1957) in one of the early studies of this type, where heart rate and skin temperature measures were recorded and a manually operated signaling device permitted the observer to code on the polygraph the social interactions of the participants. Instances of tension release and tension increase on the part of the patient were noted. Examples of tension release were when the patient joked or laughed, or showed satisfaction. Tension increase was indicated when the patient asked for help, withdrew out of the field, expressed disagreement, showed passive rejection, or indicated antagonism by responses that deflated the other participant's status.

An intensive analysis was made of an extended series of therapy sessions with one patient. The primary measure of interest was the correlation between the physiological measure and the social-interaction ratings. These correlations were employed to describe the interaction process graphically as is shown in Figure 2.7. Among the conclusions observable for the patient were that tension release was accompanied by a decrease in heart rate (r = −.58) whereas an increase in tension was accompanied by a faster heart rate (r = +.69). For the therapist, an increase in patient's tension was accompanied by a faster heart rate for

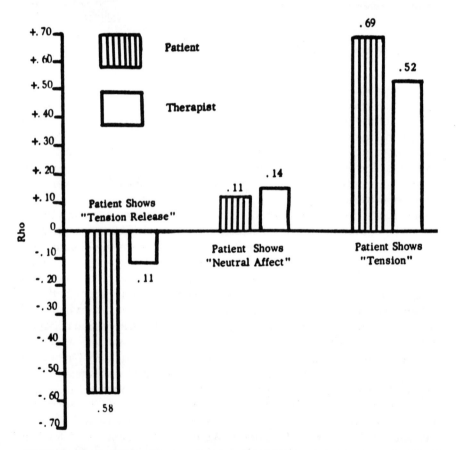

FIGURE 2.7. Correlations (measured in rho) of social interaction ratings and physiologic activity (heart rate) during psychotherapy. [From DiMascio, Boyd, & Greenblatt, 1957.]

the therapist (r = +.52). In general, the neutral interviews failed to produce any significant correlations for either the patient or the therapist.

Other researchers have emphasized other responses and have experimentally manipulated aspects of the interaction situation. For example, the effects of varying the attitude of an interviewer upon the physiological reactions of both the person being interviewed and the interviewer were investigated. The two experimental manipulations of the interviewer's attitude were intended to be either supporting or threatening. Two groups of female outpatients were matched for age and symptomatology. One of the groups was praised and the other group was criticized. Muscle action potential pickup from the chin and the neck of both the patient and the therapist were recorded, as was the heart rate.

The general procedure involved having the subjects tell a story from a standard Thematic Apperception Test (TAT) card. After the story had been completed, the experimenter read the subject the designated reactions as follows. For the group being praised:

> Excellent. Now I am going to tell you why I like your story. You had only a brief time to make up this story, but you have made unusually good use of this time. Your description of the scene aroused my curiosity and your interpretation showed imagination of the sort which is required in composing good fiction, in which the action moves along fast enough to keep your interest alive until the end. Do you see why I liked your story?

For the group being criticized:

> Well, now I am going to criticize your story. The beginning of a good short story arouses your curiosity about something. The rest of the story then moves along fast enough to keep your interest alive until the end. Your story, however, was not that kind of a story. That is, I don't think it would be the kind of story that you would enjoy reading in a magazine. Do you agree with that?

Immediately after the patients replied to the reaction, a rest period was introduced for a period of about 40 seconds. Then another set of reactions was given. After that, another person, introduced as the interviewer and also connected for physiological measurements, came into the room and interviewed the subject.

The muscle potentials recorded from the neck did not yield differential responding, whereas those recorded from the chin did. In the patient, there was a falling curve of tension immediately after the patient's reply to the praise reaction but a flat curve of sustained tension was obtained following the response to the criticism reaction. For the examiner, there was also a decrease in the muscle tension following the praise reaction and there was no such decrease following criticism. For the heart rate measure, the criticized group showed a rise in heart rate following the reactions whereas the praised group showed a reduction. This difference in heart rate was sustained during the subsequent interview.[6] Thus, criticism produced sustained muscle tension and elevated heart rate while praise led to decreased muscle tension and decreased heart rate.

Kaplan (1963) extended these types of observations to small group psychotherapy. A total of 37 therapy sessions between a therapist and two schizophrenic patients were studied, employing electrodermal recordings on all three persons. The measures were the number of spontaneous SCRs and the total amplitude of electrodermal activity in a prescribed time. An observer rated the types of interactive behaviors. The results indicated that the more the therapist participated and asked questions of the patients, the more she responded. She also responded more as her patients expressed more negative reactions and more tension responses. In turn, the patients responded more as they participated more and responded less when they gave more positive responses. They gave more responses when the group as a whole gave more negative responses.

Extending these observations to normal subjects in small peer group arrangements, Kaplan, Burch, Bloom, and Edelberg (1963) tested the notion that when a strong affective relationship exists between members of a peer group, the affective responses of group members to a pattern of interpersonal activity will vary together and will be reflected in correlated autonomic activity within the group. They selected three groups each composed of four medical students on the basis of a questionnaire in which the students had been asked to designate those peers that they liked and those that they disliked. The groups were organized to represent (a) affectively positive, (b) affectively negative, and (c) neutral arrangements. Then the groups met for five discussion sessions of 45 minutes each during which their behavior was observed and electrodermal behavior was continuously recorded. It was learned that subjects who engaged in interpersonal relations with peers they either liked or did not like exhibited more correlated physiological activity than subjects who were neutral to each other. All of the affective pairs (positive pair members and negative pair members) gave physiological responses in reacting socially to their pair mates that were greater than those given

[6]Differential physiological reactions to supportive (praise) and threatening (criticism) situations were reported by Malmo, Boag, and Smith (1957).

by neutral pairs. In general, then, the correlated activity (social and physiological) occurred within pairs on the basis of their liking or disliking one another and were not present when the relationships among individuals were neutral.[7]

In summary, bodily responses in complex social situations seem to be related to the emotional reactions that occur in those situations. However, the results are difficult to interpret because of the very complexity of the situation. Physical exertion, or even the intensity of mental activity, might contribute as much as do emotions to the observed bodily responses. The uncontrolled nature of the social interaction makes it an interesting place in which to study bodily responses but also makes it a difficult situation. The controlled laboratory situation has some very important advantages in understanding the bodily reactions to emotional stimuli.

THE EFFECTS OF SET AND ATTITUDE ON RESPONSES TO STIMULI

Thus far we have discussed some of the bodily responses associated with a variety of stimuli. Differences between stimuli have been emphasized. For example, we have discussed simple environmental stimuli, task stimuli, fear-producing stimuli, and complex social stimuli. However, the importance of a subject's set or attitude toward the stimulus has not been adequately emphasized.

Both a set and an attitude involve a predispostion to respond in a certain way. They can also be described as an expectancy or an anticipation of events to occur. A convenient distinction can be made between sets that are explicit and those that are implicit. In a discussion of this distinction, Sternbach (1966) defines explicit sets as those produced by the experimenter, usually through instructions or suggestions. Implicit sets, on the other hand, are inferred, rarely verbalized, and generally occur implicitly through attitudes brought into the laboratory and attitudes created by experimental conditions, such as the characteristics of the experimental situation.

In a study of explicit sets (Sternbach, 1964), six students agreed to participate in a "drug" experiment consisting of three experimental sessions. The subjects were told that they would take three different pills that would have different effects on the activity of their stomachs, that the effects would be brief in duration and there would be no residual side

---

[7]For an overview of this type of research see Shapiro and Schwartz (1970).

effects. All subjects were given a placebo that actually contained a small magnet. The magnet was used to record gastric activity. The instructions for the three pills were:

> *Relaxant.* This pill relaxes the stomach. You will feel your stomach full and heavy in a few minutes and it will reach a peak in about 15 minutes at which time you will feel bloated. Then it will wear off gradually and be gone in another 15 minutes.

> *Stimulant.* This pill is a stimulant to the stomach. You will feel your stomach churning pretty strongly in a few minutes, and it will reach a peak in about 15 minutes at which time you feel some cramps. Then it will wear off gradually and be gone in another 15 minutes.

> *Placebo.* This pill has no effect. We use it for a control, a placebo essentially, to see the effects of taking a pill on stomach activity. You won't feel anything.

For four of the six subjects, the changes in the rate of stomach contractions were dramatically in the instructed direction. The other two subjects did not show much change. However, the overall effect of the instructions was statistically significant.

Ethnic differences have been evaluated as a source of implicit sets.[8] The work was based on an earlier report that proposed differences in behavioral expression of pain among Irish, Italian, Jewish, and "Yankee" (third generation American) patients in medical situations involving pain. It was concluded that the differences were related to orientations and values (implicit sets) in the subculture groups. "Yankees" responded to pain in a matter-of-fact way. They acted as if they should be a good, noncomplaining patient. Irish have similar displays of the experience but their response appears due to a tight inhibition and tight control, more of a burden to be endured, yet the sense of suffering comes through to an observer. In contrast, Jews and Italians have ethnic group approval for overt expression of pain. Loud suffering serves to rally sympathetic responses from family and friends. The primary concern of the Jew is the meaning of the pain, what it represents, and what the future implications are. For Italians, pain is an evil, a form of suffering not to be endured but to be avoided. Outer expressions are aimed at elimination of pain.

The investigators placed classified ads in the newspaper to obtain volunteer subjects, all of whom were housewives. Electric pain threshold measurements were administered to 15 subjects in each of four groups, and recordings of skin potential were made to repeated brief shock stimulations. The skin potential habituation curves to electric shock for the four ethnic groups are illustrated in Figure 2.8. As can be

---

[8]The information on ethnic differences was taken from Sternbach and Tursky (1965).

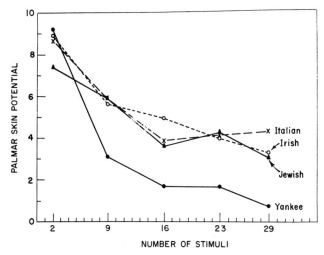

FIGURE 2.8. Habituation curves to shock stimuli for subjects of different subculture groups. [From Sternbach & Tursky, 1965.]

seen, the "Yankee" group showed faster and more complete habituation than the other groups. This finding is consistent with the "Yankee" matter-of-fact attitude of taking things in stride. These results suggest that implicit sets, or attitudes, can have an important influence on bodily responses.

One of the earliest applications of physiological response to attitude measurement involved recording skin conductance responses from white subjects while they were exposed to white and black experimenters. Subjects were engaged in a word association task and their skin conductance was measured while two experimenters made what appeared to be adjustments of apparatus upon the subject during the experiment. One experimenter was black and the other white. Subjects exhibited highly significant differences in electrodermal responses to the two experimenters, with larger responses being made to the black experimenter. However, it should be pointed out that the experimenters differed in ways other than race; one was older, taller, and heavier than the other. Therefore, in addition to skin color, other variables might have influenced the physiological responses of the subjects.

Another study attacked the problem somewhat differently. Two samples of white individuals were found, one showing scale-measured racial prejudices and the other not. The two groups were then shown photographs portraying blacks and whites in various situations while finger pulse volume and SRR activity were recorded. The data indicated

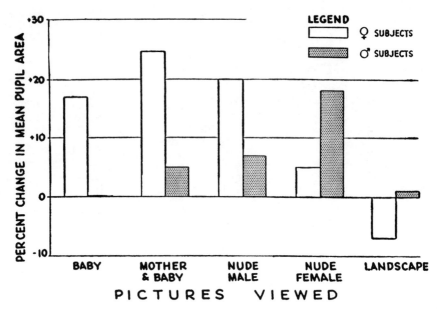

FIGURE 2.9. Changes in pupil size, in terms of percentage of decrease or increase in area, during viewing of various pictures by male and female subjects. [From Hess & Polt, 1960.]

that larger SRRs (but smaller finger pulse volume responses) were given to pictures of blacks by prejudiced subjects. However, there was evidence that the results were complicated by the sex of the subject and the sex of the person in the photographs. The authors also point out that the size of the physiological response does not necessarily indicate a negative attitude toward the stimulus. Conflicting feelings, indecision, or even positive feelings might cause large bodily responses.[9]

One of the most extensively publicized reports of measurement of attitude by physiological responses came from a report asserting that pupil size is related to interest value of visual stimuli.[10] Increases in the size of the pupil were found by these investigators to accompany the viewing of emotionally toned or interesting visual stimuli. The type of data reported are illustrated in Figure 2.9, which shows percentage changes in pupil size to different pictures predicted to have different

[9]Physiological responses and their relationship to racial attitudes were studied by Rankin and Campbell (1955) and Westie and DeFleur (1959). For a more general review see Schwartz and Shapiro (1973).

[10]The relationship between attitude and pupil size was studied by Hess and Polt (1960). For reviews, see Hess (1965, 1972).

interest value for male and female subjects. Striking differences do appear. While these data and related information were given considerable publicity, subsequent extension and replication has not appeared. This has led other researchers to state that autonomic measures, like the pupillary response, reflect only the intensity of attitudes and not the specific properties such as interest value.

CONCLUSION

The material reviewed in this chapter shows that a variety of stimuli can elicit bodily responses. The stimuli range from simple environmental changes, to task-related stimuli, to emotion-producing stimuli, to complex social stimuli. These results demonstrate that a physiological response cannot be interpreted as an indicator of a single specific psychological event. It is not possible to identify a skin conductance response as a fear response or an increase in systolic blood pressure as an anger response. The psychological significance of a physiological response is further complicated by the subject's set or attitude. Still other sources and types of individual differences in bodily responses will be discussed in the next chapter.

3
Individual Differences and Bodily Responses

Emotional behavior varies markedly from individual to individual. The same life situation may produce marked emotional reactions in one person and none in another. Under stress, physiological reactions are very different. Over a half century ago, it was proposed that individuals fall into two broad category types with regard to their autonomic behavior. It was suggested that individual differences in bodily reactions are associated with particular personality traits and proneness to certain types of illness.[1]

One type was called *vagatonic* because of a heightened readiness to respond with the vagus nerve and the entire parasympathetic branch of the autonomic nervous system. Some of the physiological characteristics

[1]In 1910 Eppinger and Hess separated individuals into two groups in terms of the effect that autonomic drugs had on their behavior. One group gave strong reactions to parasympathetic drugs like pilocarpine and atropine while being relatively insensitive to adrenalin. The second group gave strong reactions to adrenalin and minimal reactions to atropine and pilocarpine, thus emphasizing readiness to respond with a sympathetic branch of the autonomic nervous system.

This early work stimulated efforts to classify response patterns according to the anatomical divisions of the ANS. Gillilan (1954) wrote in detail about this type of classification, adding a middle group that he called amphotonic to suggest a continuum of response. Others (e.g., Kuntz, 1945, 1951) presented data from patients to show that such classification is an oversimplification (e.g., that many patients with heightened parasympathetic tonus in gastric ulcer and asthma also react strongly to adrenalin).

of the vagatonic individual are low heart rate, small pupils, and dry skin. Behaviorally, the vagatonic individual was considered to be reserved and "cold blooded" and was thought to be prone to disorders like asthma and gastric ulcers. The second type was termed *sympatheticotonic* and characterized by strong reactions with the sympathetic division of the autonomic nervous system. Such persons were believed to have rapid heart rate, large pupils, and clammy hands. The sympatheticotonic individual was thought to have a lively and excitable temperament and to be prone to illnesses such as high blood pressure and chronically high heart rate.

This early work stimulated later attempts to classify people according to which anatomical division of the autonomic nervous system was dominant for them. Several other basic approaches to the study of individual differences were also tried. There were attempts to measure bodily responses from "normal" people and to identify statistically physiological response patterns or stereotypes. Responses of people who exhibited different personality traits (e.g., high anxious versus low anxious) were also measured in order to identify physiological subtypes. Each of these approaches will be discussed in this chapter.

AUTONOMIC BALANCE

As a point of departure, we will examine a series of studies that measured 20 physiological responses from young children (ranging from 6 to 13 years of age) under resting conditions. Statistical analysis indicated that 7 of the responses were particularly useful in defining a state of *autonomic balance*. The responses were (*a*) salivary output, (*b*) skin conductance level measured from the palms, (*c*) skin conductance level measured from the forearms, (*d*) heart period, (*e*) pulse pressure, (*f*) respiration rate, and (*g*) dermographic persistence. All of the responses with the exception of dermographic persistence were defined in Chapter 1. *Dermographic persistence* refers to the length of time red marks persist on the forearm after being firmly stroked with a thin stylus. The normal range of dermographic persistence was from 3 to 30 minutes.

Values for these responses were combined into a single composite score for each individual. The score was termed an *autonomic balance score*, abbreviated Ā (pronounced "A-bar"). An average Ā score was 70 (indicative of an evenly balanced autonomic nervous system) while scores less than 70 were indicative of SNS dominance and and scores higher than 70 were indicative of PNS dominance. For example, an individual with low salivary output, high skin conductance levels (measured from the palms and forearms), low pulse pressure, short heart period (fast heart beat), short respiration period (fast respiration rate), and short dermographic persistence would get a low $\bar{A}$ score, indicative of SNS dominance. It was found that children with high $\bar{A}$ scores, indicative of PNS dominance, exhibited more emotional inhibition, less excitability, more patience, and more neatness than children with low $\bar{A}$ scores.

The relationship of the $\bar{A}$ measures to anxiety has been studied by Smith and Wenger (1965). Physiological measures were taken from 11 graduate students on two occasions: (a) a few hours before they were to take an important oral examination, and (b) approximately 1 month before or after the oral examination. It was expected that the students would be more anxious on the day of the exam than 1 month before or after the exam. Hence, it was expected that the $\bar{A}$ score would be lower on the day of the exam due to excessive SNS activity. This prediction was confirmed, the mean $\bar{A}$ score on the day of the exam was 57.02 while 1 month before or after the exam it was 69.36. In fact, every one of the students showed lower $\bar{A}$ scores on the day of the examination than on the comparison day. These results indicate a dominance of the sympathetic division of the autonomic nervous system during anxiety and demonstrate the usefulness of the $\bar{A}$ measure.

During World War II, it was suggested that the $\bar{A}$ measure might prove of value in eliminating candidates for flying duty in the U.S. Army who might exhibit extreme emotional reactions of a sort that could interfere with their military effectiveness. While autonomic balance is not openly discussed as such, mention was made of excessive apprehension and emotional instability as factors affecting flight training. Therefore, a program of measurement of aviation cadets was set up at an Army Air Force base and a battery of physiological recordings was made upon a total of 2112 cadets.[2]

Beyond identifying the basic dimension of autonomic balance, the Air Force study concentrated on applications of the information to matters of personal adjustment and psychosomatic health. For health, comparisons were made between aviation students and a sample of combat returnees convalescing from operational fatigue. Ten of the measures showed significant differences between the groups. The results were believed to support the assertion that operational fatigue is characterized

[2]A major amount of information on this military research is contained in a monograph by Wenger (1948).

TABLE 3.1
Results of the Follow-up on the Army Air Force Study:
Respondents to Questionnaire Experiencing Psychosomatic
Disorders and Their Average Original Autonomic Balance
Score[a]

Type of disorder	N	Ā Mean
High blood pressure	23	64.74
Persistent anxiety	33	66.47
Apprehension or fear	49	65.80
Excessive sweating	52	67.30
Heart trouble	21	67.66
Hay fever	52	68.27
Stomach pains	63	68.53
Allergies	78	68.55
Migraine headaches	15	68.99
Arthritis	28	69.74
Asthma	16	70.06
Peptic ulcer	40	70.38
Low blood pressure	12	73.54
No disorders reported	111	68.22

[a] Adapted from Wenger, 1966.

by excessive functioning of the SNS. It was also concluded that the data provided evidence validating the use of physiological response tests as a basis for selection of individuals unsuited for air crew duty.

The work described above was continued after World War II. Some 20 years later, questionnaires were sent to the individuals who participated in the original study. The questionnaires inquired about the occurrence of psychosomatic disorders. Table 3.1 shows the various psychosomatic disorders that were reported, the number of individuals who reported each disorder, and their mean original Ā score. People who developed high blood pressure, apprehension and anxiety, excessive sweating, and heart trouble exhibited low original Ā scores. The interested reader can find a more complete review of these results as well as more data regarding measurement properties of Ā scores (e.g., reliability and validity) and use of Ā scores in a range of medical conditions in Wenger (1966) and Wenger and Cullen (1972).

INDIVIDUAL-RESPONSE STEREOTYPY

Research conducted with the Ā measure found that many individuals do not exhibit response patterns that correspond to the simple notion of

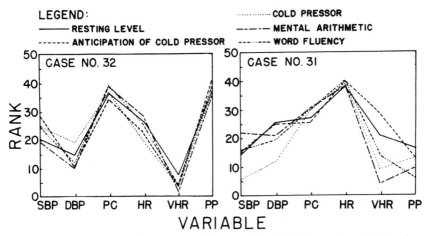

LEGEND:
············· COLD PRESSOR
——— RESTING LEVEL   ———·— MENTAL ARITHMETIC
------- ANTICIPATION OF COLD PRESSOR   ---·····--- WORD FLUENCY

FIGURE 3.1. Comparison of response patterns produced during rest and during four stressors in two individuals. [Adapted from Lacey, J. I. & Lacey, B. C. Verification and extension of the principle of autonomic response stereotypy. *The American Journal of Psychology,* 1958, 71, 50–73. Published by the University of Illinois Press. Reprinted by permission.]

SNS or PNS dominance. Some individuals show mixed patterns, for example, high heart rate and low salivary output (indicative of SNS dominance) as well as low skin conductance (indicative of PNS dominance). Thus, another approach to the study of individual differences has emphasized the existence of autonomic response patterns, or stereotypes. A *stereotype* implies the clustering of response characteristics, and several forms have been suggested. One is called *stimulus stereotypy,* where a particular pattern of response is associated with a particular stimulus situation. Another is termed *individual-response stereotypy* because the response pattern is felt to be characteristic of the individual. Still another is *symptom stereotypy,* where the responses are organized about particular somatic complaints, such as might occur in psychosomatic illness.

In one of the earliest studies of individual-response stereotypy, autonomic responses of normal subjects were measured to see if they exhibited patterns of response that were consistent within a given individual.[3] Autonomic responses were measured while subjects were at rest, while anticipating a noxious cold-pressor task (putting a foot or hand in ice water), while performing the cold-pressor task, while per-

---

[3]An introduction to questions concerning individual response stereotypy can be obtained from Lacey and Lacey (1958). This article also lists references to earlier studies.

forming a mental arithmetic test, and while performing a word fluency test. The autonomic responses that were recorded were *systolic blood pressure* (SBP), *diastolic blood pressure* (DBP), *palmar conductance* (PC), *heart rate* (HR), *variability of heart rate* (VHR), and *pulse pressure* (PP). The similarity of these responses during the different tasks was then examined for each individual. It was found that most people exhibited a consistent idiosyncratic pattern of responses to all of the tasks. As shown in Figure 3.1, Individuals 31 and 32 show different but consistent patterns of responses. Individual 31 responds most with heart rate to all of the tasks while Individual 32 responds most with palmar conductance and pulse pressure to all of the tasks. These are examples of individual stereotypy. Individuals differ from each other in the way they respond physiologically but the pattern for each individual remains consistent across a variety of different situations.

PERSONALITY TESTS AND BODILY RESPONSES

Given the possibility that patterns of autonomic response show individual stereotypy, another question is whether there are relations between personality types and autonomic responsivity. In an effort to explore this question, a variety of research approaches can be utilized. For example, scores obtained on personality inventories can be correlated with measures of autonomic responses. Or, ANS responsivity differences among groups that have been segregated on the basis of personality problems can be observed—such as comparing physiological responses of different psychiatric diagnostic groups using patient subsamples (see Chapter 4). Psychosomatic medical classifications may also be employed (see Chapter 7). This chapter will review some of the evidence regarding the relationship between scores on personality tests and autonomic responses in normal individuals.

Studies relating personality inventory scores and autonomic responses have been of two general types. In the first type, a comprehensive inventory with many scales was administered to a group of individuals on whom autonomic measures were taken under rest or stress conditions. Traits from the inventories were then correlated with the various physiological responses. The second approach has used more specialized devices to define traits of personality. Common examples of such measures have been scales of anxiety, ego-strength, hostility, and perceptual mode. Among comprehensive inventories, the Minnesota Multiphasic Personality Inventory (MMPI) has been typical of a class in which the scales are oriented around psychiatric diagnostic categories, whereas inventories such as the Guilford–Zimmerman Temperament Survey, the Eysenck Personality Inventory, Cattell Scales, and the Omnibus Personality Inventory have all defined traits of a more general nature, not as related to psychiatric diagnostic material.

The rather large number of studies relating personality and inventory scores with physiological measures have yielded low correlations at best. There are many reasons why this might be the case, without indicating the lack of a true relationship between personality and physiological responses. First of all, inventories measure a number of broad traits by means of a small sample of items on which persons designate their typical reactions. Second, there are so many other factors contributing to the variability of the measures that high correlation coefficients are not likely to be obtained.[4]

When research attention is focused on specific traits and predictions are made about particular response systems, the relationship between personality and bodily responses can be seen more clearly. As examples, nine specialized personality traits will be examined with reference to their associated physiological reactivity.

Anxiety

The trait of anxiety is well known as being associated with bodily activity. The person who is chronically anxious or worried is thought to have sweaty palms, shaky knees, and a rapid heart rate. In discussing anxiety, it is common to separate *trait anxiety* from *state anxiety*. The former is a characteristic of the individual whereas the latter is elicited by specific experiential situations. To test the relation of physiological responses to trait anxiety, an inventory measure, such as the Manifest Anxiety Scale (MAS), is commonly used. The MAS consists of items from the MMPI that refer specifically to perceptions of uneasiness and feelings of upsetness, like queasiness of the stomach or sweaty hands. Typical items ask if the individual is subject to frequent headaches, has attacks of nausea, or has cold hands.

Two studies that are typical of work in this area will be reviewed. Haywood and Spielberger (1966) administered the MAS to a large group of students and then selected 61 males to represent extreme scores for high and low trait anxiety. Physiological arousal was measured by taking sweat prints by means of a photometric technique, which indicated a palmar sweat index. Two sweat prints were taken, one before and

[4]A general theory relating personality and physiological change is contained in Roessler (1973). Also, see Arnold (1960).

another during a task of sentence construction and verbal conditioning. On both occasions, the palmar sweat index was higher for the high anxiety group. These results suggest that trait anxiety tends to be positively associated with SNS arousal in at least some situations.

In the second study, Hodges and Spielberger (1966) measured the heart rates of high and low trait anxiety subjects in high and low state anxiety situations. The high state anxiety situation involved a threat of electric shock whereas the low state anxiety situation involved no threat. The threat condition produced a significant increase in heart rate as compared to the no threat condition, but there was no difference between the HR responses of the high and low trait anxiety subjects to the threat of shock. However, differences were found in terms of whether or not the subjects had expressed a fear of shock prior to the experiment. Those expressing fear of shock showed greater heart rate change than those who reported no such fear. Hodges and Spielberger concluded that cognitive appraisal of the situation was an important determiner of the HR response. It is assumed that people who have a high fear of shock interpreted the threat of shock as more threatening than those who have little or no fear. These results indicate that state anxiety is dependent upon the cognitive interpretations of the situation and is positively associated with SNS arousal.

Hostility

Another trait that was defined by a selection of items from the MMPI was referred to as *manifest hostility*. These items ask whether people feel they are getting a raw deal much of the time, or whether they tend to feel pleased when someone is punished for getting caught in a wrongdoing. Studies on this trait have emphasized cardiovascular reactions to frustration. Physiological responses to a frustrating task were observed for individuals who consistently scored at extremes of the hostility scale.

Hokanson (1961) used the manifest hostility scale to select 40 high hostility and 40 low hostility male students, with additional selection based on different tests of hostility. They were then exposed to either high or low frustration manipulations while measurements were made of blood pressure and skin conductance. High frustration consisted of being insulted and degraded by the experimenter for presumably poor performance on a task of counting backwards from 100 by 3s; low frustration consisted of only counting backwards.

The principal physiological measures were the increases in systolic blood pressure and skin conductance during the frustration. As can be

TABLE 3.2
Effects of Frustration upon Systolic Blood Pressure (SBP)
and Skin Conductance (SC) for High Hostile and Low Hostile
Individuals[a]

	Low hostile individuals	High hostile individuals
Low frustration		
SBP (mm Hg)	+5.90	+ 5.00
SC (μmhos)	+1.18	+ 1.55
High frustration		
SBP (mm Hg)	+7.90	+15.00
SC (μmhos)	+1.42	+ 1.59

[a] Adapted from Hokanson, 1961. Copyright 1961 by Duke
University Press. Reprinted with permission.

seen in Table 3.2, the high hostility students manifested greater systolic blood pressure increases than the low hostility students under conditions of high frustration, but not under low frustration conditions. The high hostility students showed greater skin conductance changes under both high and low frustration than did the low hostility students. From this, Hokanson concluded that the highly hostile person exhibits different amounts of vascular response when frustration or anger is aroused. The high hostility subjects were viewed as showing greater anxiety about their feelings of hostility throughout the experimental session as indicated by the greater skin conductance changes.

Ego Strength

The personality trait of *ego strength* has also been assumed to reflect differences in physiological activity. This trait can be described as an "ability to accurately assess, and respond to behavior of others, while at the same time maintaining the integrity of the constellation of previously learned self-percepts called the ego."[5] Again items from the MMPI have been used to establish a scale for describing people possessing this trait. Typical behaviors might be indicated by answers to questions like whether one had a stable home environment as a child, or whether one has rather clear likes and dislikes.

[5] Roessler (1973) discusses the logic in predictions based on ego strength. The studies cited here relating responses to ego strength are referenced in his bibliography.

Since one of the functions of the ego is reality testing, differences in ego strength should be associated with differences in responsivity to environmental stimulation. Individuals with higher ego strength should be more responsive to changes occurring in their environment; those with lower ego strength should be less responsive to environmental change, resulting from more pervasive and indiscriminate use of perceptual defensive devices.

One study measured skin conductance and heart rate responses during rest, then during a stressful motion picture for subjects divided evenly on the basis of high and low ego strengths. High ego strength individuals were more responsive in skin conductance and heart rate under all conditions and showed a greater range of skin conductance values than the low ego strength persons. When subjective feelings were measured, they were found to parallel the physiological conditions; that is, high ego strength persons showed greater subjective anxiety than low ego strength individuals. The results support the notion that high ego strength people are physiologically more responsive to their environment than are low ego strength people.

Similar differences were observed when simple lights and sounds were used as the critical stimuli. In one investigation, *respiratory amplitude* (RA) and *respiration rate* (RR) were examined following stimulation with high intensities of sound and light. Thirty-two male medical student volunteers were observed, half with sound stimuli and half with light. All were given the MMPI and divided into high and low groups on the ego strength scale. High ego strength subjects responded with a greater increase in RA than did low ego strength subjects. Stimulation increased both RR and RA with the amount of change increasing with intensity. In general, the RA results are consistent with the conclusions noted previously, that high ego strength people are more responsive to environmental stimulation than are low ego strength people.

Extraversion–Introversion

Another inventory measure of personality that has been related to physiological activity is the trait of *extraversion–introversion*. In general, the extraverted person shows a strong interest in being with people, in contrast to the introvert who tends to withdraw from social contacts. One theory of personality identifies the trait of extraversion directly with the dimension of excitation and inhibition and makes specific predictions about bodily responses. The theory assumes that extraverts have greater inhibition and introverts greater excitation.

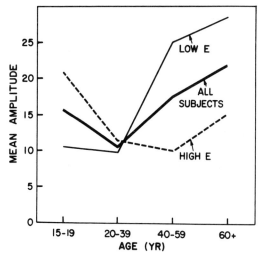

FIGURE 3.2. Mean amplitudes of evoked cortical potentials by age groups, in high and low extraversion groups. [Adapted from Shagass & Schwartz, 1965.]

Although far from conclusive, some evidence indicating greater physiological excitation among introverts has been obtained.[6] For example, one study found that introverts had chronically larger pupil diameters and also exhibited larger pupillary changes when "taboo" words were presented. These results are consistent with the theory that introverts have a higher chronic level of physiological excitation than extraverts. The complexity of these relationships can be seen from some sensory cortical evoked response data. Figure 3.2 shows the evoked response amplitude of introverts and extraverts at various age levels. The results suggest that the relationship between extraversion and introversion and the evoked brain waves is a function of the age of the individual. Note that with younger subjects (aged 15–19), high extraversion is associated with large cortical evoked responses whereas, in the older group (over age 40), high extraversion is associated with small cortical evoked responses.

[6]An extended discussion of extraversion and introversion as they related to bodily responses is contained in Eysenck (1967). Another general treatment is given by Claridge (1967). The specific data on EEG cited here were taken from Shagass and Schwartz (1965). The relationship between introversion–extraversion and the EEG indices of arousal has been reviewed by Gale (1973). The data regarding pupillary response and "taboo" words were reported by Stelmack and Mandelzya (1975).

Augmentation–Reduction

It has been hypothesized that the manner in which individuals control the intake of stimulus information operates like a trait of personality and as such may determine bodily responding. The critical notion is that people are able to control input of stimuli according to their needs. Some stimuli may be augmented for better reception whereas in other cases intensity may be reduced. Several tests have been developed to measure this assumed personality characteristic. The most common has been a kinesthetic–figural–aftereffects task, a form of size estimation test that uses a set of bars that the person handles while blindfolded. Relative sizes of a variable and standard bar are estimated. The standard bar has parallel sides whereas the comparison bar has sloping sides. The person selects a position on the tapered bar with one hand to match the size of the standard, which has been touched by the other hand. Typically, augmenters overestimate the size of the comparison bar while reducers underestimate the size of the comparison bar.

In one study, significant correlations were found between cortical evoked responses to light flashes of different intensities and the scores made by the subjects on the kinesthetic–figural–aftereffects task. The correlations indicate that augmenters show increasingly larger responses as stimulus intensity increases whereas reducers show a leveling off or decrease in response, at high stimulus-intensity levels. A related later study used the kinesthetic size estimation test to divide subjects into two groups, then compared the extreme thirds on visual cortical evoked responses to light stimulation.[7] The light stimulus fluctuated in brightness at a rate of 10 times a second. The intensity of the light fluctuations was expressed as a modulation percentage where 0% modulation meant that the light intensity remained constant and 100% modulation meant that the light varied from extremely bright to extremely dim. Figure 3.3 shows a typical set of cortical evoked responses for augmenter and reducer subjects at six levels of light modulation. As can be seen, augmenter subjects showed increased amplitude of response as the percentage of modulation increased while the reducer subjects showed a decreased response amplitude at the highest level of stimulus modulation. These results support the hypothesis that reducers tend to tune-out stimuli at high levels of intensity. This is also consis-

[7]Procedural information of the kinesthetic-figural-aftereffects test may be found in Petrie (1967). The evoked response data are from Spilker and Callaway (1969). A review of cortical evoked response differences between augmenters and reducers can be found in Buchsbaum (1976).

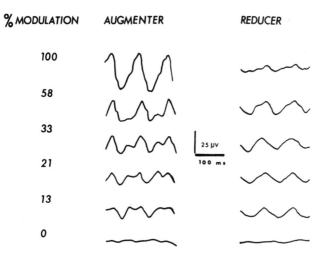

FIGURE 3.3. Typical augmenter and reducer visual evoked responses at six depths of stimulus modulation. [From Spilker & Callaway, 1969.]

tent with the finding that reducers are able to tolerate pain well while augmenters do so poorly.

Field Dependency in Perception

Another perceptual test from which physiological response predictions have been made is the rod-and-frame test. In this test, a luminescent rod and surrounding frame are presented in a dark room. The sides of the frame are tilted so that they are not actually vertical. The subject's task is to position the rod so that it is truly vertical. *Field dependent* subjects are influenced by the surrounding frame to such a degree that they cannot position the rod to a truly vertical position; while *field independent* subjects are less influenced by the frame and hence can align the rod more closely to a truly vertical position. This individual difference has been related to a number of personality characteristics—field dependent subjects are more passive, more submissive, and have lower self-esteem than field independent subjects.[8]

[8]The illustration concerning field dependence and field independence was taken from Silverman, Cohen, Shmavonian, and Greenberg (1961). More recent research has demonstrated relations of rod-and-frame scores with awareness and control over autonomic functioning (McCanne & Sandman, 1976).

Using the rod-and-frame test, some investigators reasoned that field dependent subjects should respond differently to an environment providing low sensory input than field independent persons. They used the rod-and-frame test to select two groups of male students, one highly field independent and the other highly field dependent. Both groups were placed in totally dark and quiet chambers for a period of 2 hours. The field dependent subjects showed more anxiety, more disorganization of thought, more visual and auditory imagery, and more movement than the field independent subjects. Electrodermal and EEG findings

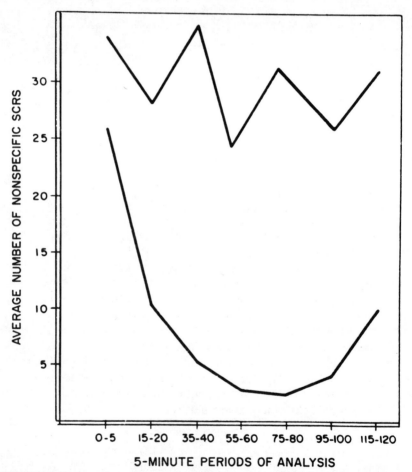

FIGURE 3.4. Average number of spontaneous electrodermal responses during the period of reduced stimulation for field dependent (upper curve) and field independent (lower curve) persons. [Adapted from Silverman, Cohen, Shmavonian, & Greenberg, 1961.]

suggested that the field dependent subjects were more aroused during the 2 hours of reduced stimulation than were the field independent subjects. Figure 3.4 shows the average number of nonspecific SCRs of the field dependent and field independent groups during the 2 hour isolation period. At the beginning of the period, the two groups were very similar in the number of nonspecific SCRs. However, the field independent group quickly showed a reduction in the number of responses while the field dependent group maintained a high level of responding. These electrodermal data are consistent with the finding that the field dependent group was more anxious and disturbed in the stimulus isolation experiment than was the field independent group. Taken together, the psychological and physiological findings are consistent with the notion that the field dependent group was more affected by the environmental situation than was the field independent group.

Body Image

Still another perceptual variable that has been studied is an individual's body image. For example, it has been hypothesized that the more definitely an individual distinguishes the right and left sides of the body, the more likely that differential bodily responses on the left versus the right sides of the body will be manifested. In one effort to study this relation, SCRs were recorded simultaneously from both sides of the body among subjects who differ in the degree of body image differentiation of the right and left sides. It was found that, among the right-handed subjects, those clearly distinguishing their right and left body sides showed more SCR reactivity on the left side than the right. Those right-handed subjects without a clear body image distinction between right and left sides either showed no SCR lateral differences or were predominantly right-reactive. For left-handed subjects there was no observable relationship between degree of differentiation and right–left SCRs.

In a further example of this type of research, it was observed that right-handed subjects who had relatively more SCR reactivity on the left side of the body than on the right side manifested fewer body image distortions than right-handed subjects showing right hand directionality or no laterality differences at all. The body image assumption has been explored in other areas such as comparing body image scores and physiological reactivity in ulcer and rheumatoid arthritis patient samples. It was shown that individuals with psychosomatic symptoms involving the exterior body layers (skin, muscle) pictured their body boundaries as more definite than did individuals with body interior (visceral) symptoms. It was concluded that an individual's body image boundaries play a part in determining the body sites in which psychosomatic symptoms develop.[9]

Repression–Sensitization

It has been suggested that individuals differ in the way they cognitively cope with threatening stimuli. The repression–sensitization scale was derived from items on the MMPI to measure this individual difference. A *repressor* is one who tries to deny or repress thinking about a threatening stimuli. A *sensitizer* is one who dwells upon and is obsessed with a threat.

Repression–sensitization scale scores were used along with electrodermal responses in a study where subjects anticipated the presentation of a strong shock. The subjects took the scale and then sat before a timer while instructed to watch the second hand. They were told that each time the hand reached 30 seconds they would receive a shock. The repressors exhibited more nonspecific SCR activity and greater reactivity to shock than the sensitizers. They also reported a stronger tendency to avoid thinking about impending shock than did the sensitizers. The attempts to not think about the shocks, however, were not successful in reducing electrodermal activity. In fact, people who showed the greatest tendency to not think about the shocks exhibited more nonspecific SCRs and larger SCRs in anticipation of the shock than did the individuals who showed less of this tendency. It may be that the mental work and effort involved in trying to not think about the shock served to produce the greater electrodermal activity.[10]

These differences between sensitizers and repressors are compatible with other research findings. For example, it has been found that repressors report feeling less subjective distress while observing a stressful motion picture than do sensitizers. However, physiological measurements indicate that the repressors are actually more reactive during the motion picture than are the sensitizers. It has also been reported that

[9]A typical early example of a study relating body image to body reactivity gradients is Fisher and Abercrombie (1958). A more recent experiment on this topic was reported by Varni, Doerr, and Varni (1975).

[10]The SCR differences during anticipation of shock between repressors and sensitizers was reported by Hare (1966). The measurement of subjective distress and physiological responses while observing an emotion-producing motion picture was reported in Opton and Lazarus (1967). Behavioral and physiological reactions in a group discussion were reported by Parsons, Fulgenzi, and Edelberg (1969).

in a group discussion situation, repressors rate themselves as less aggressive than the sensitizers. Yet, judges rated the repressors as more aggressive and physiological recordings revealed more electrodermal activity throughout the discussion among the repressors. All in all, the results indicate that repressors deny their own negative feelings and that this is associated with increased physiological responsivity.

Sensation Seeking

Individuals seem to differ in terms of their optimal level of stimulation. That is, some people are more prone to seek out environmental variety and stimulation than are other people. The sensation seeking scale (SSS) has been developed to measure this personality trait. The SSS consists of forced choices between a sensation seeking response (such as "I like to gamble for money") and a sensation reducing response.

People who score high on the SSS have been found to be more likely than those who score low to use drugs illegally and to participate in risk-taking behaviors as well as a variety of other relevant behaviors. One group of investigators hypothesized that individuals with high SSS scores would have large ORs to novel stimuli and would rapidly

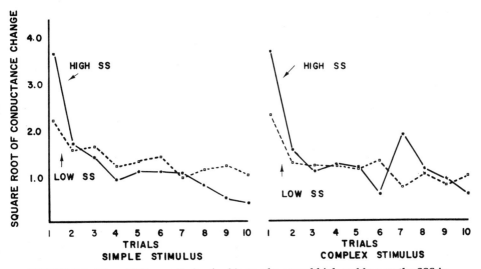

FIGURE 3.5. Mean SCR magnitude of subjects who scored high and low on the SSS in response to repeated presentations of simple and complex stimuli. [From Neary & Zuckerman, 1976.]

habituate to the repetition of such stimuli.[11] In order to test this hypothesis, 14 undergraduate students who scored high on the SSS were compared with 14 low-scoring students. The experimental procedures consisted of presenting 10 repetitions of a simple visual stimulus (a white rectangle) followed by 10 presentations of a complex visual stimulus (a colored design). The SCRs to each stimulus presentation were measured as the indices of orienting and habituation. The OR data for the high SSS and low SSS subjects for the simple and complex stimuli are shown in Figure 3.5. The high SSS group showed the predicted larger OR to the first presentation of each type of stimulus. However, contrary to prediction, the groups did not differ in their rates of habituation. Thus, the essential difference between high SSS and low SSS subjects is in terms of their initial OR to novel stimuli. The investigators concluded that this OR difference indicates that individuals who scored high on the SSS are characterized by strong internal excitatory processes.

CONCLUSION

The foregoing review of research on individual differences in bodily responding shows that the work relates to widely diverse categories of research interests. It is probable that meaningful dimensions of individual behavior may be based upon or developed from physiological responses, and it is likely that such behavior characteristics of the individual can be related to many other phenomena, ranging from psychosomatic disease to the person's method of perceiving the environment.

The empirical results already at hand demonstrate that the relations are complex and determined by many factors. In attempting to predict physiological responses from temperament inventories, the number of variables involved is probably too great to permit achievement of large correlations. Nevertheless, individual differences appear to be an important segment of psychophysiological research related to emotional behavior. It is expected that such work will continue, hopefully with an increasing measure of success.

[11]Further information regarding the measurement of sensation seeking can be found in Zuckerman (1971). The SCR data discussed were taken from Neary and Zuckerman (1976).

4

Behavior Disorders

There are several reasons for measuring bodily responses from individuals who have psychiatric or behavioral disorders. First, some of these disorders are accompanied by extreme emotional states and therefore offer a unique opportunity to study the relationship between bodily responses and emotions. Second, the measurement of bodily responses may prove to be helpful in diagnosing the nature and degree of the emotional disturbance. Third, analysis of bodily changes may help to identify those subgroups of patients who are in need of different forms of treatments. Fourth, changes in bodily responses may be useful in charting behavioral improvement following effective treatment. While some progress has been made in achieving these goals, much more work remains to be done.

Five types of psychopathological disorders are discussed in this chapter: (a) anxiety, (b) depression, (c) psychopathy, (d) hyperkinesis, and (e) schizophrenia. The emphasis will be placed on reviewing the physiological differences between individuals in each of these five

[1]This chapter emphasizes an "individual difference" approach to the study of behavior disorders. That is, bodily responses of individuals with various types of behavior disorders are compared to those of individuals without such disorders. A different approach to the subject matter might be termed a "theoretically-oriented" approach. Kietzman, Sutton, and Zubin (1975) present an example of a more theoretically-oriented approach. Alexander's (1972) work is also, in part, organized around theoretical concepts.

categories and so-called normal individuals.[1] With each disorder, the behavioral symptoms will be briefly reviewed and evidence regarding bodily responses that accompany the disorder will be presented.

ANXIETY

Life is full of uncertainties and people naturally feel anxious about what the future will bring. People may be especially susceptible to feelings of tension and anxiety in this age of "future shock" where fundamental changes seem to occur quickly and with little warning. Normally, these anxieties can be controlled and can even be useful in leading to appropriate coping behavior.

However, anxiety can become so intense and chronic that it severely disrupts the person's behavior. The term *anxiety neurosis* is used to describe individuals whose predominant complaint is chronic nervousness and who have a history of recurrent anxiety attacks. An anxiety attack is marked by overwhelming feelings of terror and panic that occur for no apparent reason or are disproportional reactions to a situation. It has been estimated that 10 million Americans suffer from anxiety neurosis.[2]

Anxiety is frequently associated with marked bodily disturbances. Subjective bodily reactions include palpitations, muscle tension, sweaty palms, trembling, etc. Therefore, anxiety neurosis would be expected to be associated with large and consistent bodily reactions that differ from the normal.

Studies that have compared the bodily reactions of anxiety neurotics with those of normal volunteers have indeed found some rather consistent differences. Tonic skin conductance level and the frequency of spontaneous skin conductance responses are higher in anxious patients than in normal groups under most testing conditions. In addition, heart rate, vasoconstriction in the fingers, forearm blood flow (a measure of blood volume in the muscles of the forearm), blood pressure, respiratory irregularities, and muscle action potentials are generally higher in chronically anxious patients than in normal controls. Moreover, there are reports that anxious patients exhibit less EEG alpha wave activity and have a higher dominant frequency in the EEG than do nonanxious controls.

[2]The clinical and behavioral symptoms of anxiety neurosis have been described by the American Psychiatric Association (1968) and, more operationally, in Feighner, Robins, Guze, Woodruff, Winokur, and Munoz (1972). The incidence, as well as chemical correlates, of anxiety can be found in Pitts (1969).

These differences between anxiety neurotics and normal individuals refer to resting tonic physiological measures and not to changes elicited by environmental stimuli. In regards to bodily changes elicited by stimuli, it has been noted that anxious patients have smaller than normal contingent negative variation responses. There is also evidence that indicates that anxiety neurotics have smaller than normal orienting responses and habituate more slowly than do normal controls. That is, anxiety neurotics give smaller physiological responses to environmental stimuli but they persist in giving these responses despite repeated presentation of the stimuli.

An example of a typical set of findings can be given. A series of brief loud tones was presented to 20 patients whose primary symptom was anxiety and 20 normal controls. The two groups were equated in terms of age and sex. Skin conductance level was measured during 10 minutes of rest preceding the tones and during the tone presentations. As can be seen in Figure 4.1, the SCL was consistently higher for the anxious patients than for the normal controls. The magnitude of the SCRs to tone presentations are shown in Figure 4.2. The anxious patients responded less to the tones during the early presentations and also habituated less to the repetition of the tones than did the normal subjects.

Some of the physiological measures, besides differing between anxious and nonanxious people, are related to the severity of anxiety. For example, the rate of spontaneous SCRs has a reasonably high relationship with the patient's assessment of degree of anxiety as well as with the psychiatrist's ratings of the patient's degree of anxiety. In addition, sedative drugs that decrease the anxiety level also tend to lower SCLs and the rate of spontaneous SCRs, while increasing the rate of habituation.

All in all, the findings indicate that anxiety is associated with diffuse overactivity of the sympathetic division of the ANS. Therefore, as discussed in Chapter 3, anxiety neurotics should have low scores on the measure of autonomic balance (Ā). This is exactly what has been found in two samples of neurotic patients who were selected on the basis of high anxiety. It has been concluded that anxious patients are in a state of sympathetic hyperactivity or, put differently, they are in a state of physiological overarousal.[3]

[3]The bodily correlates of anxiety have been reviewed by Lader and Noble (1975), Lader and Wing (1966), and Lader (1975). The electrodermal correlates of anxiety have been summarized by Stern and Janes (1973). The finding of smaller CNVs in chronic anxiety patients has been noted by Walter (1975). The Ā measure obtained from anxious patients has been summarized by Wenger (1966).

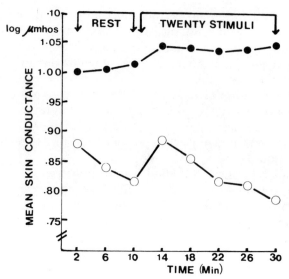

FIGURE 4.1. Comparison of mean skin conductance level for groups of 20 anxiety patients (filled-in circles) and 20 normals (opened circles) during rest and during presentation of 20 auditory stimuli. [From Lader & Wing, 1966.]

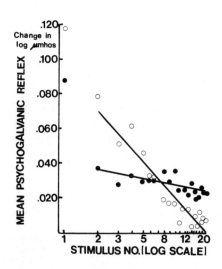

FIGURE 4.2. Electrodermal habituation curves for groups of 20 anxiety patients (filled-in circles) and 20 normals (opened circles). [Adapted from Lader & Wing, 1966.]

DEPRESSION

Although everybody feels sad sometimes, depression can also be a disabling disorder. The degree of mood disturbance is not the critical difference between normal depression and pathological depression. The critical distinguishing features are that depressive illnesses involve obsessional thoughts of self-blame, feelings of helplessness and futility, and often an inability to perform everyday functions. Depressive illness is also typically accompanied by disturbances in overall drive or motivation. There is usually a loss of interest and enjoyment in normal activities, loss of appetite, loss of sexual desire, inability to sleep soundly, and feelings of extreme fatigue.

In 1970 in the United States, nearly 24% of all newly admitted patients to a psychiatric hospital were diagnosed as depressive, making depression the national leading cause of new admissions to psychiatric hospitals. These figures do not include the estimated 4–8 million additional Americans who require treatment for depression but do not always get it. Unlike other psychological disorders, depression can have lethal consequences. It is a common symptom associated with the more than 25,000 suicides committed each year in this country.

There are a number of ways of classifying depressive disorders.[4] One division is based on the presumed cause of the depression. Cases of depression are divided into those that are thought to be caused primarily by internal factors (*endogeneous depression*) and those considered to be caused by external events (*exogeneous depression*). Another classification scheme is based on patients' activity levels. When the behavioral activity level is reduced (e.g., patients remain in bed for long periods of time and their speech is slowed) the term *retarded depression* is used. On the other hand, when the behavioral activity level is heightened (e.g., patients restlessly pace the floor and frequently wring their hands) the term *agitated depression* is used. Another distinction is between unipolar depressives and bipolar depressives. A *unipolar depressive* is a person who has no previous history of manic episodes while a *bipolar depressive* refers to a person who has had previous manic episodes.

Research findings indicate that depressed patients give smaller SCR orienting responses than nondepressed controls. Furthermore, the more

---

[4]The variety of depressive symptoms have been presented by Beck (1967), American Psychiatric Association (1968), Feighner et al. (1972), and Schuyler (1974). A strictly behavioral description and analysis of depressive symptomology can be found in Ferster (1973).

deeply depressed patients give smaller SCR orienting responses and have lower tonic SCLs than do the less depressed patients. Thus, depressed mood appears to be associated with lower electrodermal activity.

Given the lower electrodermal activity, it is surprising that depressed patients frequently have elevated heart rates. This is especially true of agitated depressives, who have been found to have higher heart rates than retarded depressives. Muscle tension has been observed to be higher than normal in depressed patients and salivation is lower than normal.

This pattern of bodily responses does not seem to fit neatly into any conventional physiological scheme. The heightened HR and EMG levels combined with the lower salivation levels suggest that the depressed patient is in a state of hyperarousal (SNS dominance) much like the anxious individual. However, the electrodermal results suggest a state of hypoarousal (PNS dominance). Thus, the pattern of bodily responses indicates that depression is a complex disorder, and in fact depression is often accompanied by anxiety.

No consistent EEG abnormalities have been found for depressed individuals. However, EEGs recorded during sleep have confirmed that depressed patients experience only shallow levels of sleep that are broken many times during the night by spontaneous awakings. Some interesting differences in average cortical evoked responses have been noted between unipolar and bipolar depressives. The bipolar patients manifested increases in their visual average evoked responses to increasing stimulus intensities (augmenting), while unipolar patients showed decreases in their evoked responses with increasing stimulus intensities (reducing) (see Chapter 3).

Facial EMGs recorded during self-generated emotional thoughts have indicated differences between depressed individuals and nondepressed controls.[5] As noted in Chapter 2, different facial muscle activity occurs when people think happy, sad, or angry thoughts. It has recently been reported that when depressed subjects are asked to "think about what

[5]The bodily responses associated with depression have been summarized by Lader (1975), Lader and Noble (1975), and a review emphasizing the electrodermal responses has been reported by Stern and Janes (1973). A recent experiment that measured electrodermal and heart rate activity in depressed patients, and recorded changes following electroconvulsive shock therapy, was reported by Dawson, Schell, and Catania (1977). A series of EEG sleep studies in depressed patients has been presented by Mendels and Chernick (1975). A review of different theories of depression has been written by Akiskal and McKinney (1975). The facial EMG data were reported by Schwartz, Flair, Salt, Mandell, and Klerman (1976).

you do on a typical day" their facial EMGs resemble the pattern generated when asked to think sad thoughts. For nondepressed subjects, the "typical day" EMG pattern resembles that produced when asked to think happy thoughts. These EMG differences are consistent with subjective reports; the depressed individuals reported feeling more sadness during their "typical day" thoughts than did the nondepressed controls.

Effective treatment of depression (with antidepressant drugs or electroconvulsive shock treatment) is sometimes associated with a return toward normalcy in the bodily reactions. For example, as shown in Figure 4.3, the rate of salivation has been found to return toward normal following treatment. As can be seen, salivation throughout the day is lower than normal when the patient is first admitted to the hospital, increases slightly during treatment, and reaches normal levels upon discharge.

However, other studies have found that following treatment depressed patients are still deficient in deep sleep, still exhibit elevated heart rate and muscle potential, and SCRs remain smaller than normal.

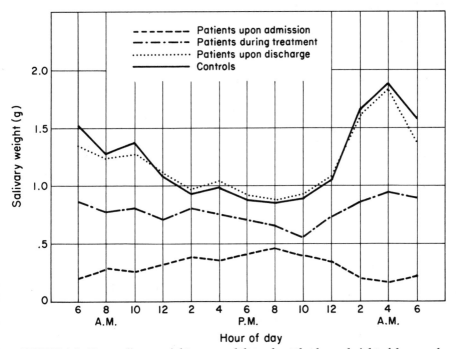

FIGURE 4.3. Mean salivary weight measured throughout the day and night of depressed patients and normal controls. [From Palmai & Blackwell, 1965.]

Since depression is often a recurrent illness, it may be that these measures are indicative of an individual's susceptibility to future depressive episodes. Longitudinal studies of individuals who are at high risk for depression (based upon a history of previous depressive episodes) need to be conducted in order to determine whether these measures are useful predictors of future depressive episodes.

PSYCHOPATHY

The term *psychopathy* (or *sociopathy*) refers to a personality disorder that is characterized by a lifelong pattern of irresponsibility, impulsivity, and emotional immaturity. The psychopath's behavior is often marked by habitual antisocial activity with no apparent remorse or guilt. Of course, not all criminals are psychopaths nor are all psychopaths criminals. For example, some individuals commit criminal acts primarily because of an affiliation with a delinquent subculture. In contrast, one of the characteristic signs of the psychopath is the inability to form genuine loyalties with any group or individual.[6]

The psychopath is considered to lack normal feelings of anxiety. This would suggest that the psychopath's physiological reactions may differ from normal in an opposite way than do anxiety neurotics. That is, the physiological responses of psychopaths and anxiety neurotics may be at opposite ends of the arousal continuum, with normals being in the middle.

Consistent with this notion, several research studies have found that psychopaths have abnormally low resting SCLs and infrequent spontaneous SCRs. Likewise, an abnormally high incidence of EEG slow-wave activity (theta waves) has been reported in some psychopaths. Although the electrodermal evidence is stronger and more consistent than the EEG evidence, both sets of findings are consistent with a state of physiological underarousal in psychopaths.

In addition, psychopaths give abnormally small SCRs in anticipation of painful stimulation and in response to the actual presentation of painful stimulation. For example, Figure 4.4 shows the skin conductance data of psychopathic (P) and nonpsychopathic (NP) criminals as well as noncriminal controls (C) while they watched the consecutive numbers 1–12 appear in the window of a memory drum. All subjects had been told that they would receive a strong electric shock when the number "8"

---

[6]The clinical and behavioral indicants of psychopathy have been described by Cleckley (1976), Hare (1970), and Ziskind, Jens, Maltzman, Parker, Slater, and Syndulko (1971).

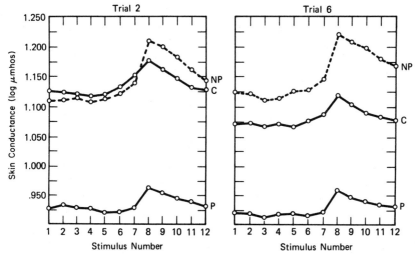

FIGURE 4.4. Skin conductance during anticipation of shock (administered at stimulus number 8) for psychopathic criminals (P), nonpsychopathic criminals (NP), and normal controls (C). [From Hare, R. D. Temporal gradient of fear arousal in psychopaths. *Journal of Abnormal Psychology*, 1965, 70. 442–445. Copyright 1965 by the American Psychological Association. Reprinted by permission.]

appeared. It can be seen that group P exhibited an overall lower SCL and a smaller SCR when the number "8" appeared than did the other groups. As shown in Figure 4.4, this difference between the groups was present after having just been told about the shock (Trial 2) and after having received several shocks (Trial 6).

The finding of small SCRs in anticipation of painful stimulation is consistent with the notion that psychopaths experience little fear or anxiety. This notion is further supported by the findings that psychopaths are poor in learning to perform tasks to avoid shock punishment, as such learning requires a certain level of fear. In other words, the psychopath may be incapable of experiencing appropriate levels of fear and this deficiency may underlie the poor avoidance learning in the laboratory. More importantly, the absence of appropriate fear of punishment may be a principal contributor to the psychopath's antisocial behavior and failure to profit from past experiences (particularly, punishing experiences).

While psychopaths are characterized by low levels of electrodermal activity, and possibly electrocortical activity, other measures of bodily states do not show the same picture. This can be described best by summarizing a study that measured several physiological responses from three types of male prison inmates. Based on examination of each prison inmate's history and an independent assessment by the prison psychiatrist, groups of primary psychopaths, nonpsychopaths, and a mixed group were selected. The mixed group was composed of individuals who were not clearly psychopathic or nonpsychopathic, and probably contained some of each type. Skin conductance, heart rate, peripheral vasomotor activity, eyeblink rate, and muscle tension (EMG) were recorded while subjects were at rest, and after an injection of adrenalin. While at rest, the only differences between the groups was that the SCL was lower in the psychopathic and mixed groups than in the nonpsychopathic group. Injection of adrenalin produced sharp and sustained increases in SCL, HR, vasoconstriction, eyeblink rate, and EMG activity. The physiological reactions to adrenalin were the same for all three groups with the exception of the SCL measure. Skin conductance levels increased less for the psychopathic and mixed groups than for the nonpsychopathic control group. Thus, the physiological hypoactivity of the psychopath compared to the nonpsychopath appears to be limited to the electrodermal (and possibly electrocortical) response system.[7]

Most of the evidence regarding bodily responses of psychopaths has been obtained while the subjects were passive recipients of stimuli. More recently, these responses have been measured during interpersonal interactions. In one experiment, pairs of subjects participated in a "game" that involved administering shocks to each other and to themselves. A 10-second tone preceded each shock, so that it was possible to evaluate physiological changes in anticipation of the shocks. Psychopaths gave smaller SCRs in anticipation of the shocks than nonpsychopaths, particularly when they themselves were about to receive the shock. However, the psychopaths exhibited larger HR responses in anticipation of the shocks, whether they themselves were about to be shocked or the other person was about to be shocked. It has been speculated that the small SCRs that preceded the shocks reflect the psychopath's deficiency in fear responding while the large HR changes reflect the psychopath's highly effective defense mechanisms in coping with forthcoming stress. The implication is that the psychopaths may be very proficient in tuning out impending stress (as indicated by the HR responsivity) and therefore they experience very little fear (as indicated by the SCRs).

[7]Some of the psychophysiological correlates of psychopathy have been reviewed by Hare (1970, 1975a,b). The reactions of psychopathic and nonpsychopathic prisoners to injections of adrenalin were investigated by Hare (1972). The electrodermal and heart rate responses during the "game" situation were reported by Hare and Craigen (1974).

HYPERKINESIS

Hyperkinesis (hyperactivity) is a relatively common childhood behavior disorder, estimated to occur in 5–10% of the general population of grade school children. The behavioral problems with the hyperkinetic children often begin in infancy and are much more common in males than females. The principal symptoms are (*a*) behavioral overactivity,

TABLE 4.1

Percentage of Positive Scores Obtained on Various Behavioral Symptoms by a Group of Hyperkinetic Patients and Normal Controls[a]

	Patients	Controls
Over active	100	33
Can't sit still	81	8
Restless in MD's waiting room	38	3
Talks too much	68	20
Wears out toys, furniture, etc.	68	8
Fidgets	84	30
Gets into things	54	11
Unpredictable	59	3
Leaves class without permission	35	0
Unpredictable show of affection	38	3
Constant demand for candy, etc.	41	6
Can't tolerate delay	46	8
Can't accept correction	35	0
Temper tantrums	51	0
Irritable	49	3
Fights	59	3
Teases	59	22
Destructive	41	0
Unresponsive to discipline	57	0
Defiant	49	0
Doesn't complete project	84	0
Doesn't stay with games	78	3
Doesn't listen to whole story	49	0
Moves from one activity to another in class	46	6
Doesn't follow directions	62	3
Hard to get to bed	49	3
Enuresis	43	28
Lies	43	3
Accident prone	43	11
Reckless	49	3
Unpopular with peers	46	0

[a] From Stewart, Pitts, Craig, and Dieruf (1966). [Reprinted with permission, from the *American Journal of Orthopsychiatry*: Copyright 1966 by the American Orthopsychiatric Association, Inc.]

(b) short attention span, (c) distractability, (d) impulsivity, and (e) low frustration tolerance. Table 4.1 lists the common behavioral symptoms reported by the parents of hyperkinetic children. These behavioral data were obtained based on interviews of the mothers of 37 hyperkinetic children and 36 nonhyperkinetic control children. As can be seen, there are striking differences between the hyperkinetic children and the control children. For example, 81% of the hyperkinetic children were described as being unable to sit still, whereas this was reported for only 8% of the controls.[8]

Given the clinical picture of behavioral overactivity, some investigators hypothesized that hyperkinetic children would exhibit hyperaroused bodily responses. However, research findings have not supported this hypothesis. In fact, a number of research reports have indicated that a sizable proportion of hyperkinetic children are physiologically underaroused.

For example, some studies have found that hyperkinetic children have lower SCLs and a number of studies have found that hyperkinetic children exhibit smaller SCRs to environmental stimuli. It has also been noted that SCRs elicited by stimuli have longer latencies, rise times, and recovery times for hyperkinetic children than for nonhyperkinetic children. In addition, hyperkinetic children reportedly have more slow wave EEG activity than do normal children. While basal heart rate levels do not differ between hyperkinetic and nonhyperkinetic children, heart rate responses elicited by stimuli are smaller among the hyperkinetic children. All in all, the data suggest a relatively low level of physiological arousal in at least some hyperkinetic children.

While the presence of low physiological arousal might not be what one would expect based upon the behavioral symptoms of hyperkinesis, it is congruent with the fact that a sizable proportion of these children (between 50 and 75%) are helped by stimulant medication. Stimulant medication increases physiological arousal but has a calming effect on the behavior of at least some hyperkinetic children. The fact that stimulant medication has a calming effect on the behavior of hyperkinetic children has been termed a paradoxical effect.

Given that stimulant medication has a beneficial effect in some but not all hyperkinetic children, it is reasonable to ask whether children who benefit from stimulant medication have a different physiological state than those who do not benefit. In one study addressed to this question, physiological measures were obtained from 31 hyperkinetic children. All of the children were boys between the ages of 6 and 9. The physiological

---

[8] Descriptions of the hyperkinetic child syndrome can be found in Cantwell (1975), Stewart, Pitts, Craig, and Dieruf (1966), and Wender (1971).

measures were resting EEG, CERs, and SCL. Behavioral improvement was rated by the children's teachers following 3 weeks of stimulant medication. Based on these teacher ratings, the six best responders (mean improvement of 71%) and the five worst responders (mean improvement 16%) were identified and compared. The best responders were found to have lower physiological arousal levels than the poor responders.

If there does exist a subgroup of hyperkinetic children who are underaroused physiologically and who respond favorably to stimulant medication, why are they behaviorally overactive? One suggestion has been that they are overactive in order to increase their stimulus input in order to compensate for their low physiological arousal level. Stimulant drugs, according to this interpretation, increase the arousal level and reduce the child's need for stimulation. Another suggestion is that they are overactive because a low level of inhibition is associated with the low level of arousal. That is, these children have insufficient inhibitory control over motor functions and sensory input. Whatever the final answer, these findings have shown that there is not a one-to-one correspondence between behavioral activation and physiological activation. These data also show the potential usefulness of measuring bodily responses in identifying subgroups of patients who respond differently to different types of treatment.[9]

SCHIZOPHRENIA

The diagnosis of schizophrenia actually covers a large group of psychotic disorders. These disorders are characterized by severe disturbances in thinking, mood, and behavior. Disturbances in thinking are marked by hallucinations, delusions, and verbal communication that is illogical and incoherent. Mood alterations include apathy, loss of em-

---

[9]Electrocortical and autonomic correlates of hyperkinesis have been presented by Satterfield (1976). A psychophysiological study of "good" and "poor" responders to stimulant medication was reported by Satterfield, Cantwell, Lesser, and Podosin (1972). Electrodermal and heart rate responses in hyperkinetic children as a function of stimulant medication has been studied by Zahn, Abate, Little, and Wender (1975). Heart rate measures of attention in hyperkinetic children were reported by Porges, Walter, Korb, and Sprague (1975). The theory of physiological low arousal has been summarized by Satterfield and Dawson (1971) and Satterfield, Cantwell, and Satterfield (1974). The belief that the effects of stimulant medication are "paradoxical" with hyperkinetic children has been challenged by Rapoport, Buchsbaum, Zahn, Weingarten, Ludlow, and Mikkelsen (1978). These investigators reported that the behavioral and cognitive effects of stimulant medication in normal children are highly similar to those observed with hyperkinetic children.

pathy for others, and inappropriate emotional reactions. Behavioral symptoms include withdrawn, regressive, and bizarre behaviors.

Traditionally, schizophrenia had been classified into several types on the basis of the predominant clinical symptoms. The four most common types are (a) *simple schizophrenia*, characterized by the predominant symptoms of apathy and social withdrawal, (b) *paranoid schizophrenia*, characterized by the predominance of persecutory and grandiose delusions, (c) *catatonic schizophrenia*, characterized by the predominance of alternations between extreme stupor and excitement, and (d) *hebephrenic schizophrenia*, characterized by the predominant symptoms of severely disorganized thinking and regression to childish behavior.

Another classification scheme has been proposed, not based on present symptoms but rather on the course of development of the disorder. When the development of the disorder is gradual, and the preillness behavior is marked by poor adjustment, the term *process schizophrenia* is used. When the development is sudden, without a long history of poor adjustment, the term *reactive schizophrenia* is used. Still other methods of classifications have been proposed. The point for our present purposes is that the symptoms can be quite varied and the term *schizophrenia* may possibly include fundamentally different types of disturbances.[10]

The preponderance of evidence indicates that schizophrenic patients exhibit higher than normal physiological arousal. That is, schizophrenics are more generally found to have higher skin conductance levels, more frequent spontaneous skin conductance responses, higher heart rate levels, greater peripheral vasoconstriction, faster respiration rates, and higher muscle tension levels than normal. However, there are a significant number of exceptions to this set of findings. The greatest source of conflicting findings comes from electrodermal measures. For example, the authors of two reviews of the electrodermal data arrived at different conclusions regarding the state of physiological arousal in schizophrenic patients.[11]

There are several possible explanations for the discrepant findings in this area. One possibility is that schizophrenic patients differ widely

[10]The clinical and behavioral symptoms of schizophrenia can be found in American Psychiatric Association (1968) and Feighner *et al*. (1972). Some of the typologies of schizophrenia have been discussed by Herron (1962). Another attempt at arriving at subtypes of schizophrenia, based on sophisticated statistical analyses of symptoms, has been reported by Carpenter, Bartko, Carpenter, and Strauss (1976).

[11]Depue and Fowles (1973) reviewed the electrodermal activity of schizophrenics and concluded that schizophrenics were overaroused. Jordan (1974) also reviewed the electrodermal activity of schizophrenics and concluded that at least some schizophrenics are underaroused.

from each other depending on factors such as diagnostic classification, stage of the disorder, etiology of the disorder, etc. In fact, recent experimentation found two rather distinct types of schizophrenic patients, one that exhibited hyperarousal and the other hypoarousal.

These experiments measured SCRs elicited by tones in schizophrenic and control groups. The normal control group showed SCRs to the initial presentations of the tone and decreased responding after the tones were repeated several times (habituation). The schizophrenics, on the other hand, showed two extreme response patterns. Of the total sample of 127 schizophrenics, 54% did not respond to the tones at all, while the remaining 46% not only responded to the tones but were extremely slow in habituating. The former group of schizophrenics is called *nonresponders*, while the latter group is called *responders*. Further analysis of these two subgroups revealed that the responders had higher SCL, more frequent spontaneous SCRs, and larger amplitude of SCRs to the tones than did a normal control group, while the nonresponders were lower than normal in these measures.

However, the distinction between responders and nonresponders was not found to be related to diagnostic classifications such as simple, paranoid, catatonic, or hebephrenic. Instead, the responder–nonresponder distinction seems to be related to the patient's behavioral activity level. Responders are rated higher than nonresponders in manic behavior, belligerence, attention-demanding behavior, and anxiety. The relationship between electrodermal measures and behavior has been examined within an individual patient. A young catatonic schizophrenic exhibited restless behavior and a euphoric mood on 2 consecutive days and then on the third day exhibited a marked change to an inert posture and dulled affect. The SCL was more than five times higher on the first 2 days than on the third day, indicating a relationship between electrodermal activity and the patient's present behavior.

The evidence indicative of two subgroups of schizophrenics, responders and nonresponders, is based solely on electrodermal measures. Can the same dichotomy be demonstrated with other physiological measures? In order to answer this question, heart rate, blood pressure, and finger skin temperature were measured from responder and nonresponder schizophrenics (initially defined in terms of their electrodermal responses). As shown in Figures 4.5, 4.6, and 4.7, the responder schizophrenics were found to have higher systolic blood pressure, heart rates, and finger skin temperature than the nonresponder schizophrenics at the beginning and end of the experimental session. In general, then, the differences found with electrodermal responding were also found with other physiological measures. However, it should be

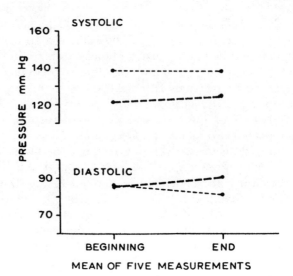

FIGURE 4.5. Systolic and diastolic blood pressure of responder (---) and nonresponder (— —) schizophrenic groups at the beginning and end of the experimental session. [Adapted from Gruzelier & Venables, 1975.]

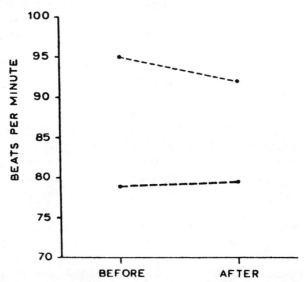

FIGURE 4.6. Heart rate of responder (---) and nonresponder (——) schizophrenic groups before and after a series of tones. [Adapted from Gruzelier & Venables, 1975.]

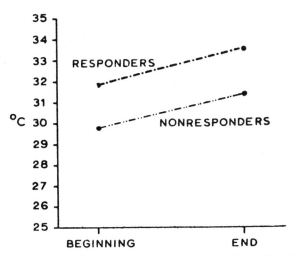

FIGURE 4.7. Skin temperature of responder and nonresponder schizophrenic groups at the beginning and end of the tone series. [From Gruzelier & Venables, 1975.]

pointed out that even though the responders had higher heart rates than the nonresponders, both subgroups had higher heart rates than the normal controls. Unfortunately, blood pressure and finger skin temperature were not recorded from the normal controls. Therefore, the differences between the subgroups and normal controls are not known. Nevertheless, the differences between the two subgroups were quite consistent and the investigators concluded that schizophrenic responders and nonresponders are two more or less distinct and homogeneous groups physiologically.[12]

Another psychophysiological difference between schizophrenic patients and normals that has been studied is the SCR rate of recovery. Early research found that electrodermal recovery rate (the time required for the SCR to return to a proportion of the preresponse level) was faster in schizophrenics than in normals. However, later findings suggest that the type of stimulus situation may be a critical determiner of the relationship between SCR recovery rate and schizophrenia. The earlier research generally used strong aversive stimuli (e.g., electric shock and loud noises). The later research employed nonaversive stimuli and found that schizophrenics have slower SCR recovery rates than nor-

[12]Data regarding responder and nonresponder schizophrenics were obtained by Gruzelier and Venables (1975). A more general review of psychophysiological studies of schizophrenia has been supplied by Venables (1975).

mals. It has been hypothesized that aversive stimuli have greater slowing effects on the recovery rates in normals than schizophrenics (hence, schizophrenics have faster recovery rates in this type of situation) but that with nonaversive stimuli, or tasks that demand goal orientation, schizophrenics have slower recovery rates. More research is needed in this relatively new area of investigation.[13]

SUMMARY AND CONCLUSIONS

A summary of the relationships between bodily responses and behavioral disorders is presented in Table 4.2. The results can be summarized as follows: (a) Anxiety neurotics exhibit high tonic levels of physiological arousal in most measures, but have small elicited SCRs (since the basal levels differ, the SCR data might be an artifact of the law of initial values, see Chapter 1). (b) Depressives have low electrodermal activity but high heart rate and EMG levels. (c) Psychopaths have low electrodermal activity and possibly low EEG activity but normal tonic heart rate and EMG levels. (d) Hyperkinetic children (at least those who respond favorably to stimulant medication) have low electrodermal and electrocortical activity levels. (e) Schizophrenics have different bodily states depending on whether they are responders or nonresponders.

Now that the research findings have been summarized, some of the difficulties of interpreting these data should be mentioned. First, there is the problem of group heterogeneity. Patients who are given the same diagnostic label may differ from each other in many important ways. This means that there may be large individual differences and therefore generalization across different studies should be made with caution since different investigators may employ different criteria for subject selection. Second, there is the problem of adequate normal control groups with which to compare the psychopathological groups. Normal control groups may differ from a psychopathological group in many significant ways. While some variables (e.g., age, sex, and race) can be equated rather easily across groups, other variables (e.g., intelligence, motivation, diet, exercise, and medication) are extremely difficult to

---

[13]The early research concerned with electrodermal recovery rates and schizophrenia was reported by Mednick and Schulsinger (1968). However, the method used to measure electrodermal recovery rates in the early research confounded response amplitude with recovery rate. Nevertheless, the basic finding of faster recovery rates in schizophrenics was later replicated when this confounding was avoided (see Ax & Bamford, 1970; Gruzelier & Venables, 1972). The later research implicating the importance of the stimulus situation was reported by Maricq and Edelberg (1975).

TABLE 4.2
Summary of Physiological Differences between Individuals with Various Behavior Disorders and Normal Individuals

Response measure	Anxiety neurotics	Depressives	Psychopaths	Hyperkinetics[a]	Schizophrenics	
					Responsive	Nonresponsive
Electrodermal						
conductance level SCL	higher[b]	lower?[c]	lower	lower?	higher	lower
spontaneous SCRs	higher	lower?	lower	same?	higher	lower
elicited SCRs	lower?	lower	lower[d]	lower	higher	lower
Heart rate level	higher	higher	same[d]	same	higher	higher
Peripheral						
vasoconstriction	higher	—	same	—	—	—
Blood pressure	higher	—	—	—	higher	lower?
Muscle potential (EMG)	higher	higher	same	—	—	—
Electroencephalogram	higher	lower?	lower?	lower	—	—

[a] Subgroup who respond favorably to stimulant medication.
[b] The word *higher* is used throughout to mean higher than normal along the arousal continuum.
[c] The word *lower* is used throughout to mean lower than normal along the arousal continuum.
[d] In stressful situations, SCRs are smaller than normal and heart rate responses are larger than normal.

equate. A third problem refers to the specificity of the physiological differences between the groups. For example, Table 4.2 indicates that elevated heart rate is found in anxiety neurotics, depressives, and both subgroups of schizophrenics. Therefore, elevated heart rate is not specific to one type of psychopathology and probably is of little use in arriving at differential diagnosis when taken as a single measure. Fourth, there is the problem of inferring cause and effect. Because a certain psychopathological group exhibits an abnormal bodily state, this does not indicate that the bodily state is related to the cause of the pathology. The abnormal bodily state could be merely a secondary side effect of the disorder.

Despite these serious difficulties, the notion of relating physiological measures with psychopathological groupings remains an intriguing one. In addition, there are certain research strategies that can minimize some of these difficulties. One strategy is to employ longitudinal studies so that the same individual can be examined when emotionally ill and emotionally healthy. An interesting longitudinal approach is to test young children who are at high risk for mental illness. For example, children who have schizophrenic mothers have about a 50% chance of eventually developing serious behavior disorders (compared to an approximate 10% chance in children who have nonschizophrenic mothers). The physiological responses of the high-risk children can be compared to those of the low-risk children. Any differences between these groups cannot be due to side effects of being psychiatrically ill since the measurements were taken before the children became ill. Furthermore, the responses of the high-risk children who eventually develop behavior disorders can be compared to those of the high-risk children who do not develop behavior problems. In this way, psychophysiological predictors of behavior disorders might be found and prove to be helpful in the early identification and prevention of mental illness. Preliminary results of this type of prospective longitudinal study are now becoming available, although it will be several years before definitive results are known.[14]

Another important experimental strategy is to measure a variety of physiological indices simultaneously. In this way, patterns of physiological abnormalities might be uncovered. Similar patterns of bodily responding may suggest similar physiological conditions that underlie dif-

---

[14]Preliminary results of prospective longitudinal studies have been reported in the following: Bell, Mednick, Ramen, Schulsinger, Smith, and Venables (1975), Erlenmeyer-Kimling (1975), and Klein and Salzman (1977). A description of the logic and advantages of longitudinal studies has been written by Mednick, Schulsinger, and Garfinkel (1975).

ferent psychopathological states. For example, as can be seen in Table 4.2, the physiological pattern is somewhat similar for psychopathy and hyperkinesis. Based on this similarity as well as other similarities in symptomatology, family histories, and response to treatment, Satterfield (1978) has suggested that childhood hyperkinesis may indicate a predisposition to adult psychopathy. Some day the identification of physiological patterns for individual patients may be an important part of determining diagnosis, prognosis, and preferred treatment. However, a great deal more research is needed before this goal is to be achieved.

5
Physiological Arousal and Performance

AROUSAL AND BODILY RESPONSES

An important feature of emotion is the effect that it has on behavior. One early interpretation about this effect was called the *emergency theory of emotion*. It suggested that the bodily reactions that accompany emotions prepare the individual for meeting emergencies by "fight or flight." Thus, the pupils dilate to allow more light to enter, the sweat glands become more active to reduce the chance of skin cuts, the blood vessels in the periphery constrict to reduce the amount of bleeding if a cut occurs, and the blood vessels in the brain and muscles dilate increasing the amount of oxygen going to these areas. All in all, many strong emotions produce a state that is optimal for "fight or flight" behavior.

Another interpretation, which has been mentioned previously, is called the *activation theory of emotion*. This theory relates the bodily reactions that accompany emotion to the level of internal activation or arousal. Variations in the internal arousal are considered to be responsible for significant variations in a person's behavior and performance. A third interpretation originated from the notion of *energy mobilization*. The concept of level of energy mobilization is roughly equivalent to the level

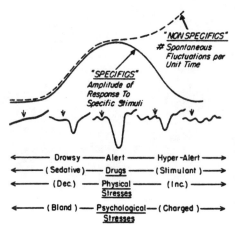

FIGURE 5.1. A proposed relationship between arousal and electrodermal data. As arousal increases, nonspecific SCRs increase while amplitude to specific stimuli (indicated by small arrows) increases and then decreases. [From Silverman, Cohen, & Shmavonian, 1959.]

of arousal notion, both of which correspond basically to what the layman calls "tension level" or "excitement level."[1]

People who use these three terms have typically sought to define them by a variety of physiological measures, chief among which are skeletal muscle tension, autonomic responses, and the electroencephalogram. These physiological indicants are assumed to reflect the motivational or emotional value of a life situation to an individual. The identification of emotion with physiological arousal and motivation has important implications for predicting relations between emotion and performance on motor tasks. An aroused individual should react faster and persevere longer, at least up to some point where too high activation might inhibit performance or increase error.

To investigate these possibilities, some objective definition of arousal or activation is essential. Early researchers equated high arousal with high levels of physiological response, such as heightened skin conductance, heart rate, blood pressure, respiration rate, muscle tension, and EEG activation. The relation of arousal to phasic skin conductance re-

---

[1]Several sources of information are useful for the history of the concepts of arousal, activation, and energy mobilization. Duffy (1957, 1962) argued for a central dimension of intensity of experience representing amount of excitation and inhibition. Lindsley (1950, 1951) used the term *activation theory of emotion* to refer to findings concerning the electroencephalogram and interaction between the lower brain-center and the cerebral cortex, particularly as they relate to phenomenon of sleep and wakefulness. This early discussion was extended in Lindsley (1957) and Malmo (1959, 1962) among others. A related point of view originated from notions of energy mobilization and behavior energetics (note particularly Freeman, 1948).

sponses has been considered to be somewhat complicated. Figure 5.1 shows the number of nonspecific SCRs and the amplitude of SCRs elicited by stimuli (called specifics) as a function of arousal levels. Silverman, Cohen, and Shmavonian (1959) reported that the number of nonspecific SCRs increases with increments in arousal while the magnitude of specific SCRs increases up to a point but then decreases.

In this chapter the relationship between arousal (as measured by physiological responses) and behavior will be examined. The relation of physiological arousal to: (a) motor performance, (b) sensory performance, (c) learning and memory, and (d) aggressive behavior will be discussed.

AROUSAL AND MOTOR PERFORMANCE

One of the earliest psychophysiological tests of an arousal–performance relation was that of Freeman (1940) who employed a reaction time task and observed some 100 paired measures of palmar skin conductance and reaction time. Low skin conductance levels were associated with slow reaction times and high skin conductance levels with fast reaction times. It was also observed that, after a certain conductance point was reached, the speed curve took a downward turn. The finding that performance improved with increased arousal to a point where it then became worse with further increases indicates an inverted-U relation between performance and arousal. Performance is optimal at moderate levels of arousal and is inferior at higher or lower levels of arousal.[2]

In order to study the effects of different levels of arousal upon motor performance it is desirable to have some means for producing a range of arousal. One approach to producing the different levels of activation is to have the subjects induce muscle tension voluntarily. One way to do this is to have them squeeze against the force of a stiff spring to a prescribed level of exertion while performing a task. A second method is to increase arousal by increasing the reward or incentive being offered for the performance of the task. When these methods are used it is important to determine whether the induced tension is reflected in changes in the physiological indices that are used to identify levels of arousal. Note the information in Figure 5.2. There it can be seen that there is a systematic relation among voluntarily induced levels of muscle tension, palmar conductance, heart rate, and respiration. These results,

[2]Other early investigators interested in these phenomena employed induced muscle tension as the determiner of arousal that influenced performance (e.g., Courts, 1942).

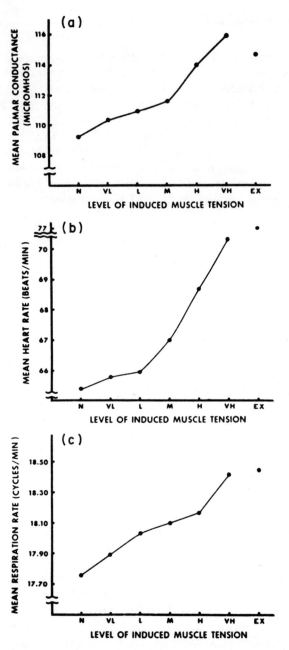

FIGURE 5.2. Relations between induced muscle tension and physiological arousal: (a) palmar conductance, (b) heart rate, and (c) respiration rate. [From Pinneo, L. R. The effects of induced muscle tension during tracking on level of activation and on performance. *Journal of Experimental Psychology,* 1961, *62,* 523–531. Copyright 1961 by the American Psychological Association. Reprinted by permission.]

reported by Pinneo (1961), support the assumption that voluntarily produced muscle tension is one way to produce physiological arousal.

Wood and Hokanson (1965) used voluntary muscle tension as a way of producing physiological arousal and then studied its effect on performance. Heart rate was used as the indicator of arousal and the digit symbol test (a speed test of matching numbers and forms) was the measure of performance. It was predicted that heart rate would increase linearly throughout the range of muscle tension, whereas performance on the test would increase up to a moderate level of tension and then would decline. As can be seen in Figure 5.3, the results supported the prediction. These results indicate an inverted-U relationship between physiological arousal and performance.

Silverman *et al.* (1959) used spontaneous skin conductance changes to measure level of arousal, and argued for the existence of an inverted-U relation between arousal and performance. As verification for the relation of arousal and performance, arousal was manipulated experimentally by having subjects ride in a human centrifuge at different gravitational force levels while performing a tracking task. When the skin conductance measures indicated moderate alerting, psychomotor performance improved; when hyperalerting was indicated by skin conductance, performance declined.

The previously mentioned studies might be interpreted to mean that arousal is directly related to a general increase in autonomic activity and

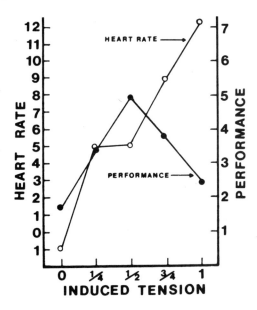

FIGURE 5.3. The relationship between mean heart rate difference scores and mean performance difference scores as a function of increasing levels of tension. [From Wood, C. G. & Hokanson, J. E. Effects of induced muscular tension on performance and the inverted U function. *Journal of Personality and Social Psychology*, 1965, 1, 506–509. Copyright 1965 by the American Psychological Association. Reprinted by permission.]

that an inverted-U relationship can be demonstrated between arousal level and performance on all tasks. This, however, is an oversimplification and overgeneralization, as has been pointed out by other investigators.

Results contrary to the inverted-U hypothesis were obtained in an experiment that studied the relationship between arousal and behavioral reaction-time in groups of young adults and kindergarten children. Physiological indicators of arousal included EEG, EMG, HR, RR, and SCL. Levels of arousal were manipulated experimentally by offering incentives (high arousal) or by not offering any incentives (low arousal) for fast reactions. It was found that the offering of incentives lead to faster behavioral reaction times among both the adults and the children. It was also found that offering incentives increased all of the physiological indicants of arousal among the adults, but increased only HR and RR among the children. Other differences between the adults and children were noted, but the most important findings for the present discussion concern the relationships between reaction speed and physiological activity. Based on the inverted-U hypothesis, it was expected that the slowest reactions would be associated with either extreme of physiological activity (either very low or very high arousal). This prediction was not confirmed for either the adults or the children. Thus, the inverted-U hypothesis was not supported.[3]

It has also been asserted that a general arousal notion is oversimplified since CNS, ANS, and behavior represent imperfectly coupled, complexly interacting systems. For this reason one cannot easily use one measure of arousal as a highly valid index of another. That is, measures of cortical arousal, autonomic arousal, and behavior arousal are not always highly correlated and may reflect different forms of arousal.[4]

Another line of research into the relationship between physiological responses and behavior has measured bodily responses during the foreperiod of a reaction-time task. Undergraduate males were presented 100 trials where each trial consisted of a 5-second ready light followed by a respond light. The subjects were instructed to release a telegraph key as quickly as possible when they saw the respond light. Heart rate, EMG (recorded from the chin and neck), and respiration amplitude were measured on each trial. The physiological changes plotted second-by-second

---

[3]The relationship of physiological arousal to performance in children and adults was studied by Elliott (1964). A review article critical of the inverted-U hypothesis was written by Näätänen (1973).

[4]A more general discussion of problems relating cortical arousal, autonomic arousal, and behavioral arousal can be obtained in Lacey (1967) and Lacey and Lacey (1970).

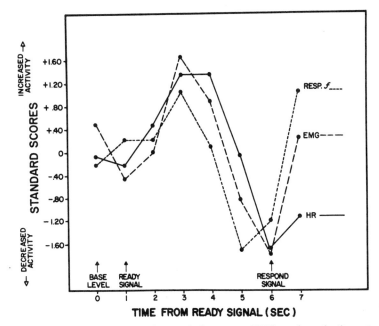

FIGURE 5.4. Second-by-second changes in heart rate, EMG, and respiration rate during the foreperiod of a simple reaction time task. [From Obrist, Webb, & Sutterer, 1969.]

are shown in Figure 5.4. As can be seen, the HR, EMG, and RR all decreased just prior to the presentation of the respond signal. In addition, the HR and EMG decreases were directly correlated with the speed of the reaction time. Subjects who showed the greatest decreases in HR and EMG tended to show the fastest motor reaction times. The authors interpret these results to indicate that these physiological changes reflect a state of general somatic inhibition that is associated with the central processes of paying close attention.[5]

The relationship between motor reaction time performance and the contingent negative variation (CNV) has also been studied. Tecce and Scheff (1969) instructed their subjects to respond quickly to a tone that would sometimes follow a light flash. The CNV was measured during

[5]The psychophysiological changes during the preparatory interval of a reaction-time task are from Obrist, Webb, and Sutterer (1969). There are two general points of view regarding the importance of the anticipatory heart rate deceleration that occurs during the preparatory interval. In one, the heart rate deceleration is considered to have a facilitatory effect on reaction-time due to afferent feedback mechanisms (Lacey, 1967). In the other, the heart rate deceleration is considered merely to be part of the general inhibition of somatic events (Obrist, Webb, Sutterer, & Howard, 1970).

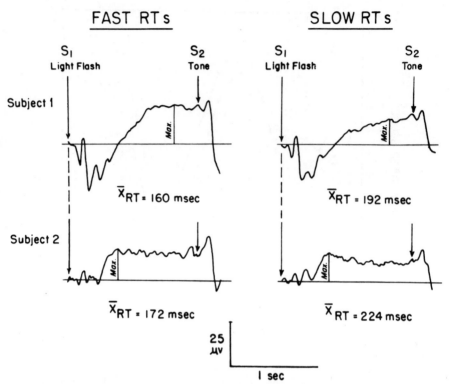

FIGURE 5.5. Average contingent negative variation for two subjects showing the relation of high contingent negative variation amplitude to fast reaction time (RT). Negativity is shown as an upward tracing. [From Tecce & Scheff, 1969.]

the 1.5-second interval between the light flash and the tone. It was found that the CNV was usually larger when the subject responded quickly to the tone than when he responded slowly. The CNVs associated with fast and slow reactions are shown for two subjects in Figure 5.5. On the basis of data such as these, it was suggested that when the subject pays close attention his CNV amplitude increases and he responds to the tone more quickly. Therefore, it was concluded that the amplitude of the CNV is a sensitive measure of attentional processes in individuals.

AROUSAL AND SENSORY PERFORMANCE

The fact that bodily responses may accompany the act of paying close attention suggests that such responses may be correlated with sensory performance. That is, if the act of paying attention is associated with greater sensory acuity and if bodily responses are associated with the act of paying attention, then the bodily responses may be related to sensory acuity. This notion is particularly interesting since the intake–rejection theory (see Chapter 2) suggests that sensory intake is associated with HR deceleration while sensory rejection is associated with HR acceleration. Thus, this theory predicts that decreased HR will be associated with greater sensory acuity than increased HR.

In order to test this hypothesis, Edwards and Alsip (1969) presented a tone 25 times to subjects while their heart rate levels (HRLs) were momentarily high and 25 times while their HRLs were momentarily low. The tones varied in intensity, some slightly above the subjects' auditory threshold and some slightly below this threshold. The subjects were instructed to push a foot pedal whenever they heard the tone. The results showed that subjects correctly detected the tone equally often when HRL was high and low. Thus, decreases in HRL were not associated with greater sensory acuity and the intake–rejection theory was not supported.

Schell and Cantania (1975) employed a warning cue before each stimulus presentation. The subjects were instructed that a 7-second warning tone would precede the dim illumination of a white dot. The illumination was adjusted so as to be near the subject's visual threshold. Heart rate was analyzed separately for trials on which the subjects reported seeing the white dot ("hits") and for trials on which subjects failed to indicate seeing the dot ("misses"). In addition, subjects were divided into good HR slowers and poor HR slowers based on the changes in HR during the warning tone. It was found that, for both groups of subjects, HR deceleration was greater on the hit trials than on the miss trials. Figure 5.6 shows the HR changes for both groups on the hit and miss trials. These results indicate a positive relationship between HR deceleration and sensory acuity. Thus, the results are consistent with the intake–rejection theory.

The results discussed thus far regarding HR and sensory performance are correlational in nature. The studies measured changes in HR and changes in sensory acuity and then determined whether there was a relationship between the two. A more convincing demonstration of a causal relationship between HR and sensory acuity would involve an experimental manipulation of HRL. Saxon and Dahle (1971) manipulated HRL by having subjects perform physical exercises. It was found that detection of the threshold level tone was better during low resting HRLs than during high exercise induced HRLs. These results are consistent with what one would expect on the basis of the intake–rejection theory. However, one difficulty with interpreting these results is that

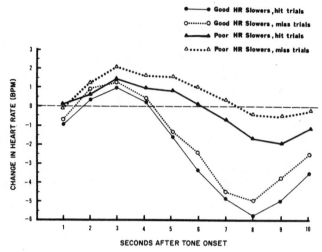

FIGURE 5.6. Second-by-second changes in heart rate following the warning tone on "hit" trials and "miss" trials for good HR slowers and poor HR slowers. [From Schell & Catania, 1975.]

some other effect of exercise (e.g., heavy breathing) may have contributed to the differences in auditory sensitivity.

Thus far we have discussed the relationship of heart rate to sensory performance. Beatty, Greenberg, Deibler, and O'Hanlon (1974) studied the effects of EEG slow waves (theta activity, 3–7 Hz) on sensory performance. Slow theta waves are considered to be an indicator of low CNS arousal and an abundance of such activity has been found previously to be correlated with poor sensory performance in a prolonged vigilance test. Nineteen undergraduate students performed a complex simulated radar vigilance test. The task was to detect small targets that appeared irregularly on a radar-type screen. The students were divided into two groups. Both groups received operant training (these training procedures are discussed more fully in Chapter 8), one group was trained to increase their occipital theta waves, while the other group was trained to decrease this activity. Sensory performance was measured by counting the number of target sweeps across the screen before the target was detected. The effects of theta wave training on sensory performance can be seen in Figure 5.7. The group trained to increase their theta waves did the poorest on the vigilance test, while the group trained to decrease their theta waves did the best. Thus, it appears that the theta rhythm is associated with low CNS arousal that determines sensory efficiency, and

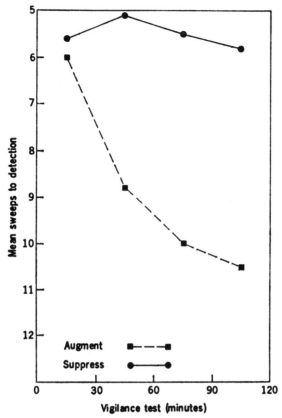

FIGURE 5.7. Detection performance (mean number of sweeps to detect targets) as a function of time in the vigilance task for the theta increase group and the theta decrease group. [Adapted from Beatty, Greenberg, Deibler, & O'Hanlon, 1974.]

experimental manipulations of this EEG rhythm have pronounced effects on sensory performance.[6]

AROUSAL, LEARNING, AND MEMORY

A typical study in which physiologically defined arousal has been used to predict performance in a learning situation was conducted with

[6]Another experiment that found that experimental variation in the EEG affected performance was reported by Woodruff (1975). The reader interested in the relationship between SCRs and performance on a vigilance task is referred to Crider and Augenbraum (1975).

eyeblink conditioning of human subjects. All of the subjects received a sharp air puff in the eye 15 times while skin conductance and heart rate were measured. The subjects were then divided into high and low emotional (drive) groups, on the basis of the physiological measures, and administered an eyeblink conditioning acquisition series. Two divisions were made, one—the single index—on the basis of the most discriminating physiological measure (either SCR or HR) and the other—the combined index—using both measures. As will be noted from Figure 5.8, significantly better eyeblink conditioning performance was obtained for the high emotionality group on a single index and an almost significant difference on the combined index. The researchers concluded that performance in the conditioning situation is a function of an emotionality drive that is definable by physiological responses.[7]

Another study related individual differences in physiological orienting response to differences in the rates of learning a tactual discrimination problem. Heart rate orienting responses to a series of tactual stimuli were measured from 128 male school children, ranging in age from 9 to 11 years. Immediately after measuring the ORs, the children were required to solve a tactual discrimination problem. In this task, subjects felt items that differed on several dimensions (e.g., shape, position, size, and texture). The subjects were required to learn the relevant dimension and ignore the irrelevant dimensions. On the basis of their performance on this task, 32 fast learners and 32 slow learners were identified. The heart rate OR data suggested that there were clear-cut differences between the two groups, with the fast learners having larger ORs and slower habituation than the slow learners. The author speculated that the fast learners may have been more highly motivated than the slow learners and that this was related to their larger ORs, slower habituation, and subsequent faster learning.

Another study relating arousal and retention involved memory for verbal materials. Subjects were presented eight paired-associate items while skin resistance responses were recorded. Each paired-associate item consisted of a stimulus (a word) and a response (a digit) member of the pair. Subjects were merely instructed to "concentrate" on the word-digit pairs, no mention was made of the subsequent retention

[7]The eyelid conditioning data were taken from Runquist and Ross (1959). The verbal retention data are from Kleinsmith and Kaplan (1963). A later review of the verbal retention research can be found in Craik and Blankstein (1975). The study dealing with the individual differences in orienting responses and subsequent learning was reported by Cousins (1976). M.W. Eysenck (1976) has made an interesting distinction between arousal induced by the learning material and arousal level of the subject at the time of learning.

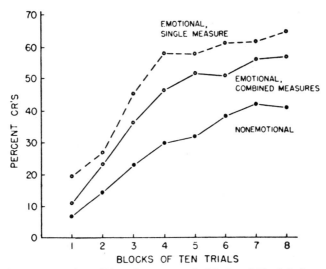

FIGURE 5.8. Percentage of conditioned responses in blocks of 10 trials for groups of subjects selected by combinations of physiological measures. [From Runquist, W. N., & Ross, L. E. The relation between physiological measures of emotionality and performance in eyelid conditioning. *Journal of Experimental Psychology*, 1959, 57, 329–332. Copyright 1959 by the American Psychological Association. Reprinted by permission.]

tests. The SRRs following the eight stimulus words were ranked for each subject from largest to smallest. The stimulus words followed by the three largest SRRs were designated as high arousal and the three smallest were designated as low arousal. Different groups of subjects were then given retention tests of the paired-associate items at 2, 20, and 45 minutes and 1 day and 1 week following the initial session. As indicated in Figure 5.9, the words accompanied by small SRRs (low arousal) were easily remembered 2 minutes after presentation, but were forgotten on the later tests. On the other hand, the high arousal words were poorly remembered on the early test, but were well remembered on the later tests. Thus, high arousal was associated with poor short-term retention but good long-term retention, while low arousal was associated with good short-term retention but poor long-term retention. The fact that high arousal words are associated with better long-term retention is not particularly surprising and, in fact, has been found by several investigators. What is surprising is that high arousal is associated with poor short-term retention, which then improves over time. This provocative result has been replicated by the original investigators as well as others, but other investigators have failed to find this effect.

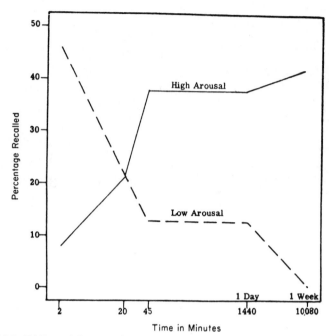

FIGURE 5.9. Differential recall of paired associates as a function of arousal level. [From Kleinsmith, L. J., & Kaplan, S. Paired-associate learning as a function of arousal and interpolated interval. *Journal of Experimental Psychology*, 1963, *65*, 190–193. Copyright 1963 by the American Psychological Association. Reprinted by permission.]

Another interesting way in which physiological responses have been used in the study of memory is as a measure of cognitive memory load. For example, dilation of the pupil has been employed as an index of the amount of material held in short-term memory storage. These findings have been extended using pupil dilation as an index of the amount of material retrieved from long-term storage and being held for processing.[8]

The role of arousal in determining learning performance has been related to the concept of reinforcement. The question is then raised whether it is an increase or decrease of arousal that is the effective element in reinforcement. Berlyne (1967) suggested that an increase in arousal is the essential element associated with positive rewards while a decrease in arousal is the essential element with negative punishment.

[8]The pupillary changes during cognitive memory load have been reviewed by Craik and Blankstein (1975).

AROUSAL AND ACTING OUT AGGRESSION

An interesting series of studies (Hokanson & Shetler, 1961; Hokanson & Burgess, 1962) employed physiological responses as an index of recovery from arousal due to frustration. The experimental paradigm provided a situation in which frustration leads to a build-up of hostility. Then the anger is reduced by aggressive acts. Blood pressure and cardiovascular responses are employed as the index of arousal during frustration and its reduction following aggression. In the early studies, a procedure was developed for frustrating subjects by having them count backward from 100 by 3s. The high frustration group was frequently interrupted while the low frustration group was not. Finally, at the end of the experiment, the subjects were given an opportunity to aggress against the experimenter by administering shocks to him. It was found that high frustration subjects gave more shocks to the experimenter than the low frustration group.

The major question was whether expression of aggression after frustration produced a greater reduction in arousal than having no opportunity to aggress. Systolic blood pressure was used as the index of arousal. The study employed a high status frustrator (an older professor) and a low status frustrator (a young student) to evaluate a social variable. The high frustration led to significantly greater systolic blood pressure increases than the low frustration condition for both the high and the low status frustrator. Persons frustrated by the high status experimenter and given an opportunity to aggress showed no significant reduction in blood pressure. Persons frustrated by the low status experimenter and given the opportunity to aggress returned rapidly to a prefrustration blood pressure level. One conclusion about the factor that produces the return is the knowledge that the experimenter is actually undergoing discomfort and that the subject feels responsible for that discomfort.

A related study sought to compare effectiveness of different types of aggression in reducing the effects of frustration hostility. Eighty subjects were divided into two major groups of high and low frustration, as before. The two subgroups were each divided into four type of aggression groups: (a) physical—given an opportunity to administer an electric shock to the experimenter; (b) verbal—filled out a questionnaire evaluating the experimenter's capabilities; (c) fantasy—created a story to a TAT card aimed at eliciting aggressive themes; and (d) no aggression. Each aggression condition took 2 minutes during which blood pressure and heart rate were measured. The results for the blood pressure and heart rate are given in Table 5.1 for the high frustration condition. As will be noted, the frustrated subjects who were given a chance to physically or

TABLE 5.1
Blood Pressure and Heart Rate Increases from Prefrustration Level during Different Types of Aggression[a]

	Immediately after frustration	During aggression			
		Physical	Verbal	Fantasy	None
Blood pressure (mm Hg)	10.3	1.2	1.8	9.2	10.8
Heart rate (BPM)	9.0	.8	−3.8	8.0	11.4

[a] From Hokanson, J. E., & Burgess, M. The effects of three types of aggression on vascular processes. *Journal of Abnormal and Social Psychology*, 1962, 64, 446–449. Copyright 1962 by the American Psychological Association. Reprinted by permission.

verbally aggress against the frustrator showed returns of both physiological measures to low levels. The frustrated persons in the fantasy and no aggression conditions exhibited significantly elevated blood pressure and heart rate at the post aggression point. It is concluded that the type of aggression is an important variable and that, at least within the 2 minute time limit, fantasy is not effective.

Numerous extensions of this basic paradigm have been made. For example, it has been found that various types of frustrations (e.g., an ego threat and a blocked goal) are capable of producing blood pressure elevation and heart rate acceleration. Another study evaluated the opportunity to physically aggress against objects varying in similarity to the frustrator. Aggression directed to the frustrator reduced systolic blood pressure but aggression to substitute targets did not. Later studies have found that aggressive behavior rapidly reduced systolic blood pressure, whereas friendly or ignoring behavior led to a slow return to base.

Other investigators provided the opportunity for angered subjects to aggress either indirectly by shocking a nonfrustrator, directly by shocking their frustrator, or not at all. Feelings of guilt among the subjects were evaluated by means of an open-ended questionnaire. The results suggested that when subjects feel guilty about the use of aggressive acts the effectiveness of the cathartic behavior is altered. Arousal reduction achieved by a subject counteraggressing alone have been compared to those with aggressive responses expressed with another individual. While significant changes in blood pressure were observed to occur with counteraggression the variable of counteraggressing alone or with another did not differ significantly.

These experiments provide a research prototype that may be extended into a variety of social, personal interaction situations. It is interesting that the previous results were found to be much more prominent among male subjects than female. The research has been applied to the development of theoretical propositions concerned with the manner in which aggressive behavior is learned.[9]

In the examples given up to this point, the emphasis has been upon actual physiological components of arousal as determiners of performance. It has also been shown that people's cognitions about their physiological state may be just as important in determining performance of various kinds. If individuals think they have physiologically responded in a certain way, they perform differently than if they think they have responded in a different way. A commonly cited example of this effect involved presenting 10 slides of seminude females to a group of male introductory psychology students. The subjects were led to believe that they could hear sounds of their own hearts beating while watching the slides. In actuality, the sounds were controlled by the experimenter and were unrelated to the subject's true heart rate. These sounds changed markedly for half of the slides and did not change for the others. Subjects rated those slides for which their "heart beats" changed as being significantly more attractive than those for which they heard no change. It was concluded that a subject's perception of a physiologically response can have an important effect on emotional behavior.[10]

CONCLUSION

The material reviewed in this chapter indicates that physiological arousal has some interesting relationships to behavior. Under certain circumstances, arousal is related to motor performance with an inverted-U function. Deceleration of heart rate tends to be positively related to sensory acuity while the occurrence of EEG slow waves is negatively related to sensory performance. The size of SRRs is nega-

---

[9]More recent discussion of this research arrangement are given in Hokanson (1970), Hokanson, DeGood, Forrest, and Brittain (1971), and Stone and Hokanson (1969).

[10]The experiment that studied the effects of false HR sounds on the rated attractiveness of slides was reported by Valins (1966). See Harris and Katkin (1975) for a review of the evidence bearing on the question of whether bodily reactions must occur for there to be an emotional experience or whether an individual merely needs to *think* that there is a bodily reaction for there to be an emotional experience.

tively related to short-term retention of verbal material but is positively related to long-term retention. Finally, aggressive behavior following frustration induction is positively associated with reduction in cardiovascular arousal. However, each of these relationships is limited by our lack of understanding of the concept *physiological arousal*. The low correlations between the physiological indices of arousal suggest that arousal is multidimensional and that we need to better understand these various dimensions.

6
General Behavioral States

In the previous chapter there was a tendency to use bodily responses to define behavioral concepts, such as motivation and drive. Individuals show faster heart rates when they are pursuing stronger incentive stimuli. Thus, heart rate gives empirical meaning to drive. The relationship between physiological indices of arousal and specific behaviors, such as learning, performance efficiency, and blocking of motives (e.g., frustration) were of central interest in the previous chapter.

The measurement of bodily responses is important to the understanding of many other, more general behavior states. While some of these behaviors would not be termed emotional in a strict sense, a kinship to emotion does exist. As an example, consider the state of sleep. It is a level of consciousness of the organism that can be evaluated by the type of brain waves emitted. It may also represent a certain phase or portion of a continuum of excitation—the low end of a scale that has excitement at the other end. Another general state is that of stress, which may be said to result from some form of threat to the organism.

The material that follows will examine some of the bodily responses that occur during four general behavior states: (a) sleep, (b) stress, (c) relaxation, and (d) fear reduction.

SLEEP

The electroencephalogram has come to play a very central role in the identification and description of sleep.[1] An early system classified EEG patterns into five groupings (labelled a through e) that were considered representative of increasing depth of sleep. That classification has more currently been modified into a system that identifies four stages of sleep depth and a fifth state labelled 1-REM. The top tracing of Figure 6.1 (Stage 0) shows the relaxed nonsleep EEG pattern. Then as the subject dozes off into sleep, the EEG shows an increasing desynchrony with occasional slow waves of less than 8 Hz (a dominant mixture of low amplitude and mixed frequencies) and the alpha waves tend to drop out and appear only intermittently. This is called Stage 1 and closely resembles the EEG of the awake subject. Stage 2 is identified by the presence of sleep spindles that are more sharply pointed than are alpha waves, and of 14–16 Hz. These waves tend to occur in intermittent and frequent bursts over a low-voltage background. Stage 3 is characterized by the appearance of high amplitude waves of 1–2 Hz. Sleep spindles continue to occur. Stage 4 is dominated by large amplitude waves of 1–3 Hz and is typically referred to as "deep sleep." Stage 1-REM shows the same EEG characteristics as Stage 1, but is accompanied by rapid eye movements (REM). To evaluate stages of sleep, the electroencephalogram is typically scored in 1-minute intervals.

It has been demonstrated that Stages 1 through 4 represent a continuum of sleep depth, as may be determined by the subject's sensitivity to external stimulation. Stage 1-REM has been shown to be associated with visual dreaming. Persons awakened during 1-REM periods report dreams 80% of the time, and less than 10% when awakened at other times. No doubt these activated REM periods suggest occurrence of vivid visual forms of imagery during sleep. Other research, however, has shown that all mental activity is not confined to these periods, but

[1]Since the earliest discussion of an activation–arousal continuum, the phenomenon of sleep has represented the low activation end of the range. (See Magoun, 1963, for an historical account.) However, empirical–behavioral studies of sleep were relatively few until the 1960s. Since then there has been an increasing amount of interest in the empirical study of sleep and several books have been published (e.g., Kleitman, 1963; Oswald, 1962; Murray, 1965; Foulkes, 1966; Kales, 1966; and Webb, 1968). Webb (1975) has briefly summarized the broad range of concepts and data pertaining to sleep for what he terms a "general readership" as contrasted to the technical expert. There is a research society named the Association for the Psychophysiological Study of Sleep under whose sponsorship a manual of electrophysiological criteria for stages of sleep has been published (Rechtschaffen & Kales, 1968).

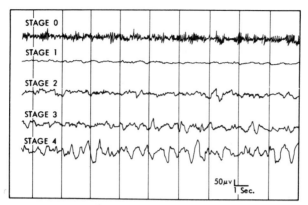

FIGURE 6.1. EEG characteristics during various stages of sleep. [Reprinted with permission of Macmillan Publishing Co., Inc. from *Sleep: An experimental approach* by W. B. Webb. Copyright © 1968 by Wilse B. Webb.]

rather that visual dreaming is more specialized during these periods. People dream several times a night for a total of 1 or 2 hours on the average, and the greatest concentration of such dream time is in the latter portion of the sleep. The dreams run their course in 20–30 minutes and stop abruptly. There does not seem to be any shortening of time during dreams; that is, a dream takes about as long as imagining the same activity would take. There is good evidence that external stimulation can be incorporated into a dream state.

A normal sleep period (e.g., throughout a night) shows clear patterning, and the times occupied by each stage can easily be represented graphically (see Figure 6.2), or percentage time determinations can be

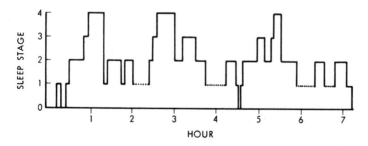

FIGURE 6.2. Stages of sleep across a night. Dotted lines identify periods of Stage 1-REM. [Reprinted with permission of Macmillan Publishing Co., Inc. from *Sleep: An experimental approach* by W. B. Webb. Copyright © 1968 by Wilse B. Webb.]

made. Individuals show consistent and characteristic patterns. Changes from stage to stage are typically in sequential order when moving toward Stage 4, but are often abrupt when moving away from Stage 4. It has been reported that certain sleep disorders (e.g., sleep walking, nightmares, and bed-wetting) usually occur during the abrupt change from deep sleep (Stage 4) to light sleep (Stage 1). Contrary to popular belief these sleep disorders are not associated with dreaming and Stage 1-REM. Stage 1-REM usually emerges from Stage 2. The different stages are distributed in a characteristic way throughout the night. One study has shown that typically 69% of the Stage 4 sleep occurs during the first third of the sleep period. In contrast, 52% of the Stage 1-REM sleep occurs in the final third of the period.

An example of a practical research problem involving psychophysiological responses is the evaluation of the effect of drugs in producing sleep. It is possible to compare the sleep stages of individuals under normal sleeping conditions and under the influence of hypnotic drugs. Studies of this type have demonstrated that most sleeping pills do not succeed effectively in mirroring the course of natural sleep.[2]

The bodily changes that occur during sleep are interesting, but also somewhat perplexing.[3] As might be expected, the tonic levels of most response systems (e.g., heart rate, respiration rate, and skin temperature) are lower during sleep than when awake. Unexpectedly, during deep sleep (Stages 3 and 4) there is an increase in spontaneous skin conductance responses and skin potential responses (SPRs). These spontaneous electrodermal responses, however, are not associated with increases in heart rate, finger pulse volume, or respiration. The cause of these spontaneous responses is not known, but they clearly demonstrate a dissociation of electrodermal and cardiovascular activity. This dissociation is further indicated when bodily responses to stimuli presented during sleep are recorded. A stimulus (e.g., tone) presented during sleep, and which the subject does not indicate awareness of, can cause EEG, HR, and finger PV responses, but not SCRs or SPRs. Elicitation of SCRs or SPRs occurs to stimuli presented during sleep only when

---

[2]Broughton (1968) has reviewed various sleep disorders, such as bed-wetting, sleepwalking, and nightmares. See Kales (1966) for a summary of research on sleeping pills.

[3]Typical curves of metabolic measures (e.g., oxygen consumption, heart and respiration rate, internal and external body temperature) as well as skin conductance and blood pressure are given by Snyder and Scott (1972). Other topics covered include arousal reactions during sleep and individual differences in sleep patterns. The chapter is an excellent summary of critical issues relating to sleep from the viewpoint of bodily responses.

there are EEG signs of awakening and the person reports awareness of the stimuli.[4]

Another extensive area of research on sleep involves the effects of sleep loss. To date there has been no general agreement as to the exact changes in the central nervous system that result from the loss of sleep, although adenosine triphosphate (ATP) the chemical responsible for the transformation of food energy into bodily energy is not produced after about 4 days of sleep deprivation.

The behavioral consequences of sleep deprivation have been reviewed by Naitoh (1975).[5] Performance deteriorates primarily as a consequence of short periods of time in which the person is incapable of responding, rather than as a result of a general decline in ability to perform. These lapses of a few seconds or less are clearly identifiable as brief sleep periods. It is probable that performance is affected by motivational changes as well as capacity to perform. Probably the most striking effects of sleep deprivation are seen in the realm of personality, for increasing sleep deprivation creates temporary personality disorganization.

Studies of partial deprivation have attempted to determine whether sleep can be reduced without a decrease in behavioral efficiency. Generally, when sleep is restricted, it leads to a differential deprivation of different stages of sleep. Thus, it is not possible to say whether a particular performance effect noted is due to reduced sleep or due to deprivation of a specific sleep stage. For this reason, the major studies have sought to deprive subjects of selected kinds or stages of sleep. Dement and Kleitman (1957) and Dement (1960) demonstrated the need for dreams. Subjects were prevented from dreaming for 6 consecutive nights by being awakened whenever indications of Stage 1-REM dreaming occurred. It became necessary to awaken the subjects more often each night. Then on a recovery night the subjects were found to dream as much as 30% more than they did before they had been deprived of dreams. Similar effects have been noted with Stage 4 deprivation. There

---

[4]More information regarding the physiological responses to stimuli while asleep can be found in Johnson (1970, 1975). Information processing during sleep is discussed by Williams (1973). Performance of previously learned physiological reactions during sleep has been studied by McDonald, Schicht, Frazier, Shallenberger, and Edwards (1975). Evidence regarding the learning of new material during sleep has been reviewed by Aarons (1976).

[5]An example of the relation between sleep deprivation and behavior can be found in Malmo and Surwillo (1960). Naitoh (1975) speaks of three kinds of sleep deprivation: total, partial (which represents a simple fraction of total), and differential (which implies deprivation of specific stages of sleep). Effects of the various types differ.

is an increased need for Stage 4 as evidenced by the appearance of increased intervals of Stage 4 when deprivation time is increased.

There are a number of variations and modifications of sleep behavior that are of interest in discussions of emotion. Among these are relations of sleep to psychopathology as well as sleep as a method of therapy.[6]

STRESS

When people are confronted with threatening stimuli or any form of disablement, like disease, they react with a nonspecific physiological pattern that is termed *stress*. Any stimulus capable of producing the reaction pattern is referred to as a *stressor*. *Physiological stress* can result from disease, exposure, or deprivation; whereas *social stress* results from an individual's threatened loss of esteem or integrity.

Hans Selye (1950, 1956), one of the earliest writers on stress, emphasized the neuroendocrine sequence of reactions, called the *general adaptation syndrome*. The first stage to occur in this syndrome is a reaction of alarm, where the organism is alerted and makes initial autonomic and hormonal adjustments. With continued exposure to the stressor, a stage of adaptation or resistance ensues. A principal feature of this stage is the organism's attempt to reduce the stress by using various coping mechanisms. Finally, after a period of persistent nonadjustive attempts, a stage of exhaustion may occur. All stages are assumed to involve a certain amount of wear and tear on the organism.

In elaborating upon the notion of stress, psychologists have emphasized that we should not think of stress as being imposed upon the organism, but rather as the organism's response to internal and external processes that reach levels that strain the physiological and psychological integrative processes to their limit. People perceive that their well-being is in danger and that they must divert special energies to their protection. A critical factor, then, in producing stress is the person's cognitive interpretation of the stimulus. It is this cognitive process that may turn a stimulus into a stressor.

Recently, the notion that a stimulus must be unpleasant or noxious to be a stressor has been challenged. Some investigators believe that any

---

[6]Insomnia is commonly reported as a symptom in neurotic and psychotic conditions. In the former, the prominent source of sleep interference is anxiety or depression, whereas in the latter a wide variety of events have been reported, ranging from emotional turmoil during sleep to forms of drowsy withdrawal from confrontations with world events. In acute manic states sleep may be almost nonexistent, requiring heavy sedation to prevent complete exhaustion and collapse.

event that requires adjustment and accommodation can be a potent stressor. Thus engagements, marriages, job promotions, vacations, etc. can all be potential stressors. Rahe (1975) has described a checklist of common life events that require adjustment (see also Liebman, 1955). Relative weightings were given to life events based on the ratings of judges in terms of the degree, intensity, and length of time required for adjustment. The result was a scale where, for example, the death of a spouse is weighted 100 (the highest point on the scale), marriage is weighted 50, and vacation is weighted 12. Research with this and similar scales has shown associations between scores on the scales and subsequent illnesses of various types. Stress, therefore, is viewed as a precipitating factor in the timing, but not necessarily the type, of illness episodes.[7]

As a general behavior state, stress has been widely studied by researchers interested in its biological and psychological aspects. One emphasis has been upon the varied aspects of the neuroendocrine pattern, particularly involving the hypothalamus, and its interrelations with the pituitary and adrenal glands. A second emphasis has been upon the effects of exposure to psychosocial stimuli. Among the responses to such stimuli that have been investigated are those considered here, namely, EEG, muscle tension, and autonomic responsivity.[8]

The stimuli investigated have varied widely and most have been selected because they persistently occur in modern living environments. A good example is the high level noise that is common in industrial

[7]A review of the literature relating stress and illness has been written by Rabkin and Struening (1976). One example of illness as a stressor that has been studied carefully is the stress of impending surgery. Janis (1958) reports extensive psychoanalytic observations of patients before and after elective surgery and noted clear relations between degree of apprehension before surgery and postoperative recovery.

[8]An interesting example of relations among chemical factors, stress, and illness is provided by Christie (1975). When a person perceives a threat, a physiological reaction of preparation for action is assumed to take place. That reaction involves phylogenetically old components—physiological reactions that are not adaptive for humans. Present customs and cultures are more likely to react symbolically than physically, hence an excess of metabolic materials occurs and builds up. One example is high levels of free fatty acids, which can increase the likelihood of lipid deposits on the walls of arteries. Other examples are mobilization of glucose in the blood and the increased use of protein for the emergency production of energy.

One chemical is singled out for special attention because of its effect on the excitability of nerve cells. It is the concentration of potassium ($K+$) in the blood, a factor which is sensitive to stress. Of particular importance in the present context is the assumption that the concentration of $K+$ can be indexed by bodily responses of the type emphasized here. One is skin potential level, which has been used as an index of intramuscular $K+$. Another is the amplitude of the T-wave of the EKG.

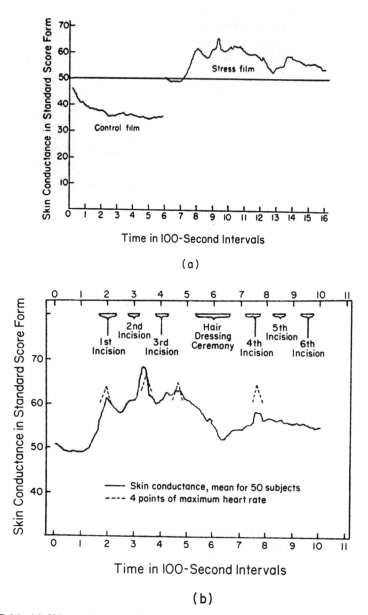

FIGURE 6.3. (a) Skin conductance during each of 100-second intervals for control and stress films. (b) Skin conductance aligned with stressor film contents. Also, four points of maximum heart rate. [From Lazarus, R. S., Spiesman, J. C., Mordkoff, A. M., & Davison, L. A. A laboratory study of psychological stress produced by a motion picture film. *Psychological Monographs*, 1962, 76 (Whole No. 34). Copyright 1962 by the American Psychological Association. Reprinted by permission.]

environments and in a number of urban situations (like residences near airports). Another example is air pollution, which, like noise, may exert a stressful threat. As population densities increase, the social stimulus of overcrowding assumes importance. Several books have been written on the stress effects of catastrophic events, such as war.[9]

The question being raised is whether such general environmental stresses have long-term deleterious effects on organ functions such as blood pressure or muscle tension level. It also becomes important to examine carefully the techniques that are developed by individuals to cope with stress. Sometimes these coping mechanisms become an important key to the total personality.

As an example of psychophysiological evaluation of stress, brief note will be taken of the use of motion pictures as a source of stress stimulus. A movie has the unique advantage of combining ingredients of both a naturalistic and a laboratory environment. In the earliest studies of this type a stress movie was taken by an anthropologist to depict an Aboriginal Australian tribe performing puberty rites on an adolescent boy. The movie contained some gory scenes involving surgery with crude flints. As a nonstressful control film a sequence of corn farming in Iowa was used. Personality measures and various forms of subjective reports were employed to determine subjective reactions; physiological measures, such as heart rate, were also recorded.

An example of skin conductance reactions during the stress film is shown in Figure 6.3, where it will be noted that the points of maximum skin conductance and heart rate coincided with the points of maximum stress in the film. Responses to the control film showed continuous adaptation or habituation throughout the film.[10]

RELAXATION

Stress as a bodily state implies tension and defensive levels of arousal or perhaps anxiety. An opposite state of affairs is assumed to exist with

---

[9]For early discussions, see Grinker and Speigel (1945), and Janis (1951). In a specific discussion on psychophysiological reactions to military stress Weybrew (1967) tabulates stressors in two major classes (primary and secondary) and relates each to a variety of physiological indices. Some examples of primary stressors that have not been discussed in this chapter are weightlessness, linear and rotary acceleration, hypobaric and hyperbaric atmospheric pressure, anoxia, radiation, and vibration. Some secondary stressors include threat to "life and limb," isolation and confinement, sustained performance, and threat to status or self-esteem. For more detail, see Weybrew (1967).

[10]The specific reference discussed here is by Lazarus, Speisman, and Mordkoff (1963). For a more extended discussion see Lazarus (1966).

relaxation. Muscular tension is at a very low level and a general pattern of conserving energy prevails. Respiration and heart rate slow down, skin conductance decreases, and peripheral arterioles dilate, as indicated by elevated hand temperature.

The importance of relaxation to general health was emphasized many years ago by a physiologist–physician (Jacobson, 1929) who developed techniques for reducing muscle tension through a procedure he called *progressive relaxation*. This procedure consists essentially of a set of responses through which individuals are taught to recognize very small muscle contractions so that they can control the contractions and eventually perceive an experience of deep relaxation. In learning to relax, a person practices flexing and relaxing muscle groups individually (e.g., hand, arm, thigh, tongue) until progressively a general relaxation state is achieved.

The progressive relaxation procedure has been compared to a wide variety of techniques subsumed under various forms of meditation, autogenic training, and self-hypnosis. An important way to demonstrate the effectiveness of any technique for producing relaxation has been to demonstrate the reduction in arousal it produces in measures like muscle potentials, alpha brain waves, heart rate, respiration rate, and skin conductance. One of the best known techniques being studied in this manner is a method termed *biofeedback*, which gets its name from the fact that information about a physiological response (e.g., muscle tension, amount of alpha EEG, or skin temperature) is fed back to the subject in some convenient form (e.g., on a meter). The basic assumption of biofeedback is that if a person is allowed to see an objective indication of bodily responses then the individual can more effectively learn to control these responses.

As examples of the role that bodily responses play in relaxation, two studies comparing physiological changes that accompany different relaxation techniques will be noted. The first compares progressive relaxation to hypnosis and a control rest situation. The second compares progressive relaxation and biofeedback procedures using muscle tension as the information fed back. Finally, note will be made of applications of these procedures to clinical psychological situations—patients with phobic anxiety and patients with headache complaints.

Paul (1969) selected three groups of 20 persons each, who were equal on scores on a test of general anxiety level. One of the groups was then administered instructions in progressive relaxation by means of a tape recorder. A second group was administered a standardized technique for inducing hypnosis. The third group was a control, given an equal period in which they were simply instructed to relax any way they wished. Heart rate, respiration rate, muscle tension, and skin conductance were measured before, during, and after the session; and the entire procedure was repeated a week later. The results for the first session are shown in Figure 6.4 where it can be seen that both relaxation training and hypnotic suggestion produced effects and that the relaxation training resulted in generally greater effects than the hypnotic suggestions. It should be noted that the anxiety test reflected subjective change in tension that agreed with the changes in physiological responses. Similar results were obtained on the second session.

Schandler and Grings (1976) in a very similar experiment, compared the effects of progressive relaxation (PR) training, a control test (CT), and two types of biofeedback training where information about muscle

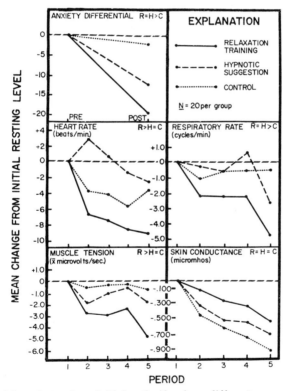

FIGURE 6.4. Mean change from initial resting levels on different measures for the various conditions. Session I. [From Paul, G. L. Physiological effects of relaxation training and hypnotic suggestion. *Journal of Abnormal Psychology,* 1969, *74,* 425–437. Copyright 1969 by the American Psychological Association. Reprinted by permission.]

potentials was fed back to subjects either visually (VFB) on a meter, or by tactile vibrations on the skin (TFB). Heart rate, EMG measured from the forearm (extensor muscle) and the forehead (frontalis muscle), and skin conductance were recorded. Progressive relaxation and the two types of feedback procedures provided significantly greater reductions than the control situation for both subjective and physiological measurements. The physiological changes are shown in Figure 6.5.

If relaxation procedures are to be applied in practical situations such as psychotherapy, it becomes desirable to determine whether patients with

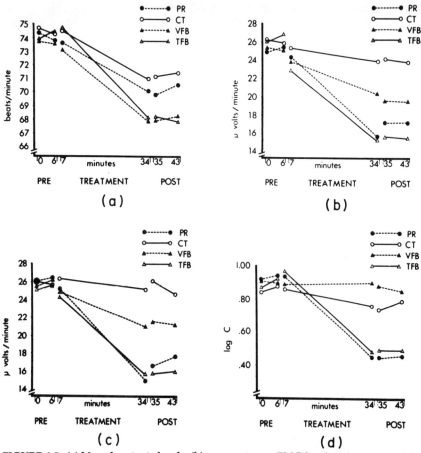

FIGURE 6.5. (a) Mean heart rate levels, (b) mean extensor EMG levels, (c) mean frontalis EMG levels, and (d) mean log skin conductance levels for each experimental group ($N = 20$) over all measurement periods for PR (progressive relaxation), CT (control test), VFB (visual feedback), and TFB (tactual feedback). [From Schandler & Grings, 1976.]

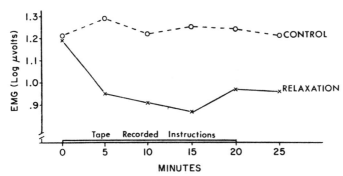

FIGURE 6.6. Average responses for phobic patients under relaxation and control conditions, frontalis EMG. [From Mathews & Gelder, 1969.]

emotional problems will respond effectively to the procedures and show the types of physiological changes present in a normal population. Matthews and Gelder (1969) administered progressive relaxation to 14 phobic patients and then measured the patients in two situations: (a) a relaxation session and (b) a control session. Frontalis EMG, skin conductance, heart rate, and respiration were measured, along with self-ratings of tension. While the EMG and skin conductance values were significantly lower during relaxation (see Figure 6.6), heart rate and respiration were not. Subjective ratings of tension were correlated with skin conductance measures. While the results of this study cannot be taken as evidence for the effectiveness of relaxation training in alleviating phobic disorders, they do show short-term significant physiological changes for the patients.

Biofeedback procedures have been widely applied to different clinical problems, ranging from the alleviation of anxiety to the treatment of specific symptoms, such as headaches, high blood pressure, and excessive sweating. It is not possible to summarize this work here, but one example will be noted. In this case, headaches were the symptom and EMG feedback from the muscles of the forehead (the frontalis muscle group) were employed. Figure 6.7 gives a diagram of the kind of instrumentation that was used to give auditory information to the patient about forehead muscle tension. As a result of the training, the patients not only learned to reduce the tension in the frontalis muscle, they also showed clear reduction in their reports of discomfort from headaches, as is shown in Figure 6.8.[11]

[11]The illustration regarding EMG feedback and tension headache levels was taken from Budzynski, Stoyva, and Adler (1970).

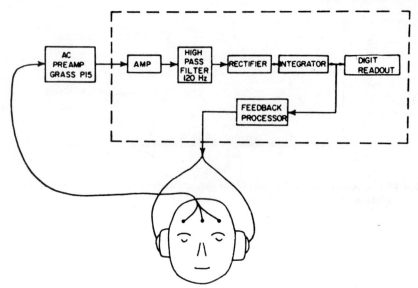

FIGURE 6.7. Functional diagram: EMG information feedback. [From Budzynski, Stoyva, & Adler, 1970.]

DESENSITIZATION OF FEARS

One example of teaching relaxation in specific stimulus situations is called *systematic desensitization*. Consider a situation in which persons express a fear of snakes and this fear of snakes is measured in some way, such as measuring how close the individual can physically come to a snake in a cage. The desensitization procedure typically consists of two parts. The first part involves relaxation training and consists of interviewing the individual to develop a hierarchy of world events that are adequate to elicit the fear behavior. In the second part, the individual imagines a situation that is low on the hierarchy while at the same time applying the procedures that have been learned for relaxation. Assuming that the relaxation is strong enough to overshadow the mild anxiety for an item low on the anxiety hierarchy, the subject then proceeds to an item of higher (or more capable of eliciting) anxiety. This continues until a hierarchy item is reached that is just strong enough to overshadow the response of relaxation. When this is done, the individual pauses and practices the application of relaxation to stimulus items at that level. Eventually it becomes possible to advance through the hierarchy to where anxiety is not perceived on imagined events, which originally were very strong in eliciting fear responses.

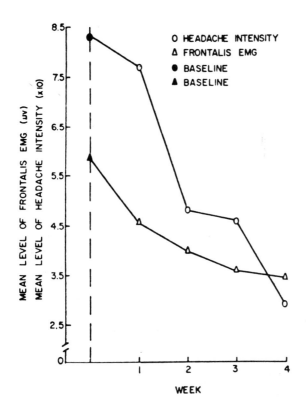

FIGURE 6.8. Mean tension headache levels and mean frontalis EMG levels for five patients over a 5-week period. [From Budzynski, Stoyva, & Adler, 1970.]

For research on desensitization it has been common practice to use college student volunteers and the phobic behavior about which they are most aware. The most common phobic behavior is the fear of snakes (others are fear of public speaking and fear of spiders). One experiment of this type is of particular interest because it used bodily responses to measure emotional arousal.[12] An apparatus for administering desensitization automatically, termed a device for automated desensitization (DAD), was constructed. The DAD consisted essentially of two magnetic tape transports. On one there were taped instructions in muscular relaxation, instructions to imagine hierarchy items, questions concerning fear evocation, and the vividness of the items, plus the subject's anxiety

[12]Lang, Melamed, and Hart (1970, 1975), and Lang (1971). The electrodermal correlates of systematic desensitization have been reviewed by Katkin and Deitz (1973).

hierarchy in the appropriate order. The other transport involved taped instructions in relaxation and a question about relative change in fear evocation of successive items. The DAD instructed the subject to relax and then to visualize the hierarchy items in order. The equipment was programmed to present each item twice before the subsequent item was presented. If the subject signalled fear by pressing a switch on the left arm of the chair, the item was immediately terminated and instructions to stop visualizing the scene and to relax were given.

Two studies were conducted utilizing this method. One assessed the effectiveness of the DAD as a therapist by comparing improvement with automated and live desensitization procedures, and evaluated physiological activity during the treatment, particularly to see (a) if hierarchy items on which the subject signalled anxiety showed higher physiological arousal levels than adjacent items, and (b) whether repetition of the items was associated with reduction of those responses. The second study evaluated the hypothesis that anxiety hierarchies constitute gradients of autonomic activity.

The first experiment used 29 female volunteers, all of whom were snake phobic. The study was explained to them as one of fear reduction. The fear of each subject was measured and rated both by the experimenter and by the subjects themselves filling out a snake-fear questionnaire. Four physiological variables were employed: (a) heart rate, (b) skin conductance, (c) respiration rate, and (d) muscle action potential (measured from the left forearm extensor). Subjects were assigned to one of three groups: (a) automated (or DAD), (b) live desensitization (LIVE), and (c) nontreatment (control). The treatment subjects had four sessions. First, they were trained in relaxation, practiced visualizing neutral scenes, and constructed the anxiety hierarchy in collaboration with the therapist. A hierarchy of 20 items was developed and arranged in ascending order. Most were based on the individual's responses but 4 standard items were used: 2 were at the top of the hierarchy (e.g., holding a live snake in your hands) and 2 were at the bottom (e.g., writing the word snake in a notebook).

Following the sessions, all subjects were given a posttreatment assessment battery. This consisted of an interview, the snake avoidance (or approach) test, and self-ratings. The automated procedure (DAD) was as effective in producing improvement as the LIVE procedure and both were superior to the control procedure. Bodily responses to hierarchy items for which anxiety was reported during training are shown in Figure 6.9 where it can be noted that heart rate, skin conductance, and respiration rate were all at a much higher level during visualized scenes which subjects signalled as fearful than during other scenes (not signalled as fearful).

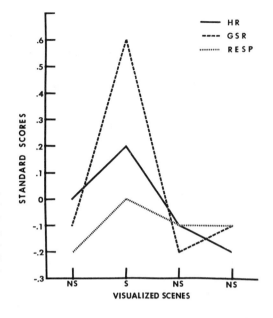

FIGURE 6.9. Heart rate (HR), skin conductance (GSR), and respiration rate (RESP) responses during visualized scenes following which subjects signaled fear (S), and the preceding and subsequent nonsignal (NS) scenes. [From Lang, Melamed, & Hart, 1970.]

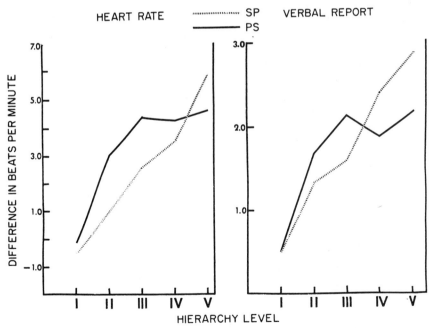

FIGURE 6.10. Heart rate and verbal report for increasing levels of anxiety hierarchy (I–V) for spider phobic (SP) and public-speaking-anxious (PS) subjects. [From Lang, Melamed, & Hart, 1970.]

In the second study an attempt was made to explore the anxiety hierarchy to determine whether the intensity of the subject's verbally reported fear following the visualization of the item was correlated with physiological responses. Subjects with either fear of public speaking or fear of spiders were employed. The results for both groups can be seen in Figure 6.10 where the ascending hierarchy levels for the stimuli are indicated with Roman numerals. The physiological responses (HR) on the left are compared with the verbal reports of intensity of anxiety on the right where it will be noted that the two curves are quite parallel. From this series of observations, the investigators conclude that the process of desensitization may be effectively investigated by automated procedures, and that concomitant psychophysiological measures add strength to the evidence for marked emotional changes.

CONCLUSION

Some of the physiological changes that occur during general states of sleep, stress, relaxation, and fear-reduction have been reviewed. The principal physiological response measured during sleep is the EEG, which is used to measure and define depth of sleep. Endocrine and autonomic changes have been measured in a variety of physically and psychologically stressful situations. Autonomic and skeletal changes have been employed as indices of relaxation following various methods of inducing relaxation (e.g., progressive relaxation, hypnosis, biofeedback, and systematic desensitization). They have also been used to indicate progress in reducing fear by the method of desensitization.

7
Psychosomatic Disorders

When a physiological dysfunction appears to result from an emotional origin the disorder is likely to be termed *psychosomatic*. More specifically, the term may refer to classes of disorders involving organs and structures regulated by the autonomic nervous system, and situations with emotional stress. In preference to the term psychosomatic, some medical classifications use the designation *psychophysiologic autonomic and visceral disorders*.[1]

Whatever the terminology used, the essential assumption is that the disorders involve visceral expressions of emotion. The list of reactions include several classes of common problems: gastrointestinal (e.g., ulcers, mucous colitis, and chronic gastritis); skin reactions (e.g., atopic dermatitis and hyperhydrosis); respiration problems (e.g., bronchial spasm, hyperventilation, and sighing syndrome); cardiovascular difficulties (e.g., tachycardia, hypertension, and migraine); musculoskeletal reactions (e.g., muscle cramps and tension headaches); genitourinary problems (e.g., dysuria); plus many others depending upon the particular criteria for classification.

---

[1]Some of the problems in classifications of psychosomatic disorders have been reviewed by Katz, Cole, and Barton (1965). For a detailed orientation to current trends in research on psychosomatic disorders, the volume edited by Lipowski, Lipsett, and Whybrow (1977) will be found to be helpful.

Conjectures about just how the reactions are linked to emotion have been numerous, and a few of the popular interpretations will be reviewed here. They include (a) a necessary conditions hypothesis; (b) a specific attitude hypothesis; and (c) a response specificity hypothesis. A few other interpretations, like a stress adaptation syndrome theory and a substitution theory will be mentioned only briefly.

NECESSARY CONDITIONS HYPOTHESIS

As its name implies, a *necessary conditions* interpretation rests on the notion that in order for a psychosomatic disorder to become manifest certain circumstances must occur. One of these is the exposure to stressful or emotion-arousing situations. Assuming prolonged exposure to such stressful events, the person who is susceptible to some sort of physiological breakdown is one who also does not have efficient mechanisms for coping with and modulating the emotional arousal. As one writer puts it, such a person does not have adequate homeostatic restraints. Finally, it is assumed that individual-response stereotypy (see Chapter 3) operates to produce strong reactions with certain response systems, thus increasing the vulnerability of that response outlet as the focus of the physiological complaint.

This form of interpretation has one clear advantage. It isolates or suggests a subprocess that can be measured and scientifically tested for its relevance. For example, it assumes that individual-response specificity can be demonstrated and that such stereotypy will be correlated with the psychosomatic symptomatology. Further, it assumes that mechanisms for modulating emotional activation can be identified and used both in terms of describing cause and effect relations and developing preventive and remedial procedures. The mechanisms may be learned and subject to investigation as methods of behavior change. Finally, the emphasis on environmental stimulus determiners is important for scientific observation and classification with an ultimate goal of improving the life environment. One proponent[2] of the above interpretation has expressed the three conditions in the form of a logical *"if-then"* statement, as follows:

	individual-		inadequate		exposure to		psychosomatic
if	response	*and*	homeostatic	*and*	activating	*then*	episodes
	stereotypy		restraints		situations		

[2]The necessary conditions interpretation is based on Chapter 10 in Sternbach (1966).

SPECIFIC ATTITUDE HYPOTHESIS

A second interpretation that is particularly relevant for the present discussion is one that asserts that (a) each psychosomatic disease is associated with its own specific attitude, and (b) each attitude has its own specific physiological characteristic. This theory defines emotion as a response consisting of a combination of an attitude and a physiological change. Put differently, the emotion is regarded as a response to an event that has two different aspects.

The first of these consists of the physiological changes occurring in the organism during the emotional response. The second aspect of the emotional response is how the person feels about the event that has produced the response. This feeling about the precipitating event has been called an *attitude*. The attitude in this usage consists of two parts: (a) what the person feels is happening to him; and (b) what he wants to do about it or what action he wants to take.[3]

It is then assumed that each psychosomatic disease is part of a specific emotion, and each emotion has its own unique physiological component. Graham (1972) relates 18 psychosomatic disorders to 18 specific attitudes. The following brief listing is taken from the Graham article.

1. Urticaria (hives): felt he was taking a beating and was helpless to do anything about it.
2. Ulcerative colitis: felt he was being injured and degraded and wished he could get rid of the responsible agent.
3. Eczema: felt he was being frustrated and could do nothing about it except take it out on himself.
4. Acne: felt he was picked on or at and wanted to be let alone.
5. Psoriasis: felt there was a constant gnawing at him and that he had to put up with it.
6. Asthma and rhinitis: felt left out in the cold and wanted to shut the person or situation out.
7. Hyperthyroidism: felt he might lose somebody or something he loved and took care of, and wanted to prevent loss of the loved person or object.
8. Vomiting: felt something wrong had happened, usually something for which he felt responsible, and wished it hadn't happened, and wanted to undo it.
9. Duodenal ulcer: felt deprived of what was due him and wanted to get even.
10. Constipation: felt in a situation from which nothing good could come but kept on with it grimly.
11. Essential hypertension: felt threatened with harm and had to be ready for anything.

[3]Elaboration of the attitude specificity hypothesis can be found in references by Graham, Stern, and Winokur (1960) and Graham, Lundy, Benjamin, Kabler, Lewis, Kunish, and Graham (1962).

12. Migraine: felt something had to be achieved and then relaxed after the effort.
13. Multiple sclerosis: felt he was forced to undertake some kind of activity, especially hard work, and wanted not to, but to have help and support.
14. Metabolic edema (idiopathic edema of females): felt she was carrying a heavy load and wanted somebody else to carry all or part of it.
15. Rheumatoid arthritis: felt tied down and wanted to get free.
16. Raynaud's disease: wanted to take hostile gross motor action.
17. Regional enteritis: felt he has received something harmful and wanted to get rid of it.
18. Low backache: wanted to run away [p. 857].

Three methods have been devised and utilized for testing the attitude hypothesis. The first used ratings by judges of interview protocols obtained on admission interviews with hospitalized patients. Two studies were conducted. The first involved 16 patients having 8 different diseases and the second employed 20 patients having 10 different diseases. The purpose of the interview was to locate events occurring close in time to the onset of the disease and to obtain a statement by the patient of his attitude toward the event. One hour tape-recorded interviews were obtained for analysis. Results of the two studies are shown in Table 7.1 where it can be seen that the judges selected the correct attitudes (i.e., the attitude predicted to be associated with the patient's disease) significantly more often than they selected the same attitude when patients had other diseases.

A second method for evaluating predictions employed cartoons intended to illustrate the attitudes. Examples of these cartoons are shown in Figure 7.1 with the associated interpretations. The cartoons were then presented to hospitalized patients having various relevant diseases. It was hypothesized that patients with a disease relevant to the cartoon would respond to that cartoon in a way different from patients who have other diseases not relevant to the cartoon. The measure of response was a verbal choice between cartoons by the patient. The subjects were asked

TABLE 7.1
Mean Percentage Predicted Choices of Attitudes Compared to the Mean Percentage Unpredicted Choices of the Same Attitudes[a]

Blind interviews	Predicted choices	Unpredicted choices
Study I	28.1	17.4
Study II	45.0	20.8
Studies I and II	37.5	19.3

[a] From Graham (1962).

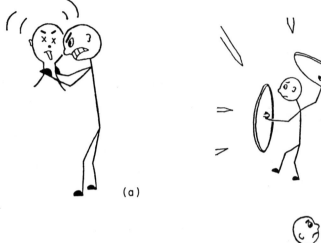

FIGURE 7.1. Cartoons designed to depict critical attitudes of (a) Raynaud's disease, (b) essential hypertension, and (c) hives. [From Graham, D. T. Research on psychophysiological specificity. In R. Roessler and N. Greenfield (Eds.), *Physiological Correlates of Psychological Disorder*. Madison: University of Wisconsin Press, 1962. Reprinted by permission.]

to compare every cartoon with every other cartoon (i.e., using a paired comparison psychophysical procedure). In one study there were 18 subjects selected from patients hospitalized for hypertension, hyperthyroidism, asthma, eczema, multiple sclerosis, ulcerative colitis, duodenal ulcer, rheumatoid arthritis, metabolic edema, or hives; and the verbal responses were scored by ranking the responses to the cartoons according to frequency of choice.

Only one of the cartoons was relevant for each patient depending upon his disease. It was then determined whether the rank assigned by the patient who did have the corresponding disease was in the first, second, third, or fourth quartile of the distribution obtained from the patients who did not have the disease. A first analysis of the results showed no significant difference in quartiles but it was noted that a possible relation to intelligence existed. Patients were, therefore, divided into groups scoring above and below the median on the Wechsler

Adult Intelligence Scale and it was found that subjects scoring above the median tended to choose the relevant cartoons significantly more often whereas the less intelligent subjects tended to reject it significantly more often. To further evaluate this finding, a new group of 29 patients was obtained and evaluated, including the subdivision on intelligence. The findings were that the verbal choice of the cartoons was such that the subjects tended either to accept or to deny their relevant cartoon depending roughly upon their intelligence level.

The third method applied experimental induction of attitudes in volunteer subjects. Healthy young men were hypnotized and given attitude suggestions. Physiological responses were measured before, during, and after the attitude suggestion. In one study (Graham, Stern, & Winokur, 1960) the attitude associated with hives and the attitude associated with Raynaud's disease were chosen because the characteristic feature of the physiological reactions associated with hives is a warming of the skin, whereas a characteristic feature of the response in Raynaud's disease is a cooling of the skin. The hypothesis was that when the hives attitude was suggested skin temperature would rise and when Raynaud's attitude was suggested the skin temperature would fall. Subjects were hypnotized and given a brief relaxation period. Then a first attitude suggestion was made and sustained for 10 minutes. Then a second period of relaxation occurred followed by the second attitude suggestion, which was also sustained for 10 minutes. The order of presentation of the two attitudes was varied.

Instructions given for the hives attitude were

> Doctor X is now going to burn your hand with a match. When he does so, you will feel very much mistreated, very unfairly treated, but you will be unable to do anything about it; and you can't even think of anything you want to do about it; you just have to take it. You were thinking only about what happened to you [p. 11].

After this the hand was touched with an unlit match and the attitude suggestion was repeated throughout the 10-minute period. The suggestion for the Raynaud's disease attitude was

> You feel mistreated, and you want to hit Doctor X. You want to hit him just as hard as you can. You want to hit him and choke him and strangle him; that's all you are thinking about—how much you want to hit him [p. 11].

This suggestion was similarly repeated throughout the 10-minute period. As will be noted from Figure 7.2, small but clear-cut differences developed after the attitude induction. The changes in skin temperature occurred as were predicted. Another way to evaluate these data is in terms of changes of hand temperature following the attitude sugges-

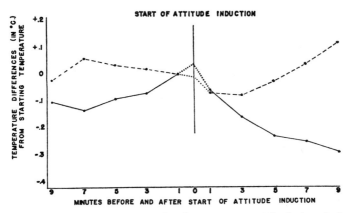

FIGURE 7.2. Mean differences between hand temperatures at the last control readings and after induction of attitudes for Raynaud's disease (——) and hives (---).

tions. A tabular presentation of this form is presented in Table 7.2. As can be seen, most of the subjects who had hives attitude showed a temperature increase whereas most who had a Raynaud's disease attitude had a temperature decrease.

In a later study (Graham, 1962), the attitudes associated with hives and with essential hypertension were examined employing five physiological measures: (a) skin temperature, (b) diastolic blood pressure, (c) systolic blood pressure, (d) heart rate, and (e) respiration rate. It was predicted that there would be a rise in skin temperature in response to hives attitude, whereas such a change would not occur with a hypertension attitude suggestion. Conversely, it was predicted that there would be a rise in diastolic blood pressure in response to hypertension attitude suggestion, whereas such changes would not accompany the hives attitude suggestion. A procedure similar to that employed in the previous study was used on 20 male subjects. The suggestion for the hypertension attitude was that the subject felt he might be attacked and hurt at any instant and had to try to be ready for whatever was going to happen. The results were in accord with the predictions. That is, temperature changes with the hives instruction were in the form of increases and exceeded changes for the hypertension suggestion. The hypertension suggestion, on the other hand, produced diastolic blood pressure increases, which did not occur under the hives attitude suggestion. From this series of studies the researchers concluded that the specific attitude hypothesis of psychosomatic disease is supported.[4]

[4]A general summary of this research is provided in Graham (1962).

TABLE 7.2
Number of Changes in Hand Temperature Following
Attitude Suggestions[a]

Attitude suggested	Temperature increases	Temperature decreases
Hives	17	6
Raynaud's disease	3	15

[a] From Graham et al. (1960).

RESPONSE SPECIFICITY HYPOTHESIS

This interpretation implies that some individuals are predisposed to develop specific response patterns in reaction to stress situations. That is, when faced with environmental stress, some individuals develop tendencies to respond with heightened cardiovascular activity, others with changes in breathing, still others with gastrointestinal activity. Empirical research examining this hypothesis has produced varied results, some supporting the hypothesis, others not. Note will be made here of three examples in the study of bronchial asthma.

One point of departure for each study was the notion that asthma is associated with an overactive parasympathetic system or with an underactive sympathetic system, since during an asthmatic attack behavior activated by the PNS appears to be dominant. In addition, an asthmatic attack can frequently be checked by an injection of epinephrine or by cutting certain branches of the vagus nerve. Early research done by Hahn and his associates (Hahn, 1966; Hahn & Clark, 1967) however, did not support this notion of parasympathetic predominance and investigators were led to study overall autonomic activity in asthmatic children as compared to nonasthmatic children. In one such comparison it was observed that asthmatic children showed a higher mean heart rate and a higher skin temperature than a group of control children when they were performing a problem solving task and anticipating an electric shock. Data comparing the two groups of asthmatic and nonasthmatic children on heart rate and skin temperature are given in Table 7.3.

A related study compared 18 asthmatic children and 21 nonasthmatic controls on self-reports about reactions to criticism. They also compared heart rate, finger and face temperature, finger blood volume, skin resistance, and respiration rate of the subjects when they were exposed to a shock, a tone, and a problem solving task. The asthmatic children showed a more negative affect to criticism than the controls, and the heart rate reactions of the asthmatics were higher. Finger temperatures

TABLE 7.3
Mean Heart Rate and Skin Temperature Measures for
Asthmatic (A) and Nonasthmatic (NA) Children during
Various Phases[a] of the Recording Session[b]

Period	Heart rate		Temperature	
	A	NA	A	NA
Initial	91.0	74.0	34.1	31.1
Resting	86.4	69.7	34.7	32.7
Prestimulus (Task 1)	88.1	73.8	34.2	31.4
Prestimulus (Task 2)	88.2	72.6	34.2	31.4

[a] All group differences except the resting temperature condition are significantly different.
[b] From Hahn (1966).

of the asthmatics were also significantly higher than for the normals. The breathing records of the two groups under task stress were quite different. The normals increased their respiration rate under the stimulus situations whereas the asthmatics did not.

The authors did not endeavor to interpret whether the differences in respiration rate were due to physiological or psychological factors. For example, it might be that the children consciously inhibited their breathing rate since they were aware that overbreathing might precipitate an attack. On the other hand, it could be that physiological factors are involved, such as faulty regulation of respiratory mechanisms due to an imbalance of autonomic discharge. The authors tended to favor the notion that lack of proper balance in the ANS is an important aspect of the asthmatic syndrome, and that when the asthmatic is subjected to psychological stress this imbalance may play an important part in the onset of the attack.

It may be of interest to note a quite different approach to the study of the psychophysiology of asthma that proceeds from a psychoanalytic point of view and assumes that the asthmatic has a respiratory system that is predisposed to respond during a particular emotional conflict. That conflict involves separation from or the loss of a loved one, usually a maternal figure. When an emotional stimulus breaks down the asthmatic's defense against the threat of loss, the asthmatic symptoms are activated. The particular study was designed to stimulate known asthmatics to react symptomatically to a movie depicting emotionally arousing scenes of separation from loved ones. An allergy potential scale that was used as an index of allergic predisposition was administered to 35 adult asthmatics. Physical measures of respiration (volume, pressure, and rate) were made as well as measures of heart rate, finger temperature, neck temperature, and skin conductance. Only the respiratory system showed differential reactivity to the stimulus situation. The authors concluded that they had demonstrated support for a theory of organ specificity.[5]

These studies are examples of the type of research conducted to evaluate bodily reaction as it relates to specific psychosomatic conditions. Related examples have involved comparisons of characteristic physiological response patterns in hypertensive patients as compared to rheumatoid arthritics, where it has been found that arthritics did not adapt in muscle tension whereas they did adapt in blood pressure. The hypertensives showed adaptation in muscle tension but demonstrated sustained elevation in blood pressure. Results were interpreted in terms of a theory of response specificity. Still another investigation compared cardiovascular responses in healthy young adults and patients with peptic ulcer and hypertension while the subjects were participating in a thematic apperception test. Major differences were found between healthy adults and both classes of patients.[6]

OTHER INTERPRETATIONS

The preceding explanations of psychosomatic disorder were similar in several respects. Each rested upon some form of individual response specificity and all emphasized relations between psychological and physiological factors. There are many other interpretations that are generally characterized by a stronger emphasis on either the physiological or the psychological features.

The general adaptation syndrome, said to result from stress, has been related to psychosomatic disorders. As noted in Chapter 6, this syndrome involves three sequential stages of reactions. The first stage of response to stress is an alarm reaction characterized by mobilization of the neural and endocrine systems of the pituitary gland and adrenal cortex. This is followed by a stage of resistance or fight against the stress. Finally, with prolonged stress, a stage of exhaustion is reached.

[5]The example of psychoanalytic predictions about physiological correlates of emotional conflict was taken from Selesnick, Malmstrom, Yonger, and Lederman (1969). For further detail on the psychoanalytic interpretations in terms of "conflict specificity" see Graham (1972).

[6]While there is common agreement that some form of response organ specificity occurs, it has been very difficult to determine the extent that such specificity antedates the disorder in a causal fashion as contrasted to being a product or result of the disorder. The example cited is typical of attempts to associate reactions and organs. It is from Moos and Engel (1962).

Among the critical tasks of this interpretation is how to define stress. While incorporating the more common notions of environmental events, which are reacted to as potentially deleterious to the organism, a more general definition is used to include any invasion by disease processes and nonspecific stresses that leads to involvement (or defensive reaction) by the pituitary–adrenal system. The kind of exhaustion that results from prolonged resistance to stress may result in irreversible physiological symptoms. This exhaustion has been described as akin to rapid aging or rapid senility, resulting from inappropriate response to (emotional) stress.

Other theories also focus on the role of stress as the source of difficulty. One argues for the importance of predisposing structural or physiological weakness, which is likely to be genetic in nature. When a person with such a "weak organ system" is submitted to prolonged stress that organ system puts up the least resistance and is, hence, the one most likely to break down. A variation on this is the notion that people are predisposed to overaction with a particular response system, which has the effect of wearing the system out with prolonged stress.

Interpretations emphasizing psychological factors may associate particular disorders with specific traits of personality, or they may assume that the dysfunction symbolizes a form of regressive adjustment to more primitive modes of reaction to stress. Particular symptoms may be associated with cultural determiners. In support of this last interpretation, data have been gathered to document the prevalence of some psychosomatic conditions in certain nations and geographical locations, as contrasted with an absence of the same conditions in other locales.

EXPERIMENTAL PSYCHOSOMATICS

Research with laboratory animals makes possible the examination of developmental aspects of psychosomatic diseases. In other words, it is possible to produce the symptoms of diseases, such as gastric ulcers and essential hypertension, in rats, monkeys, etc. Variables determining the course of such physiological changes can thus be examined and evaluated. A brief look will be taken at representative studies involving these two major conditions, hypertension and ulcers.

Henry and Ely and their associates (Henry & Ely, 1976; Henry, Ely, Watson, & Stephens, 1975) have evaluated the proposition that psychosocial stimuli are capable of inducing prolonged systolic hypertension. It was assumed that increased systolic blood pressure may result from repeated symbolic stimuli arising from the social environment. The research task became that of producing with laboratory mice appropriate stressful social stimuli. This was accomplished by playing on the animal's inborn drives for territory, survival, and reproduction. An experimental group of mice was exposed to four general classes of events: (*a*) Animals previously maintained in different boxes were mixed. (*b*) Animals were placed in groups in quite small boxes. (*c*) Groups of animals were subjected to threat from a predator. (*d*) Conflict among the animals for territory was induced by placing equal numbers of males and females in an interconnected box system. By such experimental manipulation, the investigators produced arterial blood pressure increases from 126 mm Hg to 150–160 mm Hg and observed the elevated blood pressure to sustain itself for 6 to 9 months. The effects of drugs (such as reserpine) upon the blood pressure were also studied and it was found that the elevated pressures of the animals responded to drugs in a fashion parallel to the responses of adult humans. It was concluded that social grouping of nonprimates can be used to provide an experimental approach to the study of hypertension.

The psychosomatic condition that has probably received more work in animal research than any other is the production of gastric ulcers. In fact, amount of ulceration has been a useful index of the effects of stress in studies where the production of ulcer was not the central issue and the variable was used only as a dependent index. Early studies evaluated conditioned avoidance behavior as a potential determiner of ulceration. The extent to which the animal is restrained and immobilized was considered to be relevant. Motivational and emotional conflicts can be produced readily in laboratory situations and have been examined as a crucial determiner of ulceration, and such conditions have been observed to operate differently under different amounts of deprivation of the animal and to be accompanied or influenced by hypersecretion of gastric acid and perhaps decreased tissue resistance. Later studies have emphasized the role of conditioned fear.[7]

A general conclusion from this research, only a small portion of which

---

[7]Some of these early studies had their origin in research on "experimental neurosis." Pavlov (1927) described several kinds of situations for producing neurotic behavior in dogs. They included situations containing a threat to existence or security, a danger that was not anticipated, and situations requiring the animals to make difficult discriminations. The neurotic behavior contained many of the somatic symptoms associated with psychosomatic disorders.

The variables mentioned in the text with reference to gastric ulceration are typical of those studied in the quarter century that followed. For specific references on: ulcerations and conditioned avoidance see Brady (1970); restraint and immobilization see Ader (1964) and Brodie (1963); conflict see Sawrey and Weisz (1956); conditioned fear see Sawrey and Sawrey (1964).

is noted above, suggests that many variables are relevant to the production of ulcers. On the other hand, just how influential a particular factor is may depend upon the extent to which the animal can control the environment. In general terms, the greater the degree of control by the animal the less the degree of ulceration. Two variables of this type, which determine the extent of elicitation of fear in the animal, are the predictability of noxious events and the availability of coping behavior by the animal. For example, it has been shown that rats that are shocked through the tail will show less ulceration when the shocks are preceded by a tone signal, which makes the shock's appearance predictable, than when such a signal is not present. In a parallel situation inducing shock to the tail, ulceration in animals provided with escape or avoidance possibilities was compared to that of yoked controls and it was found that the animals capable of avoiding showed less ulceration than yoked controls receiving the same number of shocks.[8]

CONCLUSION

Emotions play a significant role in psychosomatic illness. However, there is still speculation about exactly how bodily responses and psychosomatic disorders are related. One of the theories assumes that illness occurs only when three necessary conditions are met: prolonged exposure to emotional events by a person who does not have adequate mechanisms for modulating physiological reactions, yet has strong tendencies to respond to emotional stress with a characteristic response pattern.

Other theories rest on what are termed principles of specificity. In one, there is a relation between a specific attitude toward the environment and a physiological reaction characteristic of the attitude. Each psychosomatic disorder is thus associated with a specific attitude. Another form of specificity centers on the notion of associations between emotional conflicts and physiological reactions. As an example, responses of the respiration system were seen as sensitive to conflicts.

The different interpretations have been subjected to experimental test. Induced attitudes were observed to produce characteristic response changes in human subjects. Animal studies have shown that social–psychological factors are capable of producing long term systolic hypertension and gastric ulceration. Continued research with both humans and animals will clarify these subtle relations.

[8]The research described here was reported by Miller (1967). Later research emphasizing the role of coping behavior to ulceration is described by Weiss (1972).

8
Learning of Bodily Responses

TYPES OF LEARNING

We now come to the question of how changes in bodily responses in emotion are altered by learning experiences. During a life span, dramatic and complex changes occur in the kinds of stimuli that elicit emotional behavior. Such development contributes to the great varieties in behavior that occur, from the peak of happiness to the depth of despair and even to the disintegrations of personality. Such changes brought about by learning interact with genetic variables and other organic factors such as chemical changes resulting from drugs and disease.

Tradition has held that the primary means for modifying autonomically mediated behavior is a form of association learning or Pavlovian conditioning (sometimes called respondent conditioning or classical conditioning). Pavlovian conditioning is a technique of changing behavior to a *neutral conditioned stimulus* by associating or pairing that stimulus with an *emotion-producing unconditioned stimulus*. Due to that pairing procedure the neutral stimulus comes to elicit a response called a *conditioned response*. The typical arrangement of stimuli and responses in Pavlovian conditioning is summarized in Figure 8.1.

A classical illustration of such learning is the case of a child learning to fear a furry animal, like a rabbit. Beginning with the fact that a young child will give a fear response to a sudden loud noise, a series of experi-

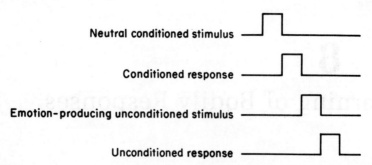

Neutral conditioned stimulus

Conditioned response

Emotion-producing unconditioned stimulus

Unconditioned response

FIGURE 8.1. Typical temporal sequence of stimuli and responses in Pavlovian conditioning.

ences are arranged in which the presence of the furry object (the *conditioned stimulus*) is followed by the appearance of the loud noise (the *unconditioned stimulus*). The loud noise will cause the child to cry or exhibit other signs of fear (the *unconditioned response*). After a few pairings the child shows definite signs of fearing the furry rabbit (the *conditioned response*).

More recently, a second general learning process has been emphasized in connection with learning bodily responses. It is *instrumental conditioning* (sometimes referred to as *operant conditioning*). Whereas in Pavlovian conditioning the association of events (conditioned and unconditioned stimuli) is not dependent upon behavior of the organism, in instrumental learning the organism must make a response in order for stimulation (reinforcement) to occur. The important point is that the frequency or magnitude of a response can be changed by following the response with an emotional stimulus or motivational event that serves as the reinforcer.[1]

There are several types of instrumental conditioning, a sampling of which is given here. One type is referred to as *reward training*. It involves the presentation of a reward following the occurrence of a response with the usual result being an increase in the likelihood of that response occurring on future occasions. Another type of instrumental conditioning is called *punishment training*. This consists of presenting an aversive punishing stimulus following the occurrence of a response with the usual result being a decreased likelihood of that response on future

[1]More information regarding the distinction between Pavlovian conditioning and instrumental conditioning can be found in most textbooks on the psychology of learning (e.g., Hall, 1976). Analyses of the various types of learning can be found in Tyron (1976) and Woods (1974).

occasions. A third type of instrumental conditioning is referred to as *avoidance learning*. Here, an aversive stimulus is withheld following the occurrence of a response, otherwise the aversive stimulus is presented. The usual result in avoidance learning is an increased likelihood of the response. It should be pointed out that each of these forms of instrumental conditioning can come under the control of an external stimulus. That is, organisms can be taught to perform responses based on these training techniques when a particular stimulus is present and not to perform the responses when the stimulus is absent.

Applications of principles of instrumental learning have had a unique history with reference to bodily responses in emotional behavior. It was assumed for many years that responses of the autonomic nervous system were not capable of being modified by such response-contingent reinforcements. The assumption was based on the notion that, since the organism is not aware of autonomic responses, reinforcements could not be applied to such responding. More recently there has been quite a change in this attitude, and instrumental modification of bodily responses has become an important field of study.

Even more recently, another type of learning has been applied successfully to the learned modification of bodily responses. This type, which developed principally as an outgrowth of instrumental conditioning procedures, is based on *biofeedback training*. It involves providing the subject information (feedback) about his biological responses. Hence, the subject has access to information normally not available to him that can be helpful in learning to control his bodily responses.

In the space available here, an attempt will be made to examine the current status of these three forms of learning as they apply to emotional behavior. First the arrangement of Pavlovian (classical) conditioning will be considered because it has been used most extensively. It will be reviewed in terms of general principles applied to the physiological responses that have been the subject of the past research discussion. Then consideration will be given to instrumental learning of emotional behavior. Lastly, the effects of biofeedback training will be reviewed.

PAVLOVIAN CONDITIONING

One of the first questions that must be faced in describing emotional learning is how to define learning so that it can be differentiated from other similar processes. For example, in Pavlovian conditioning the intent is to observe how a previously neutral environmental event acquires the capacity to elicit an emotional response. However, it is possible that the elicitation of an emotional response by a neutral stimulus after pairing with an emotional stimulus could be due simply to the organism becoming aroused or sensitized to all stimuli. It thus becomes necessary to provide a way to tell whether changes that occur are due to specific learning or just due to processes like general excitement.

One way to provide such a definition for learning is to employ a *control group*. For example, one group of individuals experiences the neutral conditioned stimulus paired with the emotional unconditioned stimulus and is subsequently tested for the capability of the conditioned stimulus to elicit the emotional response. A second group—the control group—is given the same stimulus presentations (i.e., conditioned stimuli and unconditioned stimuli) but they are not in any way temporally related. If, then, the emotional response to the conditioned stimulus is acquired by the group who had paired experiences and is not acquired by the group who did not have paired experiences, a true learning phenomenon (as opposed to a general excitatory state) is considered to be demonstrated. [2]

Another procedure that is commonly employed utilizes a *control stimulus* rather than a control group. The same organism is presented with two neutral or conditioned stimuli, but only one stimulus is paired with the emotional unconditioned stimulus. The other, or control stimulus, is presented but not paired with the unconditioned stimulus. Learning is inferred from differential responding to the two originally neutral stimuli. The organism comes to respond emotionally to the conditioned stimulus paired with the unconditioned stimulus and not to respond to the unpaired stimulus. Such learning is termed *discrimination Pavlovian conditioning*. An illustration of discrimination performance for electrodermal behavior is shown in the top of Figure 8.2 where the term TEST is employed to designate the stimulus paired with an emotional situation (shock) and CONTROL is employed to designate the unapired stimulus. As can be seen, subjects gave larger SCRs to the test stimulus paired with shock than to the control stimulus not paired with shock.

One of the first matters observed with Pavlovian conditioning is that the order of the events is quite important. When the conditioned stimulus precedes the unconditioned stimulus, the situation is termed *forward conditioning*, an arrangement that is conducive to learning. When the conditioned stimulus follows the unconditioned stimulus *backward conditioning*, an arrangement not conducive to learning, results. The interval between the stimuli is also an important factor, as are properties

[2]The issue of appropriate controls can become quite complex. See Rescorla (1967) and Seligman (1969).

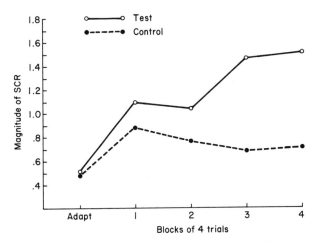

FIGURE 8.2. Electrodermal response magnitudes plotted across trials for stimuli paired with shock (TEST) and stimuli not paired with shock (CONTROL). [Adapted from Grings, W., Lockhart, R., & Dameron, L. Conditioning autonomic responses of mentally subnormal individuals. *Psychological Monographs*, 1962, 76 (39, Whole No. 558). Copyright 1962 by the American Psychological Association. Reprinted by permission.]

of the unconditioned stimulus (e.g., its intensity). The emotional stimulus may be either positive or negative in the sense that it may elicit reactions of approach and reward or it may elicit aversive reactions. Most research on emotional conditioning has emphasized aversive unconditioned stimuli, like electric shock.

Properties of the conditioned stimulus are equally significant. Learning may occur in response to a simple elemental sense impression or a complicated symbolic representation of the environment. It is likely that an infant learns predominantly through simple sense impressions. The adult, on the other hand, responds largely to a symbolic environment. Emotional conditioning to symbolic stimuli probably becomes dominant over learning to nonsymbolic stimuli in the adult, but it is likely that early learning to simple sense impressions retains an active role in expressions of adult emotional behavior. Instances have been reported of the appearance of conditioned responses many years after the original learning experience. A common example of such a situation which can be recalled by most people is the mild emotional response to a melody that had been associated with certain types of life situations many years previously.

It is also important to note that stimuli to receptors within the body (called interoceptors) may function as learning stimuli in very much the same manner as stimuli to the exterior senses (e.g., eyes, ears, etc.) but we may be much less aware of their presence. In this way bodily responses may themselves provide stimuli that can be conditioned to other emotional behavior. Association to internal stimuli resulting from bodily responses has been put forth as one basis for unconscious determination of emotion. The source of the reaction would be relatively unconscious because stimuli arising from internal organs are vague and difficult to verbalize.

Recent research results have suggested a degree of readiness or preparedness to associate certain conditioned stimuli with a specific class of unconditioned stimuli. This was illustrated in an experiment where four groups of college students were studied. The first group had potentially phobic stimuli (snakes and spiders) associated with an aversive unconditioned stimulus (shock); the second group had phobic-irrelevant stimuli (flowers and mushrooms) associated with shock; the third group had potentially phobic stimuli associated with a nonaversive unconditioned stimulus (a tone, which signaled the subject to press a key); and the fourth group had phobic-irrelevant stimuli associated with the nonaversive unconditioned stimulus. Skin conductance responses to the conditioned stimuli were measured as the conditioned response. The results indicated that the potentially phobic stimuli produced better conditioning than the phobic-irrelevant stimuli when shock was the unconditioned stimulus but not when the nonaversive stimulus was the unconditioned stimulus. The authors suggested that there is a biological preparedness to associate certain types of stimuli (e.g., snakes with aversive events) and that this leads to better and more long-lasting autonomic Pavlovian conditioning.[3]

Generalization of learning is another important property of conditioning as it relates to emotions. The crucial observation is that when learning has occurred in response to a particular stimulus, other stimuli that are similar to the learned stimulus become capable of calling forth the response. The similarity may be along a simple dimension like intensity or quality, or it may be along a dimension of meaning, such as when words are the learned stimuli.

A reduction in learned responding can be shown to occur when the neutral stimulus is presented without any longer being followed by the emotional stimulus. The conditioned stimulus loses its ability to elicit the bodily response if it is presented extensively without being accompanied

---

[3]The study that measured conditioning to potentially phobic stimuli and phobic-irrelevant stimuli was reported by Öhman, Fredrikson, Hugdahl, and Rimmö (1976). For a more general discussion of biological preparedness, see Seligman (1970).

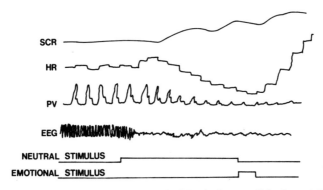

FIGURE 8.3. Responses on a typical Pavlovian conditioning trial.

by the unconditioned stimulus and *extinction* occurs. Because of the practical need to reduce undesirable emotional responses in the interest of mental health, it becomes significant to determine how organisms learn tendencies to not respond to emotional stimuli. The notion of learned inhibition implies that learning to not respond occurs in a fashion similar to the learning of tendencies to respond.

It may be informative to examine the kinds of specific bodily changes that occur when the Pavlovian conditioning arrangement is employed with specific autonomic responses. Figure 8.3 illustrates a typical conditioning trial for several bodily responses (SCR, HR, PVR, and EEG). The onset of the neutral and emotional stimuli are designated by an event-marker tracing. The time between onsets of the stimuli is 7 seconds.

Note first the skin conductance response curve. Research has suggested that the different responses reflect different functional properties. For example, the first response is felt to be evidence of alerting or orienting by the organism to the stimulus. The second response is likely to represent anticipatory or preparatory behavior for receipt of the unconditioned stimulus. The third response is either the response to the emotional stimulus, if it occurs, or a response resulting from omission of the expected emotional stimulus.[4]

Heart rate changes follow a quite different course, due in part to the nature of innervation of the heart. The response is typically multiphasic. First, there is a brief small deceleration immediately following the neutral stimulus. Second, this is followed by a somewhat larger heart rate

[4]The interpretation of the multiple skin conductance responses in Pavlovian conditioning situation is an intriguing one. For example, see Lockhart (1966). The multiple response changes in conditioned heart rate have been studied by Headrick and Graham (1969).

acceleration. Third, there is a pronounced deceleration, which becomes most marked at the time that the emotional stimulus is due to come on. Finally, the heart rate increases when the emotional stimulus is actually presented. Each of these changes in heart rate during the neutral stimulus and the emotional stimulus can be seen in Figure 8.3.

Conditioned changes in pulse volume response (PVR) are somewhat simpler. As illustrated in Figure 8.3, there is a single long-duration decrease in the PVR due to peripheral vasoconstriction during the neutral stimulus.

Numerous changes in the electroencephalogram have been described in a Pavlovian conditioning situation. One of these is the conditioned blocking of the alpha waves. The blocking of the alpha wave pattern is shown in Figure 8.3. More recently changes in cortical evoked responses have also been demonstrated to occur with Pavlovian conditioning trials.

Lest the foregoing examples imply that conditioning is studied only in reference to isolated responses it may be noted that considerable clinical interest has been shown in the modification of complex emotional symptom patterns by conditioning procedures. To cite just one example, conditioning was studied as a cause or contributor to asthmatic attacks. It was demonstrated that patients developed conditioned asthmatic attacks through the association of a neutral stimulus with the presentation of an allergen adequate to produce an attack.[5]

Pavlovian conditioning has generally been considered to be a simple, passive, and unconscious type of learning. However, recent evidence indicates that a person's thoughts and attitudes have significant effects on conditioning. For example, some studies have found that autonomic Pavlovian conditioning occurs only if the person being conditioned is consciously aware of the relationship between the conditioned stimulus and the unconditioned stimulus. Whether such awareness is absolutely necessary for the conditioning of bodily responses is an unsettled and controversial issue. Nevertheless, it is clear that the learning of bodily responses in response to neutral stimuli is greatly influenced by cognitive and symbolic processes, which are represented in a person's conscious experience. Similarly, a person's willingness to be conditioned is an important factor. If a person has a positive attitude and wants to

---

[5]The early studies on relations of conditioning and asthma were by Dekker and his associates (Dekker & Groen, 1956; Dekker, Perlser, & Groen, 1957). For later research on the same issue but using laboratory animals, see Justeen, Braun, Garrison, and Pendleton (1970).

become conditioned then he will condition better than if he has a negative or resistive attitude.[6]

INSTRUMENTAL CONDITIONING

As late as 1960, there was a predominant attitude that visceral-
emotional learning occurred entirely by the Pavlovian conditioning arrangement. More recently, there has been a change of attitude and a
great deal of emphasis has been placed on learning of emotions in situations generally described as instrumental learning.[7]

Most people are familiar with the various types of instrumental conditioning as they are applied to overt behavior. But, the question of current interest is: Can the same forms of learning be used to modify bodily
responses? For example, can reward training, punishment training, and
avoidance learning be used to increase or decrease responses like heart
rate, blood pressure, or skin conductance. Contrary to popular opinion
some years ago, the evidence suggests that the answer is yes. Some of
the evidence that supports this conclusion will now be reviewed briefly.

In one of the early human studies with reward training the illumination of a dim light was used as reinforcement for the emitting of skin
conductance changes. A *yoked control* arrangement was used such that
one group of persons had the occurrence of the light contingent upon
the giving of an SCR by the subject, whereas the other group received
the same number of lights and at the same time but not contingent upon
their behavior. The contingent group increased the frequency of electrodermal reactions and the noncontingent group decreased, as shown
in Figure 8.4. Then, during extinction when the reinforcing dim light
was no longer presented, the electrodermal responses of the two groups
converged.[8]

Similar early work proceeded with heart rate as the response. Subjects
were told that they were participating in a conditioning experiment but

[6]Various points of view regarding the role of cognitive factors in Pavlovian conditioning
of human bodily responses can be found in Baer and Fuhrer (1973), Dawson (1973),
Epstein (1973), Furedy (1973), Grant (1973), Grings (1973), Lockhart (1973), Mandel and
Bridger (1973), Ross and Nelson (1973), and Stern (1973).

[7]The changing attitude toward the possibilities of instrumentally conditioning bodily
responses has been discussed by Miller (1969) and Hall (1976).

[8]One of the earliest demonstrations of instrumental conditioning of electrodermal responses was reported by Kimmel and Kimmel (1963). A more general review of such
conditioning has been provided by H. D. Kimmel (1974).

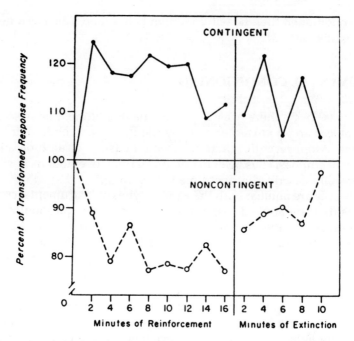

FIGURE 8.4. Frequency of electrodermal responses for persons whose response was followed by a light (contingent group) and persons receiving the same number of lights not associated with response (noncontingent). [From Kimmel, E., & Kimmel, H. D. Replication of operant conditioning of the GSR. *Journal of Experimental Psychology*, 1963, *65*, 212–213. Copyright 1963 by the American Psychological Association. Reprinted by permission.]

they were not told that heart rate was going to be used as the response to be reinforced. They were told that the correct response would turn on a light and a clock, both of which they could see. They were also told to try to keep the light on and that they would be paid at the rate of one-half cent for each second that the light was on. Ten experimental subjects and five yoked controls were studied. Five of the experimental subjects met the criterion for learned heart rate slowing and 5 did not. None of the controls learned. The investigators concluded that they had shown successful reward training of heart rate slowing, but they did not rule out the possibility that some other learned response mediated the heart rate changes. Later they repeated the study using heart rate speeding as the response and found similar results.[9]

Other studies were conducted to explore the effectiveness of

[9]Later reviews of heart rate findings may be found in Engel (1972), and Obrist, Black, Brener, and Dicara (1974).

avoidance of aversive stimuli as reinforcement. In one example, if the person gave a skin conductance change within 5 seconds after a light came on, an electric shock was withheld. If no response occurred the shock appeared at the end of the 5 seconds. The frequency of skin conductance responses for a contingent group increased as compared to a noncontingent yoked control group.

In summary, there have been many experiments on instrumental conditioning of human bodily responses and most of them have reported positive results. People can learn to increase or decrease bodily responses such as skin conductance response, heart rate, blood volume, blood pressure and salivation by means of instrumental conditioning techniques. One interesting aspect of this research is that subjects frequently do not indicate any awareness that their own bodily responses controlled the delivery of reinforcement.

It is of fundamental importance to determine whether the learning of the type just described is due to the instrumental reinforcement or due to voluntary reactions, such as tensing and relaxing muscles. An extensive program of research on animals investigated these questions. To rule out the possibility of skeletal muscle contractions accounting for heart rate changes, skeletal responses were eliminated by administration of curare, a drug that blocks the motor end plates of skeletal muscles without affecting the neural control of visceral responses. Because there are not many ways to reward an animal completely paralyzed, the early work used direct electrical stimulation of rewarding areas of the brain as reinforcement.[10]

First it was demonstrated that curarized rats rewarded for an increase in heart rate showed learned increase and those rewarded for decrease showed learned decrease. Next, attention was turned to whether the learning of the visceral responses under these conditions could be controlled by an external discriminative stimulus. They used a light to indicate "time in" and "time out" periods when the reinforcement was operative and found the stimulus to be effective.

Later these same investigators employed an electric shock to a rat's tail as an external stimulus to evaluate whether the avoidance learning procedure would produce such instrumental conditioning. For one group of curarized rats the correct response was an increase in heart rate. That is, if the animal produced an increase in heart rate it avoided the shock. For

[10]Miller (1969) has reviewed results obtained when rats are paralyzed by means of curare. In a later report by Miller and Dworkin (1974), some difficulties in interpreting and replicating the results with curarized rats are discussed. The authors urge caution in drawing conclusions at the current state of knowledge in this area.

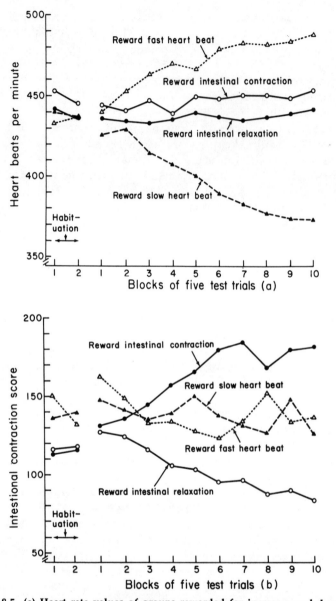

FIGURE 8.5. (a) Heart rate values of groups rewarded for increases and decreases in heart rate and groups rewarded for increases and decreases in intestinal contractions. (b) Intestinal contraction scores of groups rewarded for increases and decreases in intestinal contractions and groups rewarded for increases and decreases in heart rate. [From Miller, N. E., & Banuazizi, A. Instrumental learning by curarized rats of a specific visceral response, intestinal or cardiac. *Journal of Comparative and Physiological Psychology*, 1968, *65*, 1–7. Copyright 1968 by the American Psychological Association. Reprinted by permission.]

a second group the correct response was a decrease in heart rate. They concluded that visceral responses in curarized rats can be reinforced by rewards other than direct electrical stimulation of the brain.

Another important question to be examined was whether such visceral learning was specific to the response for which the reward was applied or whether a large number of behaviors were involved. Four groups of rats were studied in order to test the specificity of the changes in bodily responses that occurs during instrumental conditioning. All of the rats were paralyzed with curare while intestinal contractions and heart rates were recorded. The first group was rewarded with brain stimulation for intestinal contractions, the second group was rewarded for intestinal relaxation, the third group was rewarded for a fast heart rate, and the fourth group was rewarded for a slow heart rate. The results of this experiment are shown in Figure 8.5, where it can be seen that the group rewarded for increases in intestinal contraction learned an increase and the group rewarded for decreases learned a decrease; but neither of the groups showed an appreciable heart rate change. On the other hand, the group rewarded for increases in heart rate showed an increase and the group rewarded for decreases showed a decrease; yet neither of those groups showed a change in intestinal contraction. From this it was concluded that clear specificity of responding can be obtained through the appropriate application of reward.

The previously mentioned studies strongly suggest that the procedures of instrumental reward are quite applicable to modification of visceral responding and that the behavior may represent true instrumental conditioning of those responses independent of skeletal muscle mediation. The investigators are quite reserved in extending their generalizations from the animal work to explain the parallel work with human subjects. However, they suggest that adequate controls for mediated behavior may be developed sufficiently to separate the various contributors to the response changes with human subjects.

BIOFEEDBACK TRAINING

At present, one of the most popular approaches to the learning of bodily responses is the technique of biofeedback training. This technique involves giving information (feedback) to the subject regarding his bodily responses. Electronic recording devices are used so that the subject can see (e.g., on a meter) or hear (e.g., a tone) a representation of his internal responses. With this external feedback information, human subjects can be trained to voluntarily control their own heart rate, blood pressure, body temperature, muscle tension, and brain waves, to name just a few. As noted in Chapter 6, biofeedback training has been used to treat clinical problems, such as headaches. Patients were given biofeedback (in the form of a tone) regarding muscle tension in the forehead. As a result of such training, the patients learned to reduce forehead muscle tension and also showed a reduction in the number of headaches.

Another example of biofeedback training involves the learned modification of blood pressure. Male college students were told that the experiment was concerned with their ability to control their physiological responses. The students were then given a series of trials where feedback (a light and a tone) occurred whenever systolic blood pressure either increased or decreased. As an added incentive, the subjects were shown slides of a seminude girl from Playboy magazine after every 20 feedback stimuli. The blood pressure changes, grouped in blocks of five trials, are shown in Figure 8.6 for the increase and decrease training conditions. The results indicate that subjects can exert relative self-control over their blood pressure as a result of biofeedback training.

In a later investigation, simultaneous modifications of heart rate and blood pressure were observed with feedback and reward for prescribed

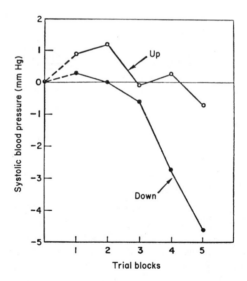

FIGURE 8.6. **Average systolic blood pressure change in persons reinforced for increasing (up) and decreasing (down) blood pressure.** [Modified from Shapiro, Tursky, Gershon, & Stern, 1969. Effects of feedback and reinforcement on the control of human systolic blood pressure. *Science*, 1969, *163*, 588–590. Copyright 1969 by the American Association for the Advancement of Science. Reprinted by permission.]

patterns of blood pressure and heart rate. People were taught to increase or decrease both responses at the same time or to differentiate between them (i.e., raise one while lowering the other). That they were able to learn such response patterns indicates that specific responses can be modified without altering other responses.[11]

The EEG alpha wave has been a popular response for biofeedback research. Early research, beginning in the 1960s, demonstrated that people can significantly increase and decrease their alpha rhythm when they are given feedback regarding this brain wave activity. Considerable attention was given to subjective reports about how the individuals felt when they had obtained control over their EEG alpha waves. Early reports suggested that increased alpha was associated with a pleasant, relaxed, and quasi-meditational state of consciousness, called an *alpha experience*. More recent research has shown that the alpha experience does not necessarily accompany the generation of alpha waves. In fact, when people are not led to expect an alpha experience, they are not likely to describe their experience as particularly unusual or enjoyable.

Laboratory biofeedback research has centered on answering questions such as: (*a*) Are the general changes mediated by skeletal behavior (e.g., changes in eye movements and respiration) or cognitive behavior (e.g., thinking about exciting or relaxing thoughts)? (*b*) Is the learning more effective when one uses analog feedback (where the information fed back is proportional to change in the critical bodily response) or binary feedback (where an on–off feedback signal designates an achievement of some specific response change)? (*c*) What are the effects of instructions on the learning process (e.g., instructing the subjects about the specific response system being monitored and the direction of the desired change)? (*d*) How specific are the learned changes (e.g., do heart rate and blood pressure change together and, if so, under what circumstances can the changes be made independently)? (*e*) What are the proper types of control comparisons that need to be used in order to assess the effects of biofeedback training (e.g., a prefeedback baseline, a nonfeedback control group, or a yoked feedback control group)? (*f*) What are the effects of incentives and motivational variables (e.g., do rewards increase the effectiveness of biofeedback training)? Finally, a large amount of research with biofeedback training has focused on its clinical usefulness in alleviating a variety of disorders (e.g., headaches, insomnia, hypertension, cardiac arrhythmias, etc.). Critical issues here

[11]The early blood pressure data were reported by Shapiro, Tursky, Gershon, and Stern (1969). Evidence regarding the learning of specific patterns of bodily responses has been reviewed by Schwartz (1975).

include the *degree* of bodily response change and the *generalizability* of these changes to life situations.[12]

CONCLUSION

This brief review of learning research and principles applied particularly to visceral emotional behavior presents strong evidence that the internal responses in emotion are susceptible to learning changes by both classical and instrumental conditioning techniques as well as biofeedback training. The temporal association of a neutral stimulus with a strong emotional stimulus may lead to the neutral stimulus producing the emotional response. Such responding may generalize to stimuli similar to the original neutral stimulus. Transfers of learning are particularly enhanced with human subjects where symbolic and cognitive processes become involved.

Contrary to a long held belief, bodily responses may be modified by the application of rewards and by arrangements that make the visceral behavior instrumental to the receipt of such rewards. A wide range of rewards have been used including avoidance of punishment. With human subjects, again, it is quite probable that these changes are very much influenced by voluntary processes and by information about contingencies and responding, which the organism possesses. On the other hand, studies with animals that have had skeletal musculature immobilized by curare suggest a basic learning mechanism in the absence of skeletal responding.

In concluding this discussion it is important to note that in addition to the basic processes of Pavlovian conditioning, instrumental learning, and biofeedback training, there are other processes of central importance to emotional learning. These include imitation and learning by modeling, both of which are referred to as forms of learning by observation. Still others involve verbal learning and the control of emotion by symbolic and language processes.[13] Such processes have not been studied as much with bodily responses as have Pavlovian conditioning, instrumental conditioning, and biofeedback training. Hence, they are not reviewed here.

---

[12]Some of the early work with alpha biofeedback training was reviewed by Kamiya (1968). For a later review see Plotkin (1976) and related comments by Hardt and Kamiya (1976). Since 1970 an annual summary of literature entitled *Biofeedback and self-control* has been published by Aldine Press, and recently the Biofeedback Research Society has begun publication of a journal by the same name. Also, see Blanchard and Young (1974).

[13]For an introduction to some of these other principles, see Kanfer and Phillips (1970) and Bandura (1977).

9
The Detection of Deception

The so-called "lie-detector" test involves the use of a polygraph machine to measure bodily responses in an attempt to determine whether a person is being deceptive. This technique takes advantage of the fact that the bodily changes that accompany emotional states are relatively involuntary. Clearly, this is an applied technique in which the measurement of physiological responses can have great social impact. Despite both the potential importance of this technique to society and the intrinsic interest in the phenomenon, relatively little research has been conducted utilizing this technique by trained psychophysiologists. However, interest in this area is increasing as indicated by three reviews written by psychophysiologists.[1] This chapter will review the following aspects of the physiological detection of deception test: (a) the procedural techniques, (b) the physiological measures, (c) the validity of the test results, (d) the theories of bodily responses during deception, and (e) the legal status of the test.

---

[1]The reviews of the detection of deception tests were written by Barland and Raskin (1973); Orne, Thackray, and Paskewitz (1972); and Podlesny and Raskin (1977).

PROCEDURES AND TECHNIQUES

Two fundamentally different techniques of using physiological measures to detect deception will be reviewed. The first technique is the *control question test* and the second is the *guilty knowledge test*. The control question test involves measuring physiological responses in order to determine if a person is lying. Guilty knowledge testing, on the other hand, involves measuring physiological responses in order to determine if a person has certain knowledge that only the guilty person could have. The difference between these techniques will become clearer in the following discussion.

The control question test[2] consists of a lengthy pretest interview (lasting usually 20–30 minutes), which is then followed by the physiological test. During the pretest interview, the examiner obtains the subject's version of the issue under investigation and, in collaboration with the subject, devises a series of questions to be used in the physiological test. The questions are thoroughly reviewed with the subject to insure that they are unambiguous before beginning the physiological test. No unreviewed surprise questions are used during the actual physiological test.

Three types of questions are devised and reviewed during the pretest interview. The first type consists of *irrelevant questions* (e.g., "Do they call you Joe?"). The purpose of the irrelevant questions is merely to ascertain the general nature of the subject's physiological responses and to serve as the innocuous lead-in items during the later physiological test. The second type consists of *relevant questions* that deal directly with the issue under investigation (e.g., "Did you steal John Doe's money on the evening of January 6th?"). The third type consists of *control questions* that deal with an issue of the same general nature as the one under investigation. The control questions do not deal directly with the issue under investigation. They are purposefully formulated so that the subject will lie to them or at least be very concerned about them. Thus, in a burglary case, a control question might be "Did you ever steal anything?" If the subject indicates during the pretest interview that he did steal something, the control question might be rephrased, "Besides what you have told me, did you ever steal anything?" The purposes of the control questions are to direct the innocent subject's "psychological set" away from the relevant issue as well as to ascertain the subject's physiological responses during an act of lying or during a state of subjective uncertainty.

---

[2]The primary reference source for the control question test is Reid and Inbau (1977). See also Backster (1962).

The physiological test is conducted following the pretest interview. This test consists of having the subject answer each of the three types of questions while physiological responses are measured. Typically, there are three or four examples of each type of question presented in an unpredictable order. The series of questions is usually presented two or three times. Deception is inferred if the subject's physiological response is consistently greater to the relevant questions than to the control questions. Nondeception is inferred if the subject consistently responds more to the control questions than to the relevant questions. The results are considered inconclusive if the subject responds inconsistently to both types of questions.

The basic assumptions underlying the control question technique are (a) if the person is being truthful in answering the relevant questions, then his psychological set will be directed toward the control question to which his attention and concern has already been drawn in the pretest interview, while (b) if the person is being untruthful in responding to the relevant questions, then his psychological set will remain directed toward those items about which he is being deceptive and the control questions will be only of secondary importance. Central to this technique is both the choice of adequate control questions for an innocent person and the skill of the examiner in directing the innocent person's psychological set toward the control questions and away from the relevant questions.

The guilty knowledge test[3] differs from the control question test in that it is directed toward uncovering the presence of guilty knowledge and not toward catching someone in the act of lying. Valid use of this technique requires that a guilty subject possesses some knowledge about an event that an innocent subject could not possess. The technique cannot be utilized when innocent subjects could have access to the relevant details, for example, from reports in the mass media.

The guilty knowledge test consists of presenting a subject a cluster of five items where only one item is relevant to the issue being investigated. The subject is typically required to listen to the cluster and is not required to answer any questions. For example, suppose a watch was stolen and only the thief could know the identity of this item. A sample cluster would then be (a) money, (b) ring, (c) watch, (d) necklace, and (e) bracelet. If the subject's physiological response is consistently greater

---

[3]The primary reference source for the guilty knowledge test is Lykken (1974). A somewhat similar test is called the *peak of tension* technique. It involves presenting items in a sequence known in advance by the subject. Changes in physiological activity leading up to the relevant item and then following the relevant item are used to detect guilty knowledge.

to the relevant items than to the irrelevant items deception is inferred, otherwise, nondeception is inferred.

The basic assumption made in the guilty knowledge test is that a guilty subject will recognize the relevant item and will respond more to it than to the irrelevant items. An innocent person will not recognize and assign a special significance to the relevant item, and therefore will not respond more to it than to the other items in the cluster.

In conclusion, it should be clear that there is no "lie-detector" machine. There is only a polygraph that can measure physiological responses and the detection of deception procedures involve the analysis of these responses to two types of stimuli. With the control question test, the comparison is between the bodily responses following relevant questions and control questions. With the guilty knowledge test, the comparison is between the bodily responses following relevant items and irrelevant items. In practice, the control question procedure is used more often than the guilty knowledge test because information about a crime is usually highly publicized and so even innocent individuals may be aware of all the details about the incident.

PHYSIOLOGICAL MEASURES

The standard detection of deception test involves the simultaneous recording of three physiological responses on a polygraph while the subject answers a series of questions. The three physiological measures are (a) skin resistance responses, (b) respiration responses, and (c) cardiovascular responses. Each of these three responses, as well as some other experimental response measures, will now be reviewed.

Skin resistance responses (SRRs) are measured from electrodes placed on the subject's palms or fingers. The magnitude and/or duration of the SRRs on response to relevant questions can be considered as indicators of deception. Figure 9.1 shows these features of the SRR.

In the field, examiners have generally believed that the SRR is not as useful an indicator of deception as are other responses. However in direct contrast, most laboratory studies have found that the SRR is the best indicator of deception. Experts in field testing procedures have put forward a hypothesis to explain this apparent discrepancy. The hypothesis is that the SRR is especially sensitive to changes in subject's attention and alertness, and these are the primary factors in laboratory detection of deception studies. In field situations, where the consequences of being found guilty are much more serious than in the laboratory, the primary factor is a deep-rooted fear of detection. Respiration

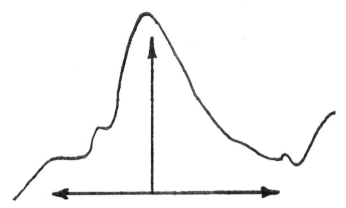

FIGURE 9.1. The magnitude (vertical arrow) and duration (horizontal arrow) of the skin resistance response which are used as indicators of deception or nondeception. [From Ponticelli & Greene, 1975.]

and cardiovascular responses are assumed to be better indicators of this fear than is the SRR. However, more recent field research has indicated that the SRR is as good or better an indicator of deception than other physiological measures.

To measure respiration responses, a pneumatic tube is placed around a subject's chest or abdomen. This response measure is considered to be one of the most reliable indicators of deception. Examiners look for a number of differences between respiration responses to the relevant questions and the control questions. Changes in breathing rhythm or amplitude are considered excellent indicators of deception. Figure 9.2 shows various forms of respiratory blocks (temporary suppressions of breathing) that are considered reliable symptoms of deception when they follow the subject's answers to relevant questions. Another advantage of the respiratory response measure is that a subject's attempt to deliberately distort the test results are considered more detectable with this measure than with other physiological recordings.

Cardiovascular responses are measured by means of applying a sphygmomanometer pressure cuff to the upper arm. A tube connects the cuff to a pressure transducer that records pressure variations. Unlike the technique used to measure blood pressure (see Chapter 1), the cuff is inflated to a point approximately halfway between systolic and diastolic blood pressure. The changes recorded are therefore not true measures of either systolic or diastolic blood pressure. Instead, the changes probably reflect a complex combination of blood volume in the arm and relative

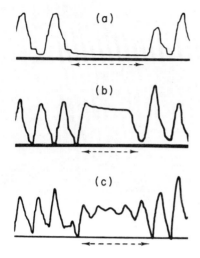

FIGURE 9.2. Examples of respiratory blocks which are considered excellent indicators of deception. [From Reid, J. E., & Inbau, F. E. *Truth and deception: The polygraph ("lie-detection") technique* (2nd ed.). Copyright © 1977 by The Williams & Wilkins Co., Baltimore. Reprinted by permission.]

blood pressure changes.[4] Pulse rate can also be observed with this technique, since each heartbeat produces a spike in the tracing. However, pulse rate cannot be very accurately quantified since a cardiotachometer is not generally employed with field polygraph instruments.

Larger and/or more persistent cardiovascular changes in response to the relevant questions than to the control questions are also used to infer deception. Figure 9.3 shows a typical tracing that is indicative of deception when it occurs following the answer to a relevant question. Notice that there is a shift in the basal level of the tracing and the spikes become somewhat smaller.

Other changes in bodily responses can be used to detect deception. For example, the finger photoelectric plethysmograph (see Chapter 1) is available with some field polygraphs.[5] Other bodily responses (e.g., muscle potential, electroencephalogram, salivation, skin temperature, etc.) may prove to be useful, but they have not been adequately studied at this time.

A response measure that has received a great deal of publicity is that of voice frequency modulations (commercially available with the

[4]The physiological meaning of the results obtained with the partially-inflated blood pressure cuff has been discussed by Geddes and Newberg (1977).

[5]Decreases in finger blood volume and finger pulse amplitude measured with a photoelectric plethysmograph show particular promise as useful indicators of deception. Raskin, Barland, and Podlesny (1977) concluded that "a properly-designed photoelectric plethysmograph would make a useful addition to field polygraph instruments."

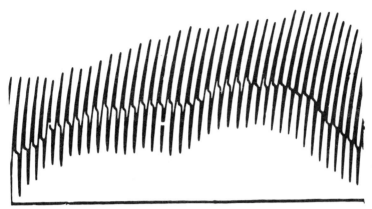

FIGURE 9.3. **Cardiovascular response considered to be indicative of deception.** [From Reid, J. E., & Inbau, F. E. *Truth and deception: The polygraph ("lie-detection") technique* (2nd ed.). Copyright © 1977 by The Williams & Wilkins Co., Baltimore. Reprinted by permission.]

psychological stress evaluator [PSE]).[6] The theory is that the vibrations of the muscles that control the vocal chords are altered by stress. It is claimed that when a person is being deceptive the voice sound waves are measurably different than when the person is not being deceptive. Research results available at the present time indicate that this measure does not work as well as the standard measures, though more research is clearly needed.

One reason why the voice measure has received a great deal of attention is its potential versatility. The measure does not require the attachment of electrodes to the subject, nor does it even require the subject's physical presence. Tape recordings of the subject's voice can be used without the subject's knowledge or consent. This technique also, then, serves to highlight some of the ethical and legal issues associated with the detection of deception tests. Some of these issues will be reviewed later in this chapter.

TEST VALIDITY

How well do the methods just described actually detect deception? As will be shown here, a definitive answer to this question is extremely

[6]The use of voice frequency modulations in the detection of deception was discussed by Holden (1975).

difficult to obtain. Nevertheless, there are three available sources of information regarding test validity: (a) estimates of field workers, (b) systematic follow-up studies of field results, and (c) laboratory studies.[7] The first two sources of information are available for the control question test but not for the guilty knowledge test. This is because the guilty knowledge testing technique has not been systematically used in field investigations. Laboratory evidence, however, is available for both techniques.

Field workers typically claim that less than 1% of the tests result in erroneous conclusions. However, this estimate is not based on scientific evidence. For example, field cases are not systematically followed-up and the definition of an error is often not specified and could range from a confession to a trial verdict. Even more critical is the fact that these estimates are not based on the number of verified cases. For example, suppose that 20,000 tests were conducted and that true guilt or innocence could be determined in 1000 of these cases. If 900 of the verified cases supported the test results and 100 did not then this would indicate a 10% error rate (100/1000). However, field examiners would typically report an error of less than 1% (100/20,000).

Some of the methodological difficulties described have been minimized in studies that objectively verified cases where detection of deception tests were employed.[8] In one study, 323 cases were randomly selected from criminal investigations conducted by various branches of the armed services. All suspects had been administered a detection of deception test using a type of control question procedure. Four attorneys independently reviewed the evidence in each case and arrived at a decision of guilty, innocent, or insufficient evidence. These decisions were made independent of legal technicalities and without the knowledge of the detection of deception test results. It was found that when all four attorneys were in agreement about guilt or innocence, the detection of deception test results agreed with the attorneys' decisions in 92.4% of the cases (a 7.6% error rate).

In a similar study, a panel of five attorneys and judges reviewed the evidence of 92 suspects who had been given detection of deception tests. Each member of the panel made a decision about guilt or innocence without knowledge of the results of the detection of deception test. The

---

[7]A more complete review of the evidence regarding test validity can be obtained from Barland (1975b) and Horvath (1976).

[8]A validation study based upon field investigations with criminal suspects as subjects has been reported by Bersh (1969). A similar validation study was conducted by Barland (1975a) and has been summarized by Raskin et al. (1977).

suspects were originally tested by a trained polygraph examiner using a type of control question procedure and the polygraph tracings were evaluated by an independent examiner who had no knowledge of the case. When the majority of panel members could agree on a decision, it was found that the polygraph results agreed with the panel decision in 86% of the cases (a 14% error rate). When the test results were compared with the judicial outcome in those cases where the judiciary was not informed of the test results, the rate of agreement was 88% (a 12% error rate). Most of the disagreements in this study occurred when the polygraph results indicated that the subject was deceptive but the panel or judiciary considered the subject innocent.

These results suggest that the field detection of deception test results are relatively valid and accurate, though certainly not perfect. However, these results must be interpreted with some caution. The attorneys and judges could agree among themselves in less than half of the cases in both studies. Therefore, the results are based on a select sample of cases that may not be entirely representative of all cases. Also, the examiners who conducted the original detection of deception tests had access to some of the evidence in the cases, this may have biased their administration of the tests. Within these limiting conditions, it appears that the decisions made (excluding inconclusive test results) by competent polygraph examiners with the field control question technique are approximately 90% accurate.

The third type of evidence regarding test validity comes from laboratory studies. Studies conducted in the laboratory have a number of advantages over those conducted in the field. For one thing, absolute truth regarding guilt and innocence can be known because subjects can be assigned to conditions of guilt or innocence on mock crimes. Also, the examiner can be uninformed of any possible biasing information. Despite these advantages, laboratory studies have a potentially serious deficiency. Namely, subjects participating in a laboratory study do not have the same intense motivation as do subjects tested in the field. Thus, laboratory results must be interpreted cautiously since their generalizability to the field situation may be quite limited.

Table 9.1 summarizes the results of these laboratory experiments in which the control question technique was employed. The typical procedure in these experiments was for one group of subjects to be guilty of taking some money from a desk drawer and for another group to be innocent of this mock theft. All subjects were then administered a control question polygraph test by a person who was unaware of the subject's true guilt or innocence. Excluding inconclusive results, it can be seen in Table 9.1 that the accuracy of the polygraph results ranges between 82%

TABLE 9.1

Percentage of Correct Decisions (Excluding "Inconclusives")
for Guilty Subjects, Innocent Subjects, and all Subjects
Combined Obtained with the Control Question Polygraph
Test in Three Laboratory Experiments

	Guilty subjects	Innocent subjects	Guilty and innocent combined
Experiment I[a]	88	71	81
Experiment II[b]	100	91	95
Experiment III[b]	82	95	89

[a] Reported by Barland and Raskin (1975).
[b] Reported by Raskin, Barland, and Podlesny (1977).

and 100% with guilty subjects, averaging approximately 90%. The analogous results for the innocent subjects ranges between 71% and 95% accuracy, averaging approximately 82%. Thus, the laboratory results suggest an overall accuracy rate (guilty and innocent subjects combined) that is similar to that reported in the field.

The polygraph detection of deception test can make two types of errors: (a) it can classify a truly guilty subject as nondeceptive (a *false negative* error) and (b) it can classify a truly innocent subject as deceptive (a *false positive* error). In two of the three studies summarized in Table 9.1, the false positive errors are more common than the false negative errors.

Table 9.2 summarizes the results of three laboratory experiments in which the guilty knowledge technique was employed. Looking first at

TABLE 9.2

Percentage of Correct Decisions for Guilty Subjects,
Innocent Subjects, and All Subjects Combined Obtained
with the Guilty Knowledge Polygraph Test in Three
Laboratory Experiments

	Guilty subjects	Innocent subjects	Guilty and innocent combined
Experiment I[a]	88	100	94
Experiment II[b]	92	100	98
Experiment III[c]	80	100	90

[a] Reported by Lykken (1959).
[b] Reported by Davidson (1968).
[c] Reported by Raskin, Barland, and Podlesny (1977).

the guilty subjects, the accuracy rate ranged from 80 to 92%, averaging approximately 87%. The analogous results for innocent subjects was 100% accurate in all three experiments. Thus, there were no false positive errors with the guilty knowledge technique. That is, there were no innocent subjects who consistently responded more to the relevant items than the irrelevant items. Of course, the experiments were arranged so that the truly innocent subjects were not aware of which items were relevant (recall that this is a necessary prerequisite for a valid guilty knowledge test).

In summary, the best available information indicates that both physiological detection of deception tests (both the control question technique and the guilty knowledge technique) are relatively valid. All of the studies indicate that the tests work significantly better than chance.[9] However, no physiological detection of deception test has been shown to be perfect. The evidence does suggest that the guilty knowledge test, when its basic assumptions are met, is virtually perfect with the truly innocent subjects. However, it must be emphasized that the guilty knowledge technique has a more limited applicability than the control question technique because it requires that the polygraph examiner be in possession of certain knowledge that the subject would have only if the subject was guilty.

THEORIES OF BODILY CHANGES
DURING DECEPTION

Why is deception usually associated with measurable bodily changes? No fully satisfactory answer to this question is currently available. If the answer were known then perhaps more valid testing techniques could be devised. But one fact seems clear, the act of lying per se does not seem to be the critical variable. This has been demonstrated in an experiment where subjects selected a numbered card and then were instructed to answer "yes" to the question "Did you choose card number —?" Hence, the subjects were lying to all of the questions except one about the card they actually selected. Yet, the electrodermal response was found to be larger to the selected number than to the nonselected numbers in the majority of subjects. These results indicate that the de-

---

[9]A question that is raised frequently is whether certain types of individuals can "beat the polygraph." For example, it is widely asserted that psychopaths (see Chapter 4) can successfully lie without being caught on the polygraph. Raskin *et al.* (1977) reviewed a study in which psychopathic and nonpsychopathic prisoners participated in a mock-crime experiment. The results indicated no differences in detectability between the psychopaths and nonpsychopaths.

tection of the selected number does not necessarily depend upon the act of lying.[10]

At least three different processes may be involved in eliciting bodily responses during detection of deception tests. First, subjects may orient or attend to the most significant questions or items. Thus, the guilty subject may orient more to the relevant questions or relevant items than to the control questions or irrelevant items while the innocent subject may not. Second, subjects may experience fear in response to the most threatening questions or items. The guilty subject may experience more fear in response to the relevant question or item than the control question or irrelevant item, while the innocent person may not. Third, the subject's mental effort or motivation to deceive may be a critical factor in eliciting differential bodily responses. The guilty person may mentally work harder during the delivery of the relevant question or item than during the delivery of the control question or irrelevant item while the innocent person may not. These three processes are not mutually exclusive. In the actual test situation, all three may be operating and interacting simultaneously to produce the physiological indices of deception.[11]

The importance of "motivation to deceive" was shown in an interesting experiment reported by Gustafson and Orne (1963). Two groups of college students selected a numbered card from a deck of cards. Electrodermal responses were then measured from the subjects while they listened to a list of numbers, including the one they had selected. One group was told that only people of superior intelligence and great emotional control could successfully conceal the number they had selected during the physiological test. The other group was not given these instructions. A subject's number was considered detected if the largest electrodermal response occurred to the selected number. Subjects in the instructed group had their selected numbers detected significantly more often than the subjects in the noninstructed group. Therefore, it was concluded that motivation to deceive is an important factor in the successful detection of deception.

---

[10]The detection of deception test conducted while subjects told the truth to the relevant item was reported by Kugelmass, Lieblich, and Bergman (1967). The fact that overt lying is not necessary in order to detect intended deception is further brought out by a technique called the *silent answer test* (Horvath & Reid, 1972). With this technique, the subject is told to merely listen to each question and answer silently to himself. Even when the subject remains completely silent, and therefore is not actually lying, the results appear to be just as valid as when the subject verbally answers the questions.

[11]The orienting theory was suggested by Lykken (1974), the fear theory was espoused by Reid and Inbau (1977), and the motivation theory was proposed by Orne et al. (1972). Other theories have been reviewed by Davis (1961).

LEGAL STATUS

There exist strong opinions and feelings regarding uses of the detection of deception test. Arguments for the use of the test may be summarized as follows:

> The technique can be of appreciable help in detecting deception and in protecting innocent people. Therefore, the test results should be considered like any other useful but imperfect source of evidence (e.g., eyewitness testimony) in arriving at just decisions.

Arguments against the test may be summarized as follows:

> This technique represents an invasion of privacy. It is a breach of a fundamental legal right that no person should be required to testify against himself. Furthermore, it usurps the function of the jury.

We certainly do not propose to settle these disagreements. However, we will review two specific issues directed toward different uses of the test. First, there is the issue of whether the test results can be admitted as evidence in a court of law. Second, there is the issue of whether an employer can require an employee or prospective employee to take such a test.

Legal Admissibility in Court

The precedent-setting court case of *Frye* v. *United States* took place in 1923. In this case, James Frye initially confessed to the murder of Dr. Robert Brown. Later, however, Frye claimed to be innocent and was given a detection of deception test by one of the pioneers in this area, the psychologist and lawyer Dr. William Marston. The test, which consisted of measuring only systolic blood pressure, indicated that Frye was innocent of the murder. However, the court refused to admit the test results and Frye was convicted. Interestingly, after Frye had served 3 years in jail, another person was arrested and confessed to the murder of Dr. Brown and Frye was released.

The reason given by the court for refusal to admit the test results was that the new technique had not yet gained "general acceptance" by the physiological and psychological scientific community. This "general acceptance" criterion set the legal precedent and is still cited today as the basis for inadmissibility of the test results. Another reason is the fear that a jury would be too greatly influenced by the test results, considering the polygraph to be infallible. The counterargument is that the polygraph expert is no different than any other expert. "His testimony is subject to cross-examination, his qualifications and methods are subject to attack, and other experts might be employed to refute his testimony [Bailey & Rothblatt, 1970, p. 299.]" See also Ansley (1975) and Altorescu (1972).

Despite the general judicial rejection of polygraph test results, a number of state appellate courts have allowed polygraph results to be admitted as evidence in a court of law if there existed "prior stipulation." That is, if both the prosecution and defense agreed to have the test results admitted regardless of the outcome then they have sometimes been ruled admissible in a court of law.[12] At least one state supreme court has encouraged trial judges to excercise discretion in admitting polygraph test results (Tarlow, 1975).

Employment Screening

There is an increasing use of detection of deception techniques in preemployment screening to aid in deciding who should be hired as well as in postemployment screening to detect individuals who may be stealing from the company. Some of the legal and ethical concerns in this area are different than those in criminal cases. For example, although no one can be sent to prison based solely on the test results, someone might be deprived of a job based solely on such results. Other concerns regarding the use of the detection of deception test in this type of situation have been reviewed by Lykken (1974).

Laws governing the use of these techniques in employment screening differ from state to state. A summary of the state laws regarding this use of the test has been prepared by Romig (1975). A total of 12 states have laws that limit to various degrees this use of the detection of deception test. The language of these laws is sometimes ambiguous. For example, a California law states that no employer may "demand or require" an employee or prospective employee to take a polygraph examination. However, the state's attorney general concluded that this did not prohibit an employer from "requesting or permitting" such tests.

---

[12]An historical review of the court decisions and an examination of the legal issues can be found in Reid and Inbau (1977). These authors take the position that, given certain conditions, "the results of a competently conducted polygraph examination should be accepted as evidence without the requirement of a preexamination agreement and stipulation [p. 365]." Among the conditions is that the examiner be required to produce the polygraph records in court for cross-examination purposes.

CONCLUSION

The physiological detection of deception test is an interesting and potentially valuable technique. In addition to its obvious potential use for law enforcement agencies and the courts, this test also has possible benefits for basic psychophysiological research. The science of psychophysiology is concerned with the complex relationships between bodily changes and psychological events such as motivation and emotion. The detection of deception test based on laboratory mock crimes offers a potentially useful technique for studying the effects of psychological events on physiological responses.

References

Aarons, L. Sleep-assisted instruction. *Psychological Bulletin,* 1976, *83,* 1–40.

Ader, R. Gastric erosions in the rat: Effects of immobilization at different points in the activity cycle. *Science,* 1964, *145,* 406–407.

Akiskal, H. J., & McKinney, W. T. Overview of recent research in depression. *Archives of General Psychiatry,* 1975, *32,* 285–305.

Alexander, A. A. Psychophysiological concepts of psychopathology. In N. S. Greenfield & R. A. Sternbach (Eds.), *Handbook of Psychophysiology.* New York: Holt, 1972.

Altorescu, H. S. Problems remaining for the "generally accepted" polygraph. *Boston University Law Review,* 1972, *53,* 375–405.

American Psychiatric Association. *Diagnostic and statistical manual of mental disorders (DSM II)* (2nd ed.). Washington, D.C.: Author, 1968.

Ansley, N. (Ed.). *Legal admissibility of the polygraph.* Springfield, Ill.: Thomas, 1975.

Appenzeller, O. *The autonomic nervous system* (2nd ed.). New York: American Elsevier, 1976.

Arnold, M. B. *Emotions and personality* (Vols. 1 and 2). New York: Columbia University Press, 1960.

Arnold, M. B. (Ed.). *The nature of emotion.* Baltimore: Penguin Books, 1968.

Arnold, M. B. (Ed.). *Feelings and emotions.* New York: Academic Press, 1970.

Ax, A. F. The physiological differentiation between fear and anger in humans. *Psychosomatic Medicine,* 1953, *5,* 433–442.

Ax, A. F. Goals and methods of psychophysiology. *Psychophysiology,* 1964, *1,* 8–25.

Ax, A. F., & Bamford, J. The GSR recovery limb in chronic schizophrenia. *Psychophysiology,* 1970, *7,* 145–147.

Backster, C. Methods of strengthening our polygraph technique. *Police,* 1962, *6,* 61–68.

Baer, P. E., & Fuhrer, M. J. Unexpected effects of masking: Differential EDR conditioning without relational learning. *Psychophysiology,* 1973, *10,* 95–99.

Bailey, F. L., & Rothblatt, H. B. *Investigation and preparation of criminal cases: Federal and state.* Rochester, N.Y.: The Lawyers Cooperative, 1970.

Bandura, A. *Social learning theory.* Englewood Cliffs, N.J.: Prentice-Hall, 1977.

Barland, G. H. *Detection of deception in criminal suspects: A field validation study.* Unpublished doctoral dissertation, University of Utah, 1975. (a)

Barland, G. H. The validity of the polygraph technique. In N. Ansley (Ed.), *Legal admissibility of the polygraph.* Springfield, Ill.: Thomas, 1975. (b)

Barland, G. H., & Raskin, D. C. Detection of deception. In W. F. Prokasy & D. C. Raskin (Eds.), *Electrodermal activity in psychological research.* New York: Academic Press, 1973.

Barland, G. H., & Raskin, D. C. An evaluation of field techniques in detection of deception. *Psychophysiology,* 1975, *12,* 321–330.

Beatty, J., Greenberg, A., Deibler, W. P., & O'Hanlon, J. F. Operant control of occipital theta rhythm affects performance in a radar monitoring task. *Science,* 1974, *183,* 871–873.

Beck, A. T. *Depression: Clinical, experimental, and theoretical aspects.* New York: Harper & Row, 1967.

Bell, B., Mednick, S., Ramen, A., Schulsinger, F., Smith, B., & Venables, P. A longitudinal psychophysiological study of three year old Mauritanian children: Preliminary report. *Developmental Medicine and Childhood Neurology,* 1975, *17,* 320–324.

Berlyne, D. E. Arousal and reinforcement. In D. Levine (Ed.), *Nebraska Symposium on Motivation.* Lincoln: University of Nebraska Press, 1967.

Bersh, P. J. A validation study of polygraph examiner judgments. *Journal of Applied Psychology,* 1969, *53,* 399–403.

Blanchard, E. G., & Young, L. D. Clinical applications of biofeedback training: A review. *Archives of General Psychiatry,* 1974, *30,* 577–589.

Brady, J. V. Endocrine and autonomic correlates of emotional behavior. In P. Black (Ed.), *Physiological correlates of emotion.* New York: Academic Press, 1970.

Brener, J. Heart rate. In P. H. Venables & I. Martin (Eds.), *A manual of psychophysiological methods.* New York: Wiley, 1967.

Brodie, D. A. Neurogenic factors in experimental peptic ulceration. In S. C. Skoryna (Ed.), *Pathophysiology of peptic ulcer.* Philadelphia: Lippincott, 1963.

Broughton, R. J. Sleep disorders: Disorders of arousal? *Science,* 1968, *159,* 1070–1078.

Brown, C. C. The techniques of plethysmography. In C. C. Brown (Ed.), *Methods in psychophysiology.* Baltimore: Williams & Wilkins, 1967.

Buchsbaum, M. Self-regulation of stimulus intensity: Augmenting/reducing and the average evoked response. In G. E. Schwartz & D. Shapiro (Eds.), *Consciousness and self regulation* (Vol. 1). New York: Plenum Press, 1976.

Budzynski, T., Stoyva, J., & Adler, C. Feedback-induced muscle relaxation: Application to tension headache. *Journal of Behavioral Therapy and Experimental Psychiatry,* 1970, *1,* 205–211.

Candland, D. K., Fell, J. P., Keen, E., Leshner, A. I., Plutchik, R., & Tarpy, R. M. *Emotion.* Monterey, Calif.: Brooks/Cole, 1977.

Cantwell, D. P. (Ed.). *The hyperactive child: Diagnosis, management, and current research.* New York: Spectrum Publications, 1975.

Carpenter, W. T., Bartko, J. J., Carpenter, C. L., & Strauss, J. S. Another view of schizophrenia subtypes: A report from the international pilot study of schizophrenia. *Archives of General Psychiatry,* 1976, *33,* 508–516.

Christie, M. J. The psychosocial environment and the precursors of disease. In P. H. Venables & M. J. Christie (Eds.), *Research in Psychophysiology.* New York: Wiley, 1975.

Claridge, G. S. *Personality and arousal.* London: Pergamon Press, 1967.

Cleckley, H. *The mask of sanity* (5th ed.). St. Louis: Mosley, 1976.

Cook, M. R. Psychophysiology of peripheral vascular change. In P. A. Obrist, A. H. Black, J. Brener, & L. V. DiCara (Eds.), *Cardiovascular psychophysiology*. Chicago: Aldine, 1974.

Cooper, R., Osselton, J. W., & Shaw, J. C. *EEG technology*. London: Butterworths, 1969.

Courts, F. A. Relations between muscle tension and performance. *Psychological Bulletin*, 1942, *39*, 347–367.

Cousins, L. R. Individual differences in the orienting reflex and children's discrimination learning. *Psychophysiology*, 1976, *13*, 479–487.

Craik, F. I. M., & Blankstein, K. R. Psychophysiology and human memory. In P. H. Venables & M. J. Christie (Eds.), *Research in psychophysiology*. New York: Wiley, 1975.

Crider, A., & Augenbraun, C. B. Auditory vigilance correlates of electrodermal response habituation speed. *Psychophysiology*, 1975, *12*, 36–40.

Davidson, P. O. Validation of the guilty knowledge technique: The effects of motivation. *Journal of Applied Psychology*, 1968, *52*, 62–65.

Davis, R. C. Physiological responses as a means of evaluating information. In A. D. Biderman & H. Zimmer (Eds.), *The manipulation of human behavior*. New York: Wiley, 1961.

Dawson, M. E. Can classical conditioning occur without contingency learning? A review and evaluation of the evidence. *Psychophysiology*, 1973, *10*, 82–86.

Dawson, M. E., Schell, A. M., & Catania, J. J. Autonomic correlates of depression and clinical improvement following electroconvulsive shock therapy. *Psychophysiology*, 1977, *14*, 569–578.

Dekker, E., & Groen, J. Reproducible psychogenic attacks of asthma. *Journal of Psychosomatic Research*, 1956, *1*, 58–67.

Dekker, E., Perlser, H. E., & Groen, J. Conditioning as a cause of asthmatic attacks. *Journal of Psychosomatic Research*, 1957, *2*, 97–108.

Dement, W. The effect of dream deprivation. *Science*, 1960, *131*, 1705–1707.

Dement, W., & Kleitman, N. The relation of eye movements during sleep to dream activity: An objective method for the study of dreaming. *Journal of Experimental Psychology*, 1957, *53*, 339–346.

Depue, R. A., & Fowles, D. C. Electrodermal activity as an index of arousal in schizophrenics. *Psychological Bulletin*, 1973, *79*, 233–238.

Deutsch, J. A., & Deutsch, D. *Physiological psychology*. Homewood, Ill.: Dorsey Press, 1966.

DiMascio, A., Boyd, R. W., & Greenblatt, M. Physiological correlates of tension and antagonism during psychotherapy. *Psychosomatic Medicine*, 1957, *19*, 99–104.

Duffy, E. The psychological significance of the concept of "arousal" or "activation." *Psychological Review*, 1957, *64*, 265–275.

Duffy, E. *Activation and behavior*. New York: Wiley, 1962.

Edelberg, R. Electrical activity of the skin: Its measurement and uses in psychophysiology. In N. S. Greenfield & R. A. Sternbach (Eds.), *Handbook of psychophysiology*. New York: Holt, 1972.

Edwards, D. C., & Alsip, J. E. Stimulus detection during periods of high and low heart rate. *Psychophysiology*, 1969, *5*, 431–434.

Elliott, R. Physiological activity and performance: A comparison of kindergarten children and young adults. *Psychological Monographs*, 1964, *78* (10, Whole No. 587).

Engel, B. T. Operant conditioning of cardiac function: A status report. *Psychophysiology*, 1972, *9*, 161–177.

Eppinger, H., & Hess, L. *Die Vagotonie*. Berlin, 1910. (*Vagotonia. Nervous and Mental Disease Monograph*. New York: Nervous and Mental Disease Publication, 1915.)

Epstein, S. Expectancy and magnitude of reaction to a noxious UCS. *Psychophysiology,* 1973, *10,* 100–107.

Epstein, S., & Fenz, W. D. Theory and experiment on the measurement of approach-avoidance conflict. *Journal of Abnormal and Social Psychology,* 1962, *64,* 97–112.

Erlenmeyer-Kimling, N. A prospective study of children at risk for schizophrenia: Methodological considerations and some preliminary findings. In. R. Wirt, G. Winokur, & M. Roff (Eds.), *Life history research in psychopathology* (Vol. 4). Minneapolis: University of Minnesota Press, 1975.

Eysenck, H. J. *The biological basis of personality.* Springfield, Ill.: Thomas, 1967.

Eysenck, M. W. Arousal, learning and memory. *Psychological Bulletin,* 1976, *83,* 389–404.

Feighner, J. P., Robins, E., Guze, J. B., Woodruff, R. A., Winokur, G., & Munoz, R. Diagnostic criteria for use in psychiatric research. *Archives of General Psychiatry,* 1972, *26,* 57–63.

Fenz, W. D., & Epstein, S. Gradients of physiological arousal in parachutists as a function of an approaching jump. *Psychosomatic Medicine,* 1967, *29,* 33–51.

Ferster, C. G. A functional analysis of depression. *American Psychologist,* 1973, *28,* 857–870.

Fisher, S. A., & Abercrombie, J. The relationship of body image distortions to body reactivity gradients. *Journal of Personality,* 1958, *26,* 320–329.

Foulkes, D. *The psychology of sleep.* New York: Scribners, 1966.

Fowles, D. C. Mechanisms of electrodermal activity. In R. F. Thompson & M. M. Patterson (Eds.), *Methods in physiological psychology.* New York: Academic Press, 1973.

Freeman, G. L. Cortical autonomous rhythms and the excitatory levels of other bodily tissues. *Journal of Experimental Psychology,* 1940, *27,* 160–171.

Freeman, G. L. *The energetics of human behavior.* Ithaca, N.Y.: Cornell University Press, 1948.

Funkenstein, D. H. The physiology of fear and anger. *Scientific American,* 1955, *192,* 74–80.

Furedy, J. J. Some limits on the cognitive control of conditioned autonomic behavior. *Psychophysiology,* 1973, *10,* 108–111.

Gale, A. The psychophysiology of individual differences: Studies of extraversion and the EEG. In P. Kline (Ed.), *New approaches to psychological measurement.* London: Wiley, 1973.

Geddes, L. A., & Newberg, D. C. Cuff pressure oscillations in the measurement of relative blood pressure. *Psychophysiology,* 1977, *14,* 198–202.

Gillilan, L. A. *Clinical aspects of the autonomic nervous system.* Boston: Little, Brown, 1954.

Glass, D. C. (Ed.). *Neurophysiology and emotion.* New York: Rockefeller University Press, 1967.

Goldstein, I. B. Electromyography: A measure of skeletal muscle response. In N. S. Greenfield & R. A. Sternbach (Eds.), *Handbook of psychophysiology.* New York: Holt, 1972.

Goldwater, B. C. Psychological significance of pupillary movements. *Psychological Bulletin,* 1972, *77,* 340–355.

Graham, D. T. Research on psychophysiologic specificity. In R. Roessler & N. Greenfield (Eds.), *Phsyiological correlates of psychological disorder.* Madison: University of Wisconsin Press, 1962.

Graham, D. T. Psychosomatic medicine. In N. S. Greenfield & R. A. Sternbach (Eds.), *Handbook of psychophysiology.* New York: Holt, 1972.

Graham, D. T., Lundy, R. M., Benjamin, L., Kabler, J. D., Lewis, W. C., Kunish, N. O., & Graham, F. K. Specific attitudes in initial interviews with patients having different "psychosomatic" diseases. *Psychosomatic Medicine,* 1962, *24,* 257–266.

Graham, D. T., Stern, J. A., & Winokur, G. The concept of a different specific set of physiological changes in each emotion. *Psychiatric Research Reports,* 1960, *12,* 8–15.

Graham, F. K. Habituation and dishabituation of responses innervated by the autonomic nervous system. In H. Peeke & M. Herz (Eds.), *Habituation: Behavioral studies and physiological substrates* (Vol. 1). New York: Academic Press, 1973.

Graham, F. K., & Clifton, R. K. Heart-rate change as a component of the orienting response. *Psychological Bulletin,* 1966, *65,* 305–320.

Grant, D. A. Cognitive factors in eyelid conditioning. *Psychophysiology,* 1973, *10,* 75–81.

Greenfield, N. S., & Sternbach, R. A. (Eds.). *Handbook of psychophysiology.* New York: Holt, 1972.

Gribbon, B., Steptoe, A., & Sleight, P. Pulse wave velocity as a measure of blood pressure change. *Psychophysiology,* 1976, *13,* 86–90.

Grings, W. W. Cognitive factors and conditioning: An overview. *Psychophysiology,* 1973, *10,* 119–120.

Grings, W. W. Recording of electrodermal phenomena. In R. F. Thompson and M. M. Patterson (Eds.), *Bioelectric recording technique, part C: Receptor and effector processes.* New York: Academic Press, 1974.

Grings, W. W., Lockhart, R. A., & Dameron, L. E. Conditioning autonomic responses of mentally subnormal individuals. *Psychological Monographs,* 1962, *76* (39, Whole No. 558).

Grinker, R. R., & Speigel, J. R. *Men under stress.* New York: McGraw-Hill, 1945.

Grossman, S. P. *A textbook of physiological psychology.* New York: Wiley, 1967.

Gruzelier, J. H., & Venables, P. H. Skin conductance orienting activity in a heterogeneous sample of schizophrenics: Possible evidence of limbic dysfunction. *Journal of Nervous and Mental Disease,* 1972, *155,* 277–287.

Gruzelier, J. H., & Venables, P. H. Evidence of high and low levels of physiological arousal in schizophrenics. *Psychophysiology,* 1975, *12,* 66–73.

Gustafson, L. A., & Orne, M. T. Effects of heightened motivation on the detection of deception. *Journal of Applied Psychology,* 1963, *47,* 408–411.

Guyton, A. C. *Textbook of medical physiology* (5th ed.). Philadelphia: Saunders, 1976.

Hahn, W. W. Autonomic responses of asthmatic children. *Psychosomatic Medicine,* 1966, *28,* 323–332.

Hahn, W. W. Attention and heart rate: A critical appraisal of the hypothesis of Lacey and Lacey. *Psychological Bulletin,* 1973, *79,* 59–70.

Hahn, W. W., & Clark, J. A. Psychophysiological reactivity of asthmatic children. *Psychosomatic Medicine,* 1967, *29,* 526–536.

Hall, J. *Classical conditioning and instrumental learning: A contemporary approach.* Philadelphia: Lippincott, 1976.

Hardt, J. V., & Kamiya, J. Some comments on Plotkin's self-regulation of electroencephalographic alpha. *Journal of Experimental Psychology: General,* 1976, *105,* 100–108.

Hare, R. D. Psychopathy. In P. H. Venables & M. J. Christie (Eds.), *Research in psychophysiology,* 1965, *70,* 442–445.

Hare, R. D. Denial of threat and emotional response to impending painful stimulation. *Journal of Consulting Psychology,* 1966, *30,* 359–361.

Hare, R. D. *Psychopathy: Theory and research.* New York: Wiley, 1970.

Hare, R. D. Psychopathy and physiological responses to adrenalin. *Journal of Abnormal Psychology,* 1972, *79,* 138–147.

Hare, R. D. Orienting and defensive responses to visual stimuli. *Psychophysiology,* 1973, *10,* 453–464.

Hare, R. D. Psychopathy. In P. H. Venables & M. J. Christie (Eds.), *Research in psychophysiology.* New York: Wiley, 1975. (a)

Hare, R. D. Psychophysiological studies of psychopathy. In D. C. Fowles (Ed.), *Clinical applications of psychophysiology.* New York: Columbia University Press, 1975. (b)

Hare, R. D., & Craigen, D. Psychopathy and physiological activity in a mixed-motive game situation. *Psychophysiology*, 1974, *11*, 197–206.

Harris, V. A., & Katkin, E. S. Primary and secondary emotional behavior: An analysis of the role of autonomic feedback on affect, arousal, and attribution. *Psychological Bulletin*, 1975, *82*, 904–916.

Haywood, H. C., & Spielberger, C. D. Palmar sweating as a function of individual differences in manifest anxiety. *Journal of Personality and Social Psychology*, 1966, *3*, 103–105.

Headrick, M. W., & Graham, F. K. Multicomponent heart rate responses conditioned under paced respiration. *Journal of Experimental Psychology*, 1969, *79*, 486–494.

Henry, J. P., & Ely, D. L. Biologic correlates of psychosomatic illness. In R. G. Grenell & S. Galay (Eds.), *Biological foundations of psychiatry*. New York: Raven Press, 1976.

Henry, J. P., Ely, D. L., Watson, F., & Stephens, P. M. Ethological methods as applied to the measurement of emotion. In L. Levi (Ed.), *Emotions—their parameters and measurement*. New York: Raven Press, 1975.

Herron, W. G. The process-reactive classification of schizophrenia. *Psychological Bulletin*, 1962, *59*, 329–343.

Hess, E. H. Attitude and pupil size. *Scientific American*, 1965, *212*, 46–54.

Hess, E. H. Pupillometrics: A method of studying mental, emotional, and sensory processes. In N. S. Greenfield & R. A. Sternbach (Eds.), *Handbook of psychophysiology*. New York: Holt, 1972.

Hess, E. H., & Polt, J. M. Pupil size as related to interest value of visual stimuli. *Science*, 1960, *132*, 349–350.

Hodges, W. F., & Spielberger, C. D. The effects of threat of shock on heart rate for subjects who differ in manifest anxiety and fear of shock. *Psychophysiology*, 1966, *2*, 287–294.

Hohmann, G. W. Some effects of spinal cord lesions on experienced emotional feelings. *Psychophysiology*, 1966, *3*, 143–156.

Hokanson, J. E. Vascular and psychogalvanic effects of experimentally aroused anger. *Journal of Personality*, 1961, *29*, 30–39.

Hokanson, J. E. Psychophysiological evaluation of the catharsis hypothesis. In E. I. Megargee & J. E. Hokanson (Eds.), *The dynamics of aggression*. New York: Harper & Row, 1970.

Hokanson, J. E., & Burgess, M. The effects of three types of aggression on vascular processes. *Journal of Abnormal and Social Psychology*, 1962, *64*, 446–449.

Hokanson, J. E., DeGood, D. E., Forrest, M. S., & Brittain, T. M. Availability of avoidance behaviors in modulating vascular-stress responses. *Journal of Personality and Social Psychology*, 1971, *19*, 60–68.

Hokanson, J. E., & Shetler, S. The effect of overt aggression on physiological arousal level. *Journal of Abnormal and Social Psychology*, 1961, *63*, 446–448.

Holden, C. Lie detectors: PSE gains audience despite critics' doubts. *Science*, 1975, *190*, 359–362.

Horvath, F. S. Detection of deception: A review of field and laboratory procedures and research. *Polygraph*, 1976, *5*, 107–145.

Horvath, F. S., & Reid, J. E. The polygraph silent answer test. *The Journal of Criminal Law, Criminology and Police Science*, 1972, *63*, 285–293.

Hunt, W. A. Recent developments in the field of emotion. *Psychological Bulletin*, 1941, *38*, 249–276.

Jacobson, E. *Progressive relaxation*. Chicago: Chicago University Press, 1929.

James, William. *The principles of psychology*. New York: Holt, 1890.

Janis, I. L. *Air war and emotional stress.* New York: McGraw-Hill, 1951.

Janis, I. L. *Psychological stress.* New York: Wiley, 1958.

Johnson, L. C. A psychophysiology for all states. *Psychophysiology,* 1970, *6,* 501–516.

Johnson, L. C. Sleep. In P. H. Venables & M. J. Christie (Eds.), *Research in psychophysiology.* New York: Wiley, 1975.

Jordan, L. S. Electrodermal activity in schizophrenics: Further considerations. *Psychological Bulletin,* 1974, *81,* 85–91.

Justeen, D. R., Braun, E. W., Garrison, R. G., & Pendleton, R. B. Pharmacological differentiation of allergic and classically conditioned asthma in the guinea pig. *Science,* 1970, *170,* 864–866.

Kagan, J., Haith, M. M., & Caldwell, C. (Eds.). *Psychology: Adapted readings.* New York: Harcourt, 1971.

Kahneman, D., Tursky, B., Shapiro, D., & Crider, A. Pupillary, heart rate, and skin resistance changes during a mental task. *Journal of Experimental Psychology,* 1969, *79,* 164–167.

Kales, A. *Sleep.* Baltimore: Lippincott, 1966.

Kamiya, J. Conscious control of brain waves. *Psychology Today,* 1968, *1,* 57–60.

Kanfer, F. H., & Phillips, J. S. *Learning foundations of behavior therapy.* New York: Wiley, 1970.

Kaplan, H. B. Social interaction and GSR activity during group psychotherapy. *Psychosomatic Medicine,* 1963, *25,* 140–145.

Kaplan, H. B., Burch, N. R., Bloom, S. W., & Edelberg, R. Affective orientation in physiological activity (GSR) in small peer groups. *Psychosomatic Medicine,* 1963, *25,* 242–252.

Karlin, L. Cognition, preparation, and sensory-evoked potentials. *Psychological Bulletin,* 1970, *73,* 122–136.

Katkin, E. S., & Deitz, S. R. Systematic desensitization. In W. F. Prokasy & D. C. Raskin (Eds.), *Electrodermal activity in psychological research.* New York: Academic Press, 1973.

Katz, M. M., Cole, J. O., & Barton, W. E. (Eds.). *The role and methodology of classification in psychopathology.* Washington, D.C.: U.S. Department of Health, Education, and Welfare, 1965.

Katz, R. A., Sutherland, G. F., and Brown, C. C. Measurement of salivation. In C. C. Brown (Ed.), *Methods in psychophysiology.* Baltimore: Williams & Wilkins, 1967.

Kietzman, M. L., Sutton, S., & Zubin, J. (Eds.). *Experimental approaches to psychopathology.* New York: Academic Press, 1975.

Kimmel, E., & Kimmel, H. D. Replication of operant conditioning of the GSR. *Journal of Experimental Psychology,* 1963, *65,* 212–213.

Kimmel, H. D. Instrumental conditioning of autonomically mediated responses in human beings. *American Psychologist,* 1974, *29,* 325–335.

Klein, R., & Salzman, L. Habituation and conditioning in high-risk children: A preliminary report. *Psychophysiology,* 1977, *14,* 105.

Kleinsmith, L. J., & Kaplan, S. Paired-associate learning as a function of arousal and interpolated interval. *Journal of Experimental Psychology,* 1963, *65,* 190–193.

Kleitman, N. *Sleep and wakefulness.* Chicago: University of Chicago Press, 1963.

Klorman, R., Weissberg, R. P., & Wiesenfeld, A. R. Individual differences in fear and autonomic reactions to affective stimulation. *Psychophysiology,* 1977, *14,* 45–51.

Kugelmass, S., Lieblich, I., & Bergman, Z. The role of "lying" in psychophysiological detection. *Psychophysiology,* 1967, *3,* 312–315.

Kuntz, A. *The autonomic nervous system.* Philadelphia: Lea & Febiger, 1945.

Kuntz, A. *Visceral innervation and its relation to personality.* Springfield, Ill.: Thomas, 1951.

Lacey, J. I. Somatic response patterning and stress: Some revisions of activation theory. In M. H. Appley & R. Trumbull (Eds.), *Psychological stress.* New York: Appleton, 1967.

Lacey, J. I., & Lacey, B. C. Verification and extension of the principle of autonomic response stereotypy. *The American Journal of Psychology,* 1958, *71,* 50–73.

Lacey, J. I., & Lacey, B. C. Some autonomic-central nervous system interrelationships. In P. Black (Ed.), *Physiological correlates of emotion.* New York: Academic Press, 1970.

Lacey, J. I., Kagan, J., Lacey, B. C., & Moss, H. A. The visceral level: Situational determinants and behavioral correlates of autonomic response patterns. In P. H. Knapp (Ed.), *Expression of the emotions in man.* New York: International Universities Press, 1963.

Lader, M. The psychophysiology of anxious and depressed patients. In D. C. Fowles (Ed.), *Clinical applications of psychophysiology.* New York: Columbia University Press, 1975.

Lader, M. H., & Noble P. The affective disorders. In P. H. Venables & M. J. Christie (Eds.), *Research in psychophysiology.* New York: Wiley, 1975.

Lader, M. H., & Wing, L. *Physiological measures, sedative drugs and morbid anxiety.* (Maudsley Monograph No. 14.) London: Oxford University Press, 1966.

Lang, P. J. The application of psychophysiological methods to the study of psychotherapy and behavior change. In A. E. Bergin & S. L. Garfield (Eds.), *Handbook of psychotherapy and behavior change: An empirical analysis.* New York: Wiley, 1971.

Lang, P. J., Melamed, B. G., & Hart, J. E. A psychophysiological analysis of fear modification using an automated desensitization procedure. *Journal of Abnormal Psychology,* 1970, *76,* 220–234.

Lang, P. J., Melamed, B., & Hart, J. Automating the desensitization procedure: A psychophysiological analysis of fear modification. In M. Kietzman, S. Sutton, & J. Zubin (Eds.), *Experimental approaches to psychopathology.* New York: Academic Press, 1975.

Lazarus, R. S. *Psychological stress and the coping process.* New York: McGraw-Hill, 1966.

Lazarus, R. S., Speisman, J. C., & Mordkoff, A. M. The relationship between autonomic indicators of psychological stress: Heart rate and skin conductance. *Psychosomatic Medicine,* 1963, *25,* 19–30.

Lazarus, R. S., Speisman, J. C., Mordkoff, A. M., & Davison, L. A. A laboratory study of psychological stress produced by a motion picture film. *Psychological Monographs,* 1962, *76* (Whole No. 553).

Liebman, S. (Ed.). *Stress situations.* Philadelphia: Lippincott, 1955.

Lindsley, D. B. Emotions and the electroencephalogram. In M. L. Reymert (Ed.), *Feelings and emotions.* New York: McGraw-Hill, 1950.

Lindsley, D. B. Emotion. In S. S. Stevens (Ed.), *Handbook of experimental psychology.* New York: Wiley, 1951.

Lindsley, D. B. Psychophysiology and motivation. In M. R. Jones (Ed.), *Nebraska Symposium on Motivation.* Lincoln: University of Nebraska Press, 1957.

Lipowski, Z. J., Lipsitt, D. R., & Whybrow, P. C. (Eds.). *Psychosomatic medicine, current trends and clinical applications.* New York: Oxford University Press, 1977.

Lockhart, R. A. Comments regarding multiple response phenomena in long interstimulus interval conditioning. *Psychophysiology,* 1966, *3,* 108–114.

Lockhart, R. A. Cognitive processes and the multiple response phenomenon. *Psychophysiology,* 1973, *10,* 112–118.

Lykken, D. T. The GSR in the detection of guilt. *Journal of Applied Psychology,* 1959, *43,* 385–388.

Lykken, D. T. Psychology and the lie detector industry. *American Psychologist,* 1974, *29,* 725–739.

Lykken, D. T., & Venables, P. H. Direct measurement of skin conductance: A proposal for standardization. *Psychophysiology*, 1971, *8*, 656–672.

Lywood, D. W. Blood pressure. In P. H. Venables & I. Martin (Eds.), *A manual of psychophysiological methods*. New York: Wiley, 1967.

Magoun, H. W. *The waking brain*. Springfield, Ill.: Thomas, 1963.

Malmo, R. B. Activation: A neuropsychological dimension. *Psychiatric Research Reports*, 1959, *11*, 86–109.

Malmo, R. B. Activation. In A. J. Bachrach (Ed.), *Experimental foundations of clinical psychology*. New York: Basic Books, 1962.

Malmo, R. B., Boag, T. J., & Smith, A. A. Psychological study of personal interaction. *Psychosomatic Medicine*, 1957, *19*, 105–119.

Malmo, R. B., & Surwillo, W. W. Sleep deprivation: Changes in performance and physiological indicants of activation. *Psychological Monographs*, 1960, *74*, (15, Whole No. 502).

Mandel, I. J., & Bridger, W. H. Is there classical conditioning without cognitive expectancy? *Psychophysiology*, 1973, *10*, 87–90.

Mandler, G. Emotion. In R. N. Brown, E. Galanter, E. H. Hess, & G. Mandler (Eds.), *New directions in psychology* (Vol. I). New York: Holt, 1962.

Maricq, H. R., & Edelberg, R. Electrodermal recovery rate in a schizophrenic population. *Psychophysiology*, 1975, *12*, 630–633.

Mathews, A. M., & Gelder, M. G. Psychophysiological investigations of brief relaxation training. *Journal of Psychosomatic Research*, 1969, *13*, 1–12.

McCanne, R., & Sandman, C. Operant autonomic conditioning and rod and frame test performance. *Journal of Personality and Social Psychology*, 1976, *34*, 821–829.

McDonald, D. G., Schicht, W. W., Frazier, R. E., Shallenberger, H. D., & Edwards, D. J. Studies of information processing in sleep. *Psychophysiology*, 1975, *12*, 624–629.

Mednick, S. A., & Schulsinger, F. Some pre-morbid characteristics related to breakdown in children with schizophrenic mothers. In D. Rosenthal & S. S. Kety (Eds.), *The transmission of schizophrenia*. New York: Pergamon Press, 1968.

Mednick, S. A., Schulsinger, F., & Garfinkel, R. Children at high risk for schizophrenia: Predisposing factors and intervention. In M. L. Kietzman, S. Sutton, & J. Zubin (Eds.), *Experimental approaches to psychopathology*. New York: Academic Press, 1975.

Mendels, J., & Chernick, D. A. Psychophysiological studies of sleep in depressed patients: An overview. In D. C. Fowles (Ed.), *Clinical application of psychophysiology*. New York: Columbia University Press, 1975.

Miller, N. E. *Psychosomatic effects of specific types of training*. New York: New York Academy of Sciences, 1967.

Miller, N. E. Learning of visceral and glandular responses. *Science*, 1969, *163*, 434–445.

Miller, N. E., & Banuazizi, A. Instrumental learning by curarized rats of a specific visceral response, intestinal or cardiac. *Journal of Comparative and Physiological Psychology*, 1968, *65*, 1–7.

Miller, N. E., & Dworkin, B. R. Visceral learning: Recent difficulties with curarized rats and significant problems for human research. In P. A. Obrist, A. H. Black, J. Brener, & L. V. DiCara (Eds.), *Cardiovascular psychophysiology*. Chicago: Aldine, 1974.

Moos, R. H., & Engel, B. T. Psychophysiological reactions in hypertensive and arthritic patients. *Journal of Psychosomatic Research*, 1962, *6*, 227–241.

Morgan, C. T. *Physiological psychology* (3rd ed.). New York: McGraw-Hill, 1965.

Murray, E. J. *Sleep, dreams and arousal*. New York: Appleton, 1965.

Näätänen, R. The inverted-U relationship between activation and performance: A critical review. In S. Kornblum (Ed.), *Attention and performance* (Vol. IV). New York: Academic Press, 1973.

Näätänen, R. Evoked potentials and selective attention in humans: A critical review. *Biological Psychology*, 1975, 2, 237–307.

Naitoh, P. Sleep deprivation in humans. In P. H. Venables & M. J. Christie (Eds.), *Research in psychophysiology*. New York: Wiley, 1975.

Neary, R. S., & Zuckerman, M. Sensation seeking, trait and state anxiety, and the electrodermal orienting response. *Psychophysiology*, 1976, 13, 205–211.

Netter, F. H. *The Ciba collection of medical illustrations* (Vol. 1). New York: Ciba Foundation, 1962.

Obrist, P. A., Black, A. H., Brener, J., & DiCara, L. V. (Eds.). *Cardiovascular psychophysiology*. Chicago: Aldine, 1974.

Obrist, P. A., Webb, R. A., & Sutterer, J. R. Heart rate and somatic change during aversive conditioning and a simple reaction time task. *Psychophysiology*, 1969, 5, 696–723.

Obrist, P. A., Webb, R. A., Sutterer, J. R., & Howard, J. L. Cardiac deleceleration and reaction time: An evaluation of two hypotheses. *Psychophysiology*, 1970, 6, 695–706.

Öhman, A., Fredrikson, M., Hugdahl, K., & Rimmö, P. A. The premise of equipotentiality in human classical conditioning: Conditioned electrodermal responses to potentially phobic stimuli. *Journal of Experimental Psychology, General*, 1976, 105, 313–337.

Opton, E. M, & Lazarus, R. S. Personality determinants of psychophysiological response to stress. *Journal of Personality and Social Psychology*, 1967, 6, 291–303.

Orne, M. T., Thackray, R. E., & Paskewitz, D. A. On the detection of deception—a model for the study of the physiological effects of psychological stimuli. In N. S. Greenfield & R. A. Sternbach (Eds.), *Handbook of psychophysiology*. New York: Holt, 1972.

Oswald, I. *Sleeping and waking: Physiology and psychology*. Amsterdam: Elsevier, 1962.

Palmai, G., & Blackwell, B. The diurnal pattern of salivary flow in normal and depressed patients. *British Journal of Psychiatry*, 1965, 111, 334–338.

Parsons, O. A., Fulgenzi, L. B., & Edelberg, R. Aggressiveness and psychophysiological responsivity in groups of repressors and sensitizers. *Journal of Personality and Social Psychology*, 1969, 12, 235–244.

Paul, G. L. Physiological effects of relaxation training and hypnotic suggestion. *Journal of Abnormal Psychology*, 1969, 74, 425–437.

Pavlov, I. P. *Conditioned reflexes*. London: Oxford University Press, 1927.

Petrie, A. *Individuality in pain and suffering*. Chicago: University of Chicago Press, 1967.

Picton, T. W., & Hillyard, S. A. Human auditory evoked potentials II: Effects of attention. *Electroencephalography and Clinical Neurophysiology*, 1974, 36, 191–199.

Pinneo, L. R. The effects of induced muscle tension during tracking on level of activation and on performance. *Journal of Experimental Psychology*, 1961, 62, 523–531.

Pitts, F. N. The biochemistry of anxiety. *Scientific American*, 1969, 220, 69–75.

Plotkin, W. B. On the self-regulation of the occipital alpha rhythm: Control strategies, states of consciousness, and the role of physiological feedback. *Journal of Experimental Psychology: General*, 1976, 105, 66–99.

Podlesny, J. A., & Raskin, D. C. Physiological measures and the detection of deception. *Psychological Bulletin*, 1977, 84, 782–799.

Ponticelli, T. P., & Greene, W. H. *Chart interpretations and reference guide, Phase I*. Los Angeles: California Academy of Polygraph Sciences, 1975.

Porges, S. W., Walter, G. F., Korb, R. J., & Sprague, R. L. The influences of methylphenidate on heart rate and behavioral measures of attention in hyperkinetic children. *Child Development*, 1975, 46, 727–733.

Prokasy, W. F., & Raskin, D. C. (Eds.). *Electrodermal activity in psychological research*. New York: Academic Press, 1973.

Rabkin, J. G., & Struening, E. L. Life events, stress, and illness. *Science*, 1976, *194*, 1013–1020.

Rahe, R. H. Life changes and near-future illness reports. In L. Levi (Ed.), *Emotions—their parameters and measurement*. New York: Raven Press, 1975.

Rankin, R. E., & Campbell, D. T. Galvanic response to Negro and White experimenters. *Journal of Abnormal and Social Psychology*, 1955, *51*, 30–33.

Rapoport, J. L., Buchsbaum, M. J., Zahn, T. P., Weingartner, H., Ludlow, C., & Mikkelsen, E. J. Dextroamphetamine: Cognitive and behavioral effects in normal prepubertal boys. *Science*, 1978, *199*, 560–563.

Raskin, D. C., Barland, G. H., & Podlesny, J. A. Validity and reliability of detection of deception. *Polygraph*, 1977, *6*, 1–39.

Rechtschaffen, A., & Kales, A. *A manual of standardized terminology, techniques and scoring system for sleep stages of human subjects*. Washington, D.C.: U. S. Government Printing Office, 1968.

Reid, J. E., & Inbau, F. E. *Truth and deception: The polygraph ("lie-detection") technique* (2nd ed.). Baltimore: Williams & Wilkins, 1977.

Rescorla, R. A. Pavlovian conditioning and its proper control procedures. *Psychological Review*, 1967, *74*, 71–80.

Reymert, M. L. *Feeling and emotions*. New York: McGraw-Hill, 1950.

Roessler, R. Personality, psychophysiology, and performance. *Psychophysiology*, 1973, *10*, 315–327.

Roessler, R., & Greenfield, N. S. *Physiological correlates of psychological disorders*. Madison: University of Wisconsin Press, 1962.

Romig, C. H. A. Status of state polygraph legislation in July, 1972. In N. Ansley (Ed.), *Legal admissibility of the polygraph*. Springfield, Ill.: Thomas, 1975.

Ross, L. E. & Nelson, M. N. The role of awareness in differential conditioning. *Psychophysiology*, 1973, *10*, 91–94.

Runquist, W. N., & Ross, L. E. The relation between physiological measures of emotionality and performance in eyelid conditioning. *Journal of Experimental Psychology*, 1959, *57*, 329–332.

Satterfield, J. H. Auditory evoked cortical response studies in depressed patients and normal control subjects. In T. A. Williams, M. M. Katz, & J. A. Shield (Eds.), *Recent advances in the psychobiology of the depressive illnesses*. Washington, D.C.: U. S. Government Printing Office, 1972.

Satterfield, J. H. The hyperactive child syndrome: A precursor of child psychopathy? In R. D. Hare & D. Schalling (Eds.), *Psychopathic Behavior, Proceedings of the NATO Advanced Study Institute on Sociopathic Behavior, Les Arcs, France, 1975*. New York: Wiley, 1978.

Satterfield, J. H., Cantwell, D. P., Lesser, L. I., & Podosin, R. L. Physiological studies of the hyperkinetic child: I. *American Journal of Psychiatry*, 1972, *128*, 1418–1423.

Satterfield, J. H., Cantwell, D. P., & Satterfield, B. T. Psychophysiology of the hyperactive child syndrome. *Archives of Child Psychiatry*, 1974, *31*, 839–844.

Satterfield, J. H., & Dawson, M. E. Electrodermal correlates of hyperactivity in children. *Psychophysiology*, 1971, *8*, 191–197.

Sawrey, W. L., & Sawrey, J. M. Conditioned fear and restraint in ulceration. *Journal of Comparative Physiological Psychology*, 1964, *57*, 150–151.

Sawrey, W. L., & Weisz, J. D. An experimental method of producing gastric ulcers. *Journal of Comparative and Physiological Psychology*, 1956, *49*, 269–270.

Saxon, S. A., & Dahle, A. J. Auditory threshold variations during periods of induced high and low heart rates. *Psychophysiology*, 1971, *8*, 23–29.

Schachter, S. *Emotion, obesity, and crime.* New York: Academic Press, 1971.

Schachter, S., & Singer, J. E. Cognitive, social and physiological determinants of emotional state. *Psychological Review,* 1962, *69,* 379–399.

Schacter, J. Pain, fear, and anger in hypertensives and normotensives. *Psychosomatic Medicine,* 1957, *19,* 17–29.

Schandler, S. L., & Grings, W. W. An examination of methods for producing relaxation during short-term laboratory sessions. *Behavior Research and Therapy,* 1976, *14,* 419–426.

Schell, A. M., & Catania, J. The relationship between cardiac activity and sensory acuity. *Psychophysiology,* 1975, *12*(2), 147–151.

Schuyler, D. *The depressive spectrum.* New York: Aronson, 1974.

Schwartz, G. E. Biofeedback, self-regulation, and the patterning of physiological processes. *American Scientist,* 1975, *63,* 314–324.

Schwartz, G. E., Flair, P. L., Salt, P., Mandell, M. R., & Klerman, G. L. Facial muscle patterning to affective imagery in depressed and nondepressed subjects. *Science,* 1976, *192,* 489–491.

Schwartz, G. E., & Shapiro, D. Social psychophysiology. In W. F. Prokasy & D. C. Raskin (Eds.), *Electrodermal activity in psychological research.* New York: Academic Press, 1973.

Selesnick, S. T., Malmstrom, E. J., Yonger, J., & Lederman, A. Induced somatic reactions in asthmatic adults. *Diseases of the Nervous System,* 1969, *30,* 385–391.

Seligman, M. E. P. Control group and conditioning: A comment on operationism. *Psychological Review,* 1969, *76,* 484–491.

Seligman, M. E. P. On the generality of the laws of learning. *Psychological Review.* 1970, *77,* 406–418.

Selye, H. *The physiology and pathology of exposure to stress.* Montreal: Acta, 1950.

Selye, H. *The stress of life.* New York: McGraw-Hill, 1956.

Shagass, C. Electrical activity of the brain. In N. S. Greenfield & R. A. Sternbach (Eds.), *Handbook of psychophysiology.* New York: Holt, 1972.

Shagass, C., & Schwartz, M. Age, personality and somato-sensory cerebral evoked responses. *Science,* 1965, *148,* 1359–1361.

Shapiro, D., & Schwartz, G. Psychophysiological contributions to social psychology. *Annual Review of Psychology,* 1970, *21,* 87–112.

Shapiro, D., Tursky, G., Gershon, E., & Stern, M. Effects of feedback and reinforcement on the control of systolic blood pressure. *Science,* 1969, *163,* 588–589.

Silverman, A. J., Cohen, S. I., & Shmavonian, B. M. Investigation of psychophysiologic relationships with skin resistance measures. *Journal of Psychosomatic Research,* 1959, *4,* 65–87.

Silverman, A. J., Cohen, S. I., Shmavonian, B. M., & Greenberg, G. Psychophysiological investigations in sensory deprivation. *Psychosomatic Medicine,* 1961, *23,* 48–61.

Smith, D. B. D., & Wenger, M. A. Changes in autonomic balance during phasic anxiety. *Psychophysiology,* 1965, *1,* 267–271.

Snyder, F., & Scott, J. The psychophysiology of sleep. In N. S. Greenfield & R. A. Sternbach (Eds.), *Handbook of psychophysiology.* New York: Holt, 1972.

Sokolov, E. N. Neuronal models and the orienting reflex. In M. A. Brazier (Ed.), *The central nervous system and behavior.* New York: Macy, 1960.

Spilker, B., & Callaway, E. "Augmenting" and "reducing" in averaged visual evoked responses to sine wave light. *Psychophysiology,* 1969, *6,* 49–57.

Stein, M., & Luparello, T. J. The measurement of respiration. In C. C. Brown (Ed.), *Methods in psychophysiology.* Baltimore: Williams & Wilkins, 1967.

Stelmack, R. M., & Mandelzya, N. Extraversion and pupillary response to affective and taboo words. *Psychophysiology,* 1975, *12,* 536–540.

Stern, J. A. Toward a definition of psychophysiology. *Psychophysiology*, 1964, *1*, 90–91.

Stern, J. A. Cognitive factors and conditioning: Comments on papers. *Psychophysiology*, 1973, *10*, 121–122.

Stern, J. A., & Janes, C. L. Personality and psychopathology. In W. F. Prokasy & D. C. Raskin (Eds.), *Electrodermal activity in psychological research*. New York: Academic Press, 1973.

Sternbach, R. A. The effects of instructional sets on autonomic responsivity. *Psychophysiology*, 1964, *1*, 67–72.

Sternbach, R. A. *Principles of psychophysiology*. New York: Academic Press, 1966.

Sternbach, R. A., & Tursky, B. Ethnic differences among housewives in psychophysical and skin potential responses to electric shock. *Psychophysiology*, 1965, *1*, 241–246.

Stewart, M. A., Pitts, F. N., Craig, A. G., & Dieruf, W. The hyperactive child syndrome. *American Journal of Orthopsychiatry*, 1966, *5*, 861–867.

Stone, L. J., & Hokanson, J. E. Arousal reduction via self-punitive behavior. *Journal of Personality and Social Psychology*, 1969, *12*, 72–79.

Strongman, K. T. *The psychology of emotion*. London: Wiley, 1973.

Tarlow, B. Admissibility of polygraph evidence in 1975: An aid in determining credability in a perjury-plagued system. *The Hastings Law Journal*, 1975, *26*, 917–974.

Tecce, J. J. Contingent negative variation (CNV) and psychological processes in man. *Psychological Bulletin*, 1972, *77*, 73–108.

Tecce, J. J., & Scheff, N. Attention reduction and suppressed direct-current potentials in the human brain. *Science*, 1969, *164*, 331–333.

Thompson, R. F., & Patterson, M. M. (Eds.). *Bioelectric recording techniques* (Parts B and C). New York: Academic Press, 1974.

Trolander, H. W. The measurement of biological temperatures. In C. C. Brown (Ed.), *Methods in psychophysiology*. Baltimore: Williams & Wilkins, 1967.

Tryon, W. W. Models of behavior disorder: A formal analysis based on Wood's taxonomy of instrumental conditioning. *American Psychologist*, 1976, *31*, 509–518.

Tursky, B. The indirect recording of human blood pressure. In P. A. Obrist, A. H. Black, J. Brener, & L. V. DiCara (Eds.), *Cardiovascular psychophysiology*. Chicago: Aldine, 1974.

Uno, T., & Grings, W. W. Autonomic components of orienting behavior. *Psychophysiology*, 1965, *1*, 311–321.

Valins, S. Cognitive effects of false heart-rate feedback. *Journal of Personality and Social Psychology*, 1966, *4*, 400–408.

Varni, J. G., Doerr, H. O., & Varni, J. R. Relationships between bilateral differences in body perception and bilateral differences in skin conductance levels. *Psychophysiology*, 1975, *12*, 179–181.

Venables, P. H. Psychophysiological studies of schizophrenic pathology. In P. H. Venables & M. J. Christie (Eds.), *Research in psychophysiology*. New York: Wiley, 1975.

Venables, P. H., & Christie, M. J. (Eds.). *Research in psychophysiology* New York: Wiley, 1975.

Venables, P. H., & Martin, I. (Eds.). *Manual of psychophysiological methods*. New York: Wiley, 1966.

Walter, W. G. The contingent negative variation as an aid to psychiatric diagnosis. In M. L. Kietzman, S. Sutton, & J. Zubin (Eds.), *Experimental approaches to psychopathology*. New York: Academic Press, 1975.

Webb, W. B. *Sleep: An experimental approach*. New York: Macmillan, 1968.

Webb, W. B. *Sleep: The gentle tyrant*. Englewood Cliffs, N. J.: Prentice-Hall, 1975.

Weil, J. L. *A neurophysiological model of emotional and intentional behavior*. Springfield, Ill.: Thomas, 1974.

Weiss, I. M. Influence of psychological variables on stress-induced pathology. In Ciba

Foundation. Symposium 8: *Physiology, emotion and psychosomatic illness*. Amsterdam: Associated Scientific Publishers, 1972.

Wender, P. H. *Minimal brain dysfunction in children*. New York: Wiley, 1971.

Wenger, M. A. Studies of autonomic balance in Army Air Forces personnel. *Comparative Psychology Monographs*, 1948, *19*(4, Serial No. 101).

Wenger, M. A. Studies of autonomic balance: A summary. *Psychophysiology*, 1966, *2*, 173–186.

Wenger, M. A., & Cullen, T. D. Studies of autonomic balance in children and adults. In N. S. Greenfield & R. A. Sternbach (Eds.), *Handbook of psychophysiology*. New York: Holt, 1972.

Westie, F., & DeFleur, M. Autonomic responses and their relationship to race attitudes. *Journal of Abnormal and Social Psychology*, 1959, *58*, 340–347.

Weybrew, B. B. Patterns of psychophysiological response to military stress. In M. H. Appley & R. Trumbull (Eds.), *Psychological stress*. New York: Appleton, 1967.

White, K. D. Salivation: A review and experimental investigation of major techniques. *Psychophysiology*, 1977, *14*, 203–212.

Williams, H. L. Information processing during sleep. In W. P. Koella & P. Levin (Eds.), *Sleep*. Basel, Switzerland: Karger, 1973.

Wolf, S., & Welsh, J. D. The gastrointestinal tract as a responsive system. In N. S. Greenfield & R. A. Sternbach (Eds.), *Handbook of psychophysiology*. New York: Holt, 1972.

Wood, C. G., & Hokanson, J. E. Effects of induced muscular tension on performance and the inverted U function. *Journal of Personality and Social Psychology*, 1965, *1*, 506–509.

Woodruff, D. S. Relationships among EEG alpha frequency, reaction time and age: A biofeedback study. *Psychophysiology*, 1975, *12*, 673–681.

Woods, P. J. A taxonomy of instrumental conditioning. *American Psychologist*, 1974, *29*, 584–597.

Young, P. T. *Motivation and emotion*. New York: Wiley, 1961.

Young, P. T. *Emotion in man and animal*. Huntington, N. Y.: Krieger, 1973.

Zahn, T. P., Abate, F., Little, B. C., & Wender, P. H. Minimal brain dysfunction, stimulant drugs, and autonomic nervous system activity. *Archives of General Psychiatry*, 1975, *32*, 381–387.

Ziskind, E., Jens, R., Maltzman, I., Parker, D., Slater, G., & Syndulko, K. Psychophysiological, chemical, and therapeutic research on sociopaths: A search for a homogenous sociopath population. *Proceedings V World Congress of Psychiatry*. (Excerpta Medica International Congress Series No. 274.) Amsterdam: Excerpta Medica, 1971.

Zuckerman, M. Dimensions of sensation seeking. *Journal of Consulting and Clinical Psychology*, 1971, *36*, 45–52.

Author Index

A

Aarons, L., 109
Abate, F., 77
Abercrombie, J., 62
Ader, R., 134
Adler, C., 118, 120
Akiskal, H. J., 70
Alexander, A. A., 65
Alsip, J. E., 95
Altorescu, H. S., 166
Ansley, N., 166
Appenzeller, O., 11
Arnold, M. B., 53
Augenbraum, C. B., 97
Ax, A. F., 2, 6, 82

B

Backster, C., 154
Baer, P. E., 145
Bailey, F. L., 166
Bamford, J., 82
Bandura, A., 152
Banuazizi, A., 148
Barland, G. H., 153, 158, 160, 162–163

Bartko, J. J., 78
Barton, W. E., 123
Beatty, J., 96
Beck, A. T., 69
Bell, B., 84
Benjamin, L., 125
Bergman, Z., 164
Berlyne, D. E., 100
Bersh, P. J., 160
Blackwell, B., 71
Blanchard, E. G., 151
Blankstein, K. R., 98, 100
Block, A. H., 146
Bloom, S. W., 40
Boag, T. J., 40
Boyd, R. W., 37–38
Brady, J. V., 134
Braun, E. W., 144
Brener, J., 12, 146
Bridger, W. H., 145
Brittain, T. M., 103
Brodie, D. A., 134
Broughton, R. H., 108
Brown, C. C., 15, 23
Buchsbaum, M. J., 58, 77
Budzynski, T., 118, 120

Burch, N. R., 40
Burgess, M., 101–102

C

Caldwell, C., 35
Callaway, E., 58–59
Campbell, D. T., 44
Candland, D. K., 11
Cannon, W., 3
Cantwell, D. P., 76–77
Carpenter, C. L., 78
Carpenter, W. T., 78
Catania, J. J., 70, 95–96
Chernick, D. A., 70
Christie, M. J., 111
Claridge, G. S., 57
Cleckley, H., 72
Clifton, R. K., 28
Cohen, S. I., 59–60, 88–89, 91
Cole, J. O., 123
Cook, M. R., 15
Cooper, R., 20
Courts, F. A., 89
Cousins, L. R., 98
Craig, A. G., 75–76
Craigen, D., 74
Craik, F. I. M., 98, 100
Crider, A., 31–32, 97
Cullen, T. D., 50

D

Dahle, A. J., 95
Dameron, L. E., 141
Davidson, P. O., 162
Davis, R. C., 164
Dawson, M. E., 70, 77, 145
DeFleur, M., 44
DeGood, D. E., 103
Deibler, W. P., 96
Dekker, E., 144
Dement, W., 109
Depue, R. A., 78
Deutsch, D., 11
Deutsch, J. A., 11
Dicara, L. V., 146
Dieruf, W., 75–76
DiMascio, A., 37–38
Doerr, H. O., 62

Duffy, E., 88
Dworkin, B. R., 147

E

Edelberg, R., 16, 40, 62, 82
Edwards, D. C., 95
Edwards, D. J., 109
Elliott, R., 92
Ely, D. L., 133
Engel, B. T., 132, 146
Eppinger, H., 47
Epstein, S., 34–35, 145
Erlenmeyer-Kimling, N., 64
Eysenck, H. J., 57
Eysenck, M. W., 98

F

Feighner, J. P., 66, 69, 78
Fell, J. P., 11
Fenz, W. D., 34–35
Ferster, C. G., 69
Fisher, S. A., 62
Flair, P. L., 70
Forrest, M. S., 103
Foulkes, D., 106
Fowles, D. C., 16, 78
Frazier, R. E., 109
Fredrikson, M., 142
Freeman, G. L., 88–89
Fuhrer, M. J., 145
Fulgenzi, L. B., 62
Funkenstein, D. H., 6
Furedy, J. J., 145

G

Gale, A., 57
Garfinkel, R., 84
Garrison, R. G., 144
Gelder, M. G., 117
Geddes, L. A., 158
Gershon, E., 150–151
Gillilan, L. A., 47
Glass, D. C., 4
Goldstein, I. B., 19
Goldwater, B. C., 24
Graham, D. T., 125–126, 128–130, 132
Graham, F. K., 28, 125, 143

Grant, D. A., 145
Greenberg, A., 96
Greenberg, G., 59–60
Greenblatt, M., 37–38
Greene, W. H., 157
Greenfield, N. S., 127
Gribbin, B., 14
Grings, W. W., 16–17, 29, 115, 141, 145
Grinker, R. R., 113
Groen, J., 144
Grossman, S. P., 4, 11
Gruzelier, J. H., 80–82
Gustafson, L. A., 164
Guyton, A. C., 9
Guze, J. B., 66, 69, 78

H

Hahn, W. W., 32, 130–131
Haith, M. M., 35
Hall, J., 138, 145
Hardt, J. V., 151
Hare, R. D., 30–31, 62, 72–74
Harris, V. A., 103
Hart, J. E., 119, 121
Haywood, H. C., 53
Headrick, M. W., 143
Henry, J. P., 133
Herron, W. G., 78
Hess, E. H., 24, 44, 47
Hillyard, S. A., 33
Hodges, W. F., 54
Hokanson, J. E., 54–55, 91, 101–103
Holden, C., 159
Horvath, F. S., 160, 164
Howard, J. L., 93
Hugdahl, K., 142
Hunt, W. A., 2

I

Inbau, F. E., 154, 158–159, 164, 166

J

Jacobson, E., 114
Janes, C. L., 67, 70
Janis, I. L., 111, 113
Jens, R., 72
Johnson, L. C., 109

Jordan, L. S., 78
Justeen, D. R., 144

K

Kabler, J. D., 125
Kagan, J., 32, 35
Kahneman, D., 31–32
Kales, A., 106, 108
Kamiya, J., 151
Kanfer, F. H., 152
Kaplan, H. B., 40
Kaplan, S., 98, 100
Karlin, L., 33
Katkin, E. S., 103, 119
Katz, M. M., 123
Katz, R. A., 23
Keen, E., 11
Kietzman, M. L., 65
Kimmel, E., 145–146
Kimmel, H. D., 145–146
Klein, R., 84
Kleinsmith, L. J., 98, 100
Kleitman, N., 106, 109
Klerman, G. L., 70
Klorman, R., 31
Korb, R. J., 77
Kugelmass, S., 164
Kunish, N. O., 125
Kuntz, A., 47

L

Lacey, B. C., 32, 51, 92
Lacey, J. I., 32, 51, 92–93
Lader, M. H., 67–68, 70
Lang, P. J., 119, 121
Lazarus, R. S., 62, 112–113
Lederman, A., 132
Leshner, A. I., 11
Lesser, L. I., 77
Lewis, W. C., 125
Lieblich, I., 164
Liebman, S., 111
Lindsley, D. B., 88
Lipowski, Z. J., 123
Lipsett, D. R., 123
Little, B. C., 77
Lockhart, R. A., 141, 143, 145
Ludlow, C., 77

Lundy, R. M., 125
Luparello, T. J., 23
Lykken, D. T., 16, 155, 162, 164, 166
Lywood, D. W., 14

M

McCanne, R., 59
McDonald, D. G., 109
McKinney, W. T., 70
Magoun, H. W., 106
Malmo, R. B., 40, 88, 109
Malmstrom, E. J., 132
Maltzman, I., 72
Mandel, I. J., 145
Mandell, M. R., 70
Mandelzya, N., 57
Mandler, G., 5
Maricq, H. R., 82
Matthews, A. M., 117
Mednick, S. A., 82, 84
Melamed, B. G., 119, 121
Mendels, J., 70
Mikkelsen, E. J., 77
Miller, N. E., 135, 145, 147–148
Moos, R. H., 132
Mordkoff, A. M., 112–113
Morgan, C. T., 7
Moss, H. A., 32
Munoz, R., 66, 69, 78
Murray, E. J., 106

N

Näätänen, R., 33, 92
Naitoh, P., 109
Neary, R. S., 63–64
Nelson, M. N., 145
Netter, F. H., 11
Newberg, D. C., 158
Noble, P., 67, 70

O

Obrist, P. A., 93, 146
O'Hanlon, 96
Öhman, A., 142
Opton, E. M., 62
Orne, M. T., 153, 164
Osselton, J. W., 20
Oswald, I., 106

P

Palmai, G., 71
Parker, D., 72
Parsons, O. A., 62
Paskewitz, D. A., 153, 164
Paul, G. L., 114–115
Pavlov, I. P., 134
Pendleton, R. B., 144
Perlser, H. E., 144
Petrie, A., 58
Phillips, J. S., 152
Picton, T. W., 33
Pinneo, L. R., 90–91
Pitts, F. N., 66, 75–76
Plotkin, W. B., 151
Plutchik, R., 11
Podlesny, J. A., 153, 160, 162–163
Podosin, R. L., 77
Polt, J. M., 44
Ponticelli, T. P., 157
Porges, S. W., 77
Prokasy, W. F., 16

R

Rabkin, J. G., 111
Rahe, R. H., 111
Ramen, A., 84
Rankin, R. E., 44
Rapoport, J. L., 77
Raskin, D. C., 16, 153, 158, 162–163
Rechtschaffen, A., 106
Reid, J. E., 154, 158–159, 164, 166
Reitz, S. R., 119
Rescorla, R. A., 140
Rimmö, P. A., 142
Robins, E., 66, 69, 78
Roessler, R., 53, 55, 127
Romig, C. H., 166
Ross, L. E., 98–99, 145
Rothblatt, H. B., 166
Runquist, W. N., 98–99

S

Salt, P., 70
Salzman, L., 84
Sandman, C., 59
Satterfield, B. T., 77
Satterfield, J. H., 21, 77

Sawrey, J. M., 134
Sawrey, W. L., 134
Saxon, S. A., 95
Schacter, J., 6
Schachter, S., 5
Schandler, S. L., 115
Scheff, N., 93–94
Schell, A. M., 70, 95–96
Schicht, W. W., 109
Schulsinger, F., 82, 84
Schuyler, D., 69
Schwartz, G. E., 36–37, 41, 44, 70
Schwartz, M., 57
Scott, J., 108
Selesnick, S. T., 132
Seligman, M. E. P., 140, 142
Selye, H., 110
Shagass, C., 21, 57
Shallenberger, H. D., 109
Shapiro, D., 31–32, 41, 44, 150–151
Shaw, J. C., 20
Shetler, S., 101
Shmavonian, B. M., 59–60, 88–89, 91
Silverman, A. J., 59–60, 88–89, 91
Singer, J. E., 5
Slater, G., 72
Sleight, P., 14
Smith, A. A., 40
Smith, B., 84
Smith, D. B. D., 49
Snyder, F., 108
Sokolov, E. N., 28
Speigel, J. R., 113
Speisman, J. C., 112–113
Spielberger, C. D., 53–54
Spilker, B., 58–59
Sprague, R. L., 77
Stein, M., 23
Stelmack, R. M., 57
Steptoe, A., 14
Stern, J. A., 2, 67, 70, 125, 128, 130, 145
Stern, M., 150–151
Sternbach, R. A., 10, 25, 41–43, 124
Stewart, M. A., 75–76
Stone, L. J., 103
Stoyva, J., 118, 120
Strauss, J. S., 78
Struening, E. L., 111
Surwillo, W. W., 109
Sutherland, G. F., 23
Sutterer, J. R., 93

Sutton, S., 65
Syndulko, K., 72

T

Tarlow, B., 166
Tarpy, R. M., 11
Tecce, J. J., 21, 93–94
Thackray, R. E., 153, 164
Trolander, H. W., 23
Tryon, W. W., 138
Tursky, B., 14, 31–32, 42–43
Tursky, G., 150–151

U

Uno, T., 29

V

Valins, S., 103
Varni, J. G., 62
Varni, J. R., 62
Venables, P. H., 16, 80–82, 84

W

Walter, G. F., 77
Walter, W. G., 67
Webb, R. A., 93
Webb, W. B., 8, 106–107
Weil, J. L., 11
Weingarten, H., 77
Weim, J. M., 135
Weissberg, R. P., 31
Weisz, J. D., 134
Welsh, J. D., 24
Wender, P. H., 76–77
Wenger, M. A., 49–50, 67
Westie, F., 44
Weybrew, B. B., 113
White, K. D., 23
Whybrow, P. C., 123
Wiesenfeld, A. R., 31
Williams, H. L., 109
Wing, L., 67–68
Winokur, G., 66, 69, 78, 125, 128, 130
Wolf, S., 24
Wood, C. G., 91
Woodruff, D. S., 97

Woodruff, R. A., 66, 69, 78
Woods, P. J., 138

Z

Zahn, T. P., 77
Ziskind, E., 72
Y   Zubin, J., 65

Yonger, J., 132
Young, L. D., 151
Young, P. T., 2

Subject Index

A

Ā, *see* Autonomic balance score
Acetylcholine, 11
Ach, *see* Acetylcholine
Adenosine triphosphate, 109
Adrenal gland
  innervation, 10-11
  stress, 111, 132
Adrenalin, 4, 74
Adrenergic system, 11
Aggression, 101-103
Alpha wave
  biofeedback, 151
  definition, 19
  during sleep, 106
Anger, *see also* Aggression
  physiological difference from fear, 6
  spinal cord lesion, 4
ANS, *see* Autonomic nervous system
Anxiety
  autonomic balance score, 48-50, 67
  hierarchy, 118-122
  neurosis, 66-67, 82-84
  phobic, 117-122
  state versus trait, 53-54

Arousal
  aggression, 101-103
  bodily responses, 87-89
  learning and memory, 97-100
  motor performance, 89-94
  sensory performance, 94-97
Asthma, bronchial, 130-132
ATP, *see* Adenosine triphosphate
Attention
  contingent negative variation, 93-94
  detection of deception, 164
  inward versus outward, 31-33
  orienting response, 28
  sensory performance, 94-97
Attitude, 41-45
  hypnotic induction, 128-129
  Pavlovian conditioning, 144-145
  psychosomatic disorders, 125-129
Average evoked potential, *see* Cortical
  evoked response
Average evoked response, *see* Cortical
  evoked response
Avoidance learning
  in curarized rats, 147
  gastric ulcers, 134
  type of instrumental conditioning, 139

Augmentation, of stimulus, 58–59, 70
Autonomic balance score, 48–50, 67
Autonomic nervous system, 9–11

B

Beta wave, 19
Biofeedback, 149–151
  alpha wave, 151
  blood pressure, 150
  compared to relaxation procedures,
    114–117
  headaches and frontalis muscles, 117–118
  heart rate, 150
Blood pressure
  aggression, 101–103
  biofeedback, 150–151
  detection of deception, 157–159
  hostility, 54–55
  measurement, 13–14, 22
  schizophrenia, 79–81
Blood volume, 14–16, 22, see also Pulse volume, measurement
Body image, 61–62
BV, see Blood volume

C

Cannon–Bard theory, 4
Cardiotachometer, 13
Central nervous system, 7–9
CER, see Cortical evoked response
Cerebral cortex, 7–8
Cholinergic system, 11
Classical conditioning, see Pavlovian condi-
  tioning
CNS, see Central nervous system
CNV, see Contingent negative variation
Conditioned response, 138–145
Conditioned stimulus, 137–145
Contingent negative variation
  measurement, 21
  reaction-time, 94
Coping mechanisms, 74, 113, 135
Cortical evoked response
  attention, 33
  augmentation–reduction, 58–59
  extraversion–introversion, 56–57

hyperkinesis, 76–77
measurement, 20–22
Criticism
  asthmatic reaction to, 130
  physiological reaction to, 39–40
Curare, 147–149

D

DAD, see Device for automated desensitization
Deception, detection of
  cardiovascular response, 157–159
  control question test, 154–155
  employment screening, 166
  guilty knowledge test, 155–156
  legal status, 165
  respiration response, 157–158
  skin resistance response, 156–157
  test validity, 159–163
  theories of bodily changes, 163–164
  type of error, 162
Defensive response, 28–31
Delta wave, 19
Depression, 69–72, 82–84
Dermographic persistance, 48
Device for automated desensitization,
  119–121
DR, see Defensive response
Dreaming, 106–109

E

ECG, see Electrocardiogram
EEG, see Electroencephalogram
Ego strength, 55–56
EKG, see Electrocardiogram
Electrocardiogram, 12
Electrodermal response, measurement,
    16–18, see also Skin conductance level;
    Skin conductance response; Skin po-
    tential response; Skin resistance re-
    sponse
Electroencephalogram
  anxiety, 66
  depression, 70
  hyperkinesis, 76–77
  measurement, 19–22
  Pavlovian conditioning, 142–144

psychopathy, 72
sensory performance, 96–97
sleep stages, 106–110
Electromyogram
  biofeedback, 115–118
  depression, 70–71
  facial muscles, 36–37
  measurement, 18–19, 22
  praise and criticism, reaction to, 39–40
  psychopathy, 74
  reaction time, 92–93
EMG, see Electromyogram
Emotion
  activation theory, 5, 87
  Cannon–Bard theory, 3–4
  cognitive factors, 5
  contemporary theories, 4
  definition, 2
  emergency theory, 87
  James–Lange theory, 3–4
Energy mobilization theory, 87
Epinephrine, 5, 130
Extraversion, 56–57
Eyeblink conditioning, 98

F

Fear, see also Anxiety
  conditioned, 134, 137–138
  desensitization of, 118–122
  detection of deception, 164
  of parachuting, 33–36
  physiological difference from anger, 6
  in psychopaths, 73–74
  of public speaking, 121–122
  of snakes, 118–120
  of spiders, 28–31, 121–122
Field dependence, 59–61
Field independence, 59–61
Frustration, 54–55, 101–103

G

Galvanic skin response, see Skin conductance response; Skin resistance response
Gastric motility
  measurement, 24
  placebo effect, 41–42
General adaptation syndrome, 110, 132

H

Habituation
  anxiety, 67–68
  definition, 28
  different subculture groups, 42–43
  individual difference in learning, 98
  schizophrenia, 79–81
  sensation-seeking, 63–64
Heart period, 13, 48
Heart rate
  aggression, 101–103
  arousal, 89–91
  asthma, 130–131
  defensive response versus orienting response, 28–30
  depression, 70
  fear, 120–121
  instrumental conditioning, 145–149
  intake–rejection hypothesis, 33, 95
  measurement, 12–13
  Pavlovian conditioning, 143–144
  psychopathy, 74
  reaction time, 91–92
  relaxation, 114–116
  schizophrenia, 79–80
  sensory performance, 94–96
  social interaction, 37–39
  state anxiety, 54
Hives, 127–129
Homeostatic restraints, see Coping mechanisms
Hostility, 54–55
HP, see Heart period
HR, see Heart rate
Hyperactivity, see Hyperkinesis
Hyperkinesis, 75–77, 82–83, 85
Hypertension, 14, 125–129, 132–134, see also Blood pressure
Hypnosis
  attitude suggestion, 128–129
  relaxation procedure, 114–115
Hypothalamus, 8, 11

I

IBI, see Interbeat interval
Instrumental conditioning, 96, 138–139, 145–149
  awareness, role of, 147

Instrumental conditioning (*cont.*)
  bodily responses, modification of, 145
  heart rate, 145–146
  muscle contractions, role of, 147
  skin conductance, 145–146
  specificity of responding, 149
  types of training, 138–139
Intake–rejection hypothesis, 32–33, 95
Intelligence, psychosomatic disorder, role
    in, 127–128
Interbeat interval, 13
Introversion, 56–57
Inverted-U hypothesis, 89–92

J

James–Lange theory, 3–4

K

Kinesthetic–figural-aftereffects task, 58
Korotkoff sounds, 14

L

Law of initial values, 25, 82
Learning, arousal, relation to, 97–100, *see
    also* Biofeedback; Instrumental condi-
    tioning; Pavlovian conditioning
Lesions, spinal cord, 4
Lie-detector test, *see* Deception, detection
    of
Limbic system, 9–10

M

Manifest Anxiety Scale, 53
MAP, *see* Muscle action potential
MAS, *see* Manifest Anxiety Scale
Memory
  arousal, role of, 97–100
  cognitive load, 100
  verbal materials, 98
Mental task, 31–33
Minnesota Multiphasic Personality Inven-
    tory, 52–56, 62
MMPI, *see* Minnesota Multiphasic Person-
    ality Inventory
Motion pictures
  asthma, 131–132
  stress source, 56, 62, 113
Motivation, to deceive, 164

Motor performance, 89–94
Muscle action potential, measurement,
    18–19, *see also* Electromyogram
Muscle potentials, *see* Electromyogram

N

Neocortex, *see* Cerebral cortex
Nerve impulse, 7
Neuron, 7
Noradrenaline, 11
Norepinephrine, *see* Noradrenaline

O

Operant conditioning, *see* Instrumental
    conditioning
Operational fatigue, 49–50
OR, *see* Orienting response
Organ specificity, theory of, 132
Orienting response
  anxiety, 67–68
  definition, 27–29
  depression, 69–70
  detection of deception, 164
  individual differences in learning, 98
  sensation seeking, 63–64

P

P_3 component, 33
Pain
  augmentation–reduction, 58
  ethnic differences, 42–43
  psychopaths, 72
Parasympathetic nervous system, 9–11, 22
  dominance of, 47–51
Patient–therapist interaction, 37
Pavlovian conditioning, 137–145
  alpha wave, 144
  backward, 140
  cognitive factors, 144–145
  discrimination type, 140
  extinction, 143
  forward, 140
  generalization, 142
  heart rate, 143–144
  pulse volume response, 144
  skin conductance, 143
Phobic stimuli, conditioning of, 142
Pituitary gland, 11, 111, 132

Placebo, 5, 42
Plethysmograph, 15
   detection of deception, 158
Pneumograph, 23
PNS, see Parasympathetic nervous system
Polygraph, 12, 156
Postganglionic fibers, 9
PP, see Pulse pressure
Praise, physiological reaction to, 39–40
Preganglionic fibers, 9
Prejudices, racial, 43–45
Psychobiology, 1–2
Psychological stress evaluator, 159
Psychopathy, 72–74, 82, 85
Psychophysiology, 1–3
Psychosomatic disorders, 49–50, 123–135
   necessary conditions hypothesis, 124
   response specificity hypothesis, 130–132
   specific attitude hypothesis, 125–130
   stress, 132–133
Psychotherapy
   relaxation techniques in, 116
   small group, 40
Pulse pressure
   autonomic balance score, 48
   individual response stereotype, 51–52
   measurement, 13, 22
Pulse volume
   measurement, 16, 22
   Pavlovian conditioning, 143–144
Pulse wave velocity, 14
Pupil size
   cognitive memory load, 100
   interest value relation, 44–45
   measurement, 24
   during mental task, 31–32
PV, see Pulse volume

R

R waves, electrocardiogram, 12
RA, see Respiratory amplitude
1-Rapid eye movements, 106, 108–109
Raynaud's disease, 128–129
Reaction-time task, 92–94
Reduction, of stimulus, 58–59, 70
Reinforcement, relation to arousal, 100
Relaxation, 113–117
   hypnotic suggestion, 114–115
   progressive, 114–117
   training, 114–120

1-REM, see 1-Rapid eye movements
Repression–sensitization scale, 62
Repressor, 62–63
Reserpine, 134
Respiratory amplitude
   detection of deception, 157–158
   ego-strength, 56
   measurement, 23
   reaction time, 92–93
Respiration rate
   arousal, 89–90
   asthma, 130–131
   autonomic balance score, 48
   detection of deception, 157–158
   ego strength, 56
   fear, 35–36, 121
   measurement, 23
   relaxation and hypnosis, 115
Respondent conditioning, see Pavlovian
   conditioning
Rod-and-frame test, 59–60
RR, see Respiration rate

S

Salivation
   autonomic balance score, 48
   depression, 71
   measurement, 23
Schizophrenia, 77–84
   responders, nonresponders, 79–82
   types of, 78
SCL, see Skin conductance level
SCR, see Skin conductance response
Sensation seeking scale, 63–64
Sensitizer, 62–63
Sensory performance
   arousal, relation to, 94–97
   electroencephalogram, relation to, 96
   heart rate relation to, 95
Set, see Attitude
Sham rage, 7
Skin conductance level
   anxiety, 67–68
   arousal, 89–90
   autonomic balance score, 48
   depression, 69–70
   fear, 35–36, 121
   hyperkinesis, 76
   individual response stereotypy, 51–52
   measurement, 16–18

Skin conductance level (*cont.*)
  psychopathy, 72–74
  relaxation, 115–116
  schizophrenia, 79
  stress, 113
Skin conductance response
  anxiety, 67–68
  body image, 61
  depression, 69–70
  field independent versus field depen-
    dent, 60–61
  hyperkinesis, 75
  instrumental conditioning, 145–146
  measurement, 16–17
  Pavlovian conditioning, 143
  psychopathy, 72–74
  repression–sensitization, 62
  schizophrenia, 79
  sensation seeking, 63–64
Skin potential response
  habituation, 28–29
  measurement, 17–18
  subculture differences, 42–43
Skin resistance response
  detection of deception, 156–157
  measurement, 16
  during mental task, 32
  racial prejudice, 43–44
Sleep
  bodily changes during, 108
  depression, 70–71
  deprivation, 109–110
  disorders, 108
  drug effects, 108
  loss, 109
  stages, 106–107
SNS, *see* Sympathetic nervous system
Sociopathy, *see* Psychopathy
Sphygmomanometer, 13, 157
SPR, *see* Skin potential response
SRR, *see* Skin resistance response
SSS, *see* Sensation seeking scale
Stereotypy
  individual-response, 51–52, 124
  stimulus, 51
  symptom, 51
Stimulant, drug, 76–77
Stimulus
  environmental, 27–31
  fear-producing, 33–36

  self-generated, 36
  social, 37–41
  task-related, 31–33
Stimulus control
  instrumental conditioning, 139
  Pavlovian conditioning, 140
Stimulus isolation, 60–61
Stress, 110–113, 131–133
  definition, 133
  physiological, 110
  social, 110
Sympathetic chain, 9
Sympathetic ganglia, *see* Sympathetic chain
Sympathetic nervous system, 9–11
  dominance of, 48–51
Sympatheticotonic, 48
Synapse, 7
Systematic desensitization, 118–122

T

TAT, *see* Thematic Apperception Test
Temperature
  measurement, 23
  psychosomatic disorders, 128–130
  schizophrenia, 79–81
Thematic Apperception Test, 39, 101
Theta wave, 19, 72, 96

U

Ulcer, 134–135
Unconditioned response, 137–145
Unconditioned stimulus, 137–145

V

Vagatonic, 47–48
Vagus nerve, 3, 10–11, 47, 130
Vasoconstriction, 14
Vasodilation, 15

W

Wechsler Adult Intelligence Scale, 128

Y

Yoked control, 135, 145, 151

A
B
C 8
D 9
E 0
F 1
G 2
H 3
I 4
J 5